Sowing Faith in a Catholic Frontier:
a Condensed History of the Diocese of Richmond

A Grain of Wheat and Rocky Ground: Introduction

"Once we reached this bay, the military governor ordered us to search for Alonso, the boy who came with Father Baptista, whom we were told had not been killed."[1]

In 1572, Father Juan Rogel, a Spanish Jesuit priest, gave this account of his missionary work around the *baía de la Madre de Dios* (Bay of the Mother of God, today the Chesapeake Bay) to the superior of his religious order in Rome. Rogel's letter contained a portent and a parable: the Catholic Church in Virginia had begun with nine people in a vast country.

Like the grain of wheat (John 12:24), or the seed on rocky ground (Matt. 13:5–6, 20–21), the Church in this territory would grow slowly under adverse conditions. Here, Catholics would contend with low membership, religious and secular hostility, geographic isolation, economic deprivation, and a chronic lack of priests. Furthermore, events in Virginia, the United States, and the wider Church would have an impact on the community's development. The presence of the Diocese of Richmond four-and-a-half centuries later bears witness to the perseverance of Virginia's Catholics, who overcame hardship, and who experienced both successes and failures, as they carried out the Church's work.

Seed Among Thorns:
Inauspicious Beginnings
(1570-1794)

Catholics faced tribulation during their first two centuries in Virginia, as a band of Spanish missionaries suffered martyrdom in that territory (1571), and religious intolerance permeated the English colony (1607–1794). These developments formed part of the broader narrative of the European colonization of North America, during which sectarian concerns shaped national interests.

Spanish Jesuit Mission (1570–1571)

Two years before Father Rogel wrote his letter, on September 10, 1570, eight Jesuit missionaries, led by Father Juan Baptista de Segura (1529–1571), and a boy, Alonso de Olmos, disembarked near the future site of Williamsburg. To Spanish ears, the native word for the region sounded like "Ajacán"; Spain claimed this land as part of *la Florida* (North America). Indians of the Chiskiack tribe, led by Don Luis de Velasco (formerly Paquiquineo), an indigenous guide who betrayed the priests and religious brothers, killed these men between February 4 and 9, 1571. Only the boy survived, having been rescued after living with his captors for a year after the massacre. Three of the missionaries—Cristóbal Redondo, Gabriel de Solís, and Juan Baptista Méndez—made their Jesuit profession sometime between their arrival and the attack. These were the first religious vocations in what became Virginia.[1] The cause

for the canonization of the Jesuit Martyrs of Virginia was introduced in 2002.

The short-lived Jesuit mission was one of many difficulties Spain encountered in its colonization of North America. Unlike Central and South America, North America lacked precious metals, its terrain and climate were sometimes harsh, and its inhabitants proved more resistant to conquest and conversion. Spain eventually controlled what is today the southwestern and southeastern United States. On the Atlantic coast, the fort of St. Augustine—the site of several battles and a base for launching operations against Spain's enemies—encapsulated the region's strategic role. (Founded in 1565 on the Florida peninsula, St. Augustine was the first permanent European and Catholic settlement in what became the United States.) Ultimately, *la Florida* was a barrier for protecting Spain's more lucrative southern colonies against potential incursions by France or England.

Catholics at Jamestown (1607–1619)

In the decades following the collapse of the Jesuit mission in Ajacán (1571), England advanced upon North America (1584), intent on gaining a foothold in the territory it called "Virginia," likely in honor of its virgin queen, Elizabeth I (1558–1603). After two attempts at colonization failed (Roanoke Island off the coast of present-day North Carolina, in 1585 and 1587), the first permanent English settlement in America was established in 1607 at Jamestown. The colony was named after the reigning king, James I (1603–1625). (Jamestown was coincidentally located in the vicinity of the earlier Spanish mission.)

Since religion, national identity, and foreign policy were closely associated at that time, Virginia became decidedly Protestant. The Reformation had begun in England in 1534, when King Henry VIII renounced the authority of the pope. The movement continued during the reign of Henry's son, Edward VI (1537–1553). Following a brief restoration of Catholicism under Mary I (1553–1558), Henry's daughter and Edward's half-sister, England became Protestant once more during the long reign of Elizabeth (1558–1603). The Church of England had been reinstituted for nearly fifty years at the time Jamestown was founded. The Anglican Church was officially established in the colony (1606) and Catholicism was formally outlawed there (1609), as in the mother country (1558–1559).[2]

In this religiously hostile environment, one of Virginia's original settlers may have been a Catholic in secret: Captain Gabriel Archer (ca. 1574–ca. 1610), a prominent leader in the Jamestown community. Two reasons support this claim. First, Archer's parents and others living in his family's home in Mountnessing (Essex), England, were known Catholic recusants. The term "recusant" designated a person who refused (Latin: *recusare*) to adhere to the Church of England, and who was fined for not attending Anglican worship services. Second, an archaeological dig at Jamestown in 2015 yielded a remarkable discovery. In the grave beneath the chancel (sanctuary) of the church, a reliquary—usually a token of Catholic devotion—lay on top of Archer's coffin.[3]

Some three years after Archer's death, a French Jesuit priest arrived at Jamestown as a prisoner (1613). Captain Samuel Argall (ca. 1580–1672) had captured Father Pierre Biard (1576–1622), along with fourteen soldiers, in a raid on the fledgling French outpost of St. Sauveur (Holy Savior) on Mount Desert Island, off the coast of present-day Maine. (St. Sauveur was one of several attempted French colonies in North America; it followed the establishment of Quebec in 1608, France's first permanent settlement on the continent.) Argall brought the captives to Jamestown, where they were eventually released. Father Biard wrote an account of these events in which he narrated that Argall's doctor had treated another French Jesuit priest who was wounded in the attack and who later died. According to Biard, this unnamed physician was "a Catholic and known as such."[4] This report, together with the clues surrounding Gabriel Archer, suggests a Catholic presence early in Jamestown's history.

The next Catholics who came to Jamestown may have been slaves. The first Africans arrived in 1619 from the Portuguese colony of Angola. Since Portugal had mandated that slaves be baptized before leaving Africa (1607, 1619), it is likely that these men and women were at least nominally Catholic. Portuguese law also required baptized slaves to receive religious instruction during the passage to the Americas, although this norm was often disregarded.[5]

The slaves who came to Jamestown were transported on the *São João Bautista* (St. John the Baptist), a vessel bound for Veracruz in New Spain (present-day Mexico). But off the coast of Campeche in the Gulf of Mexico, two privateer ships attacked the *São João Bautista* and seized approximately fifty slaves. British captains commanded the corsairs, which were operating under the authority, respectively, of the Netherlands and Savoy (a duchy comprising parts of present-day France and Italy).

The first ship, *White Lion*, which flew the Dutch flag, eventually brought "20. and odd Negroes" to Point Comfort (today Fort Monroe, Hampton), at the mouth of the James River on the Chesapeake Bay. The slaves were traded for provisions and then taken to Jamestown.[6] Some of the other slaves, transported on the second ship, *Treasurer*, arrived later. At least one of the original slaves is known by name: Angelo (probably Angela), a woman on the *Treasurer* who became a household servant at Jamestown.[7]

These first slaves were bartered in late August 1619. Astonishingly, this odious transaction took place just one month after the House of Burgesses—the forerunner of today's Virginia General Assembly, the oldest democratic institution in the Western Hemisphere—met for the

first time (July 30, 1619). This juxtaposition of events marked a contradiction at the outset of American history that would affect the Catholic Church in Virginia: the acceptance of a system, amid the development of democracy, that oppressed persons of African descent for centuries.

Catholic Communities in Virginia: The Colony and Early Republic (1619–1794)

It was illegal to be a Catholic in Virginia throughout the colonial era (1607–1783) and for the first years of American independence (1783–1786). However, Virginia enforced its laws against Catholics unevenly, as two examples demonstrate. On the one hand, the Brent family, which came from Maryland and settled in Stafford County (1651), managed to advance in Virginia society for over a century. The Brents were known recusants, but they probably avoided legal trouble because they lived in a rural area and were discreet about their faith. On the other hand, court records mention the arrest of two priests in Norfolk—a Father Edmonds and a Father Raymond, who may have been the same person—for performing a marriage and for celebrating a Mass (1687).[8]

Jesuits and Franciscans in neighboring Maryland ministered to Virginia's Catholic families during the colonial period. An English Catholic, George Calvert (1580–1632), the first Lord Baltimore, had requested a charter from King Charles I of England to establish the colony of Maryland. The charter was granted just after Calvert's death (1632). His son, Cecil Calvert (1605–1675), the second Lord Baltimore, who was also a Catholic, subsequently founded Maryland on the principle of religious freedom (1634).

Priests in Maryland made clandestine visits to Virginia. Then, in a strange turn of events, Virginia became a refuge for a number of them. The English Civil War (1642–1651) and the Glorious Revolution (1688) emboldened Protestant colonists to overthrow the Maryland government on three occasions and to persecute Catholics, with the result that several Jesuits and some Franciscans fled to Virginia (1645, 1654–1655, 1689).[9]

Thomas Jefferson

Bishop John Carroll of Baltimore

largely determine where most people, including Catholics, settled in Virginia.

In the following century, the American Revolution (1775–1783) helped to lessen anti-Catholicism in Virginia, as the British colonies were allied with Catholic France.[10] Following the Revolution, Virginia enacted the Statute of Religious Liberty (1786), written by Thomas Jefferson. This law finally allowed Catholics and others to practice their faith openly in the Commonwealth of Virginia.

The first organized Catholic communities in Virginia appeared in short order: St. Mary's in Alexandria (which was then part of the new federal capital of Washington), and St. Patrick's in Norfolk, both around 1794. Significantly, each city was a port with a sizable population.[11] Developments in transportation—shipping ports, canals, railroads, trolley cars, and highways—would

A property record from 1794 indicates that lay Catholics in Norfolk owned a parcel of land used for religious purposes. The community built a small church named St. Patrick's around this time (ca. 1795). The lay trustees' ownership of the property sparked a conflict with Bishop John Carroll of Baltimore, the country's first Catholic bishop (1789–1815), and with his successors (1815–1821), whose area of jurisdiction at that time included Virginia. The trustees asserted their right to hold property in the name of the Church. They also claimed authority to appoint pastors, just like Protestants (and some Catholic European monarchs and nobles). This dispute came to be known as the Norfolk Schism (ca. 1794–1821), which led to the creation of a diocese in Virginia.[12]

Virginia Statute of Religious Liberty, 1786

Table of Contents

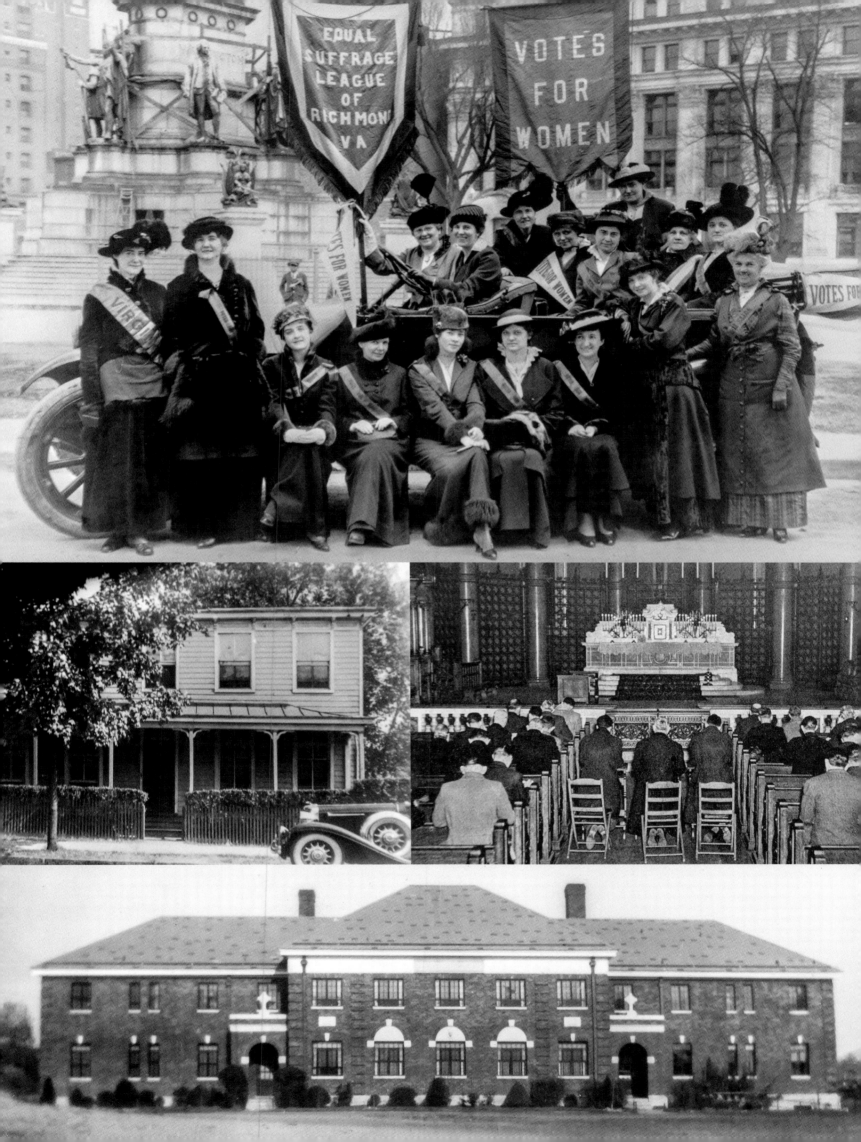

July 22, 2019

Dear Faithful of the Diocese of Richmond,

It is a joy to greet you on the occasion of the 200th anniversary of the founding of the Catholic Diocese of Richmond.

Established by Pope Pius VII on July 11, 1820, Richmond is one of the oldest dioceses in the country. The first Catholics had arrived in Virginia one hundred and fifty years earlier when a group of Spanish Jesuits were sent to evangelize the native peoples. Although short-lived, this mission produced the region's first martyrs when the Jesuits were killed within six months of their arrival. A permanent Catholic presence was not established until the English settlement of the Chesapeake in the seventeenth century and the arrival of the Brent family, who had emigrated to Virginia from Maryland. Thus began a close relationship between the Catholics of Virginia and Maryland that continues to this day. From the English Jesuit missionaries who came from Maryland to visit Virginia's Catholic families over the colonial period, to the state's inclusion in the boundaries of the nation's first diocese established at Baltimore in 1789, to the sons of Maryland (James Gibbons, Peter L. Ireton, and John J. Russell) appointed bishops of Richmond to the diocese's status as a suffragan in the Province of Baltimore, the history of these two communities has been closely intertwined.

As you celebrate your bicentennial, may this be an opportunity to learn about the rich and diverse heritage of Catholic Virginia. May you be inspired by the stories of the men and women that have gone before you and learn from their experiences to grow together as a community of faith.

Please know of my prayers for you as you celebrate this great milestone in your long and privileged history.

With kindest personal regards, I am

Faithfully in Christ,

Most Reverend William E. Lori
Archbishop of Baltimore

APOSTOLIC NUNCIATURE
UNITED STATES OF AMERICA

Prot. N. 8638/19

June 30, 2019

Your Excellency,

As the Diocese of Richmond celebrates its bicentennial, it is my special privilege to convey to Your Excellency and to your family of faith the warm greetings, heartfelt congratulations, and paternal affection of His Holiness Pope Francis.

The Holy Father gladly unites himself with you and your clergy, religious and laity in giving thanks to Almighty God for the abundant blessings of these two centuries, especially for the zeal with which the Gospel has been proclaimed and for the generosity of countless souls whose sacrifices have paved the way for the milestone you are marking today, including those early missionaries, who planted the seeds of faith.

His Holiness prays that the commemoration of this anniversary will inspire in all of the faithful a renewed awareness of their baptismal dignity as sons and daughters of God, recommitting themselves to the pursuit of authentic holiness in daily life and work. Indeed, it is the Holy Father's fervent hope that many young people will hear and answer the Lord's call to follow Him in the priesthood and consecrated life.

An anniversary such as this provides an opportunity to be grateful for the blessings of the past and the opportunity for the Church in Richmond to renew its commitment to be in a permanent state of mission, something heartily recommended by Pope Francis in *Evangelii Gaudium.* It is my fervent hope that renewed by these celebrations, the clergy and people of the Diocese of Richmond may be transformed into joyful, missionary disciples.

Commending the Diocese of Richmond to the maternal protection of Mary Immaculate and to the prayerful intercession of its patron, Saint Vincent de Paul, our Holy Father cordially imparts his Apostolic Blessing as a pledge of joy and strength in the Lord Jesus Christ.

Offering my own personal best wishes, I remain,

Sincerely yours in Christ,

+ Christophe Pierre

Archbishop Christophe Pierre
Apostolic Nuncio

My dear Brothers and Sisters:

Praised be Jesus Christ!

I am filled with joy and offer my heartiest congratulations to all in the Diocese of Richmond as together we mark the Bicentennial Anniversary of our founding as the Catholic Diocese of Richmond in the Commonwealth of Virginia.

The story of the growth and development in the eastern region of the United States stretches back to a time when the seeds of faith were planted at a great cost in the late 16th century by the Spanish Jesuits, followed by Catholics who settled in Jamestown, Norfolk, and Northern Virginia. The history recorded at that time reveals a story of the faithful proclamation of the Gospel and the extraordinary courage of our saintly ancestors.

We give thanks to God for their perseverance and all those who came after them to settle and develop this land. We owe our deepest gratitude to those faithful and devoted souls who, in their great charity, brought forth the magnificent life of this Church we celebrate today.

I commend you to the care of our Blessed Mother Mary, the Immaculate Conception, and our diocesan patron, Saint Vincent de Paul, as we mark the historic foundation of the Diocese of Richmond on July 11, 1820. May God give us peace and wisdom to pass the faith we treasure to a new generation.

Filled with confidence in the blessings of Almighty God, I remain

Sincerely, in Christ

Most Reverend Barry C. Knestout
Bishop of Richmond

Given at the Pastoral Center
July 11, 2019

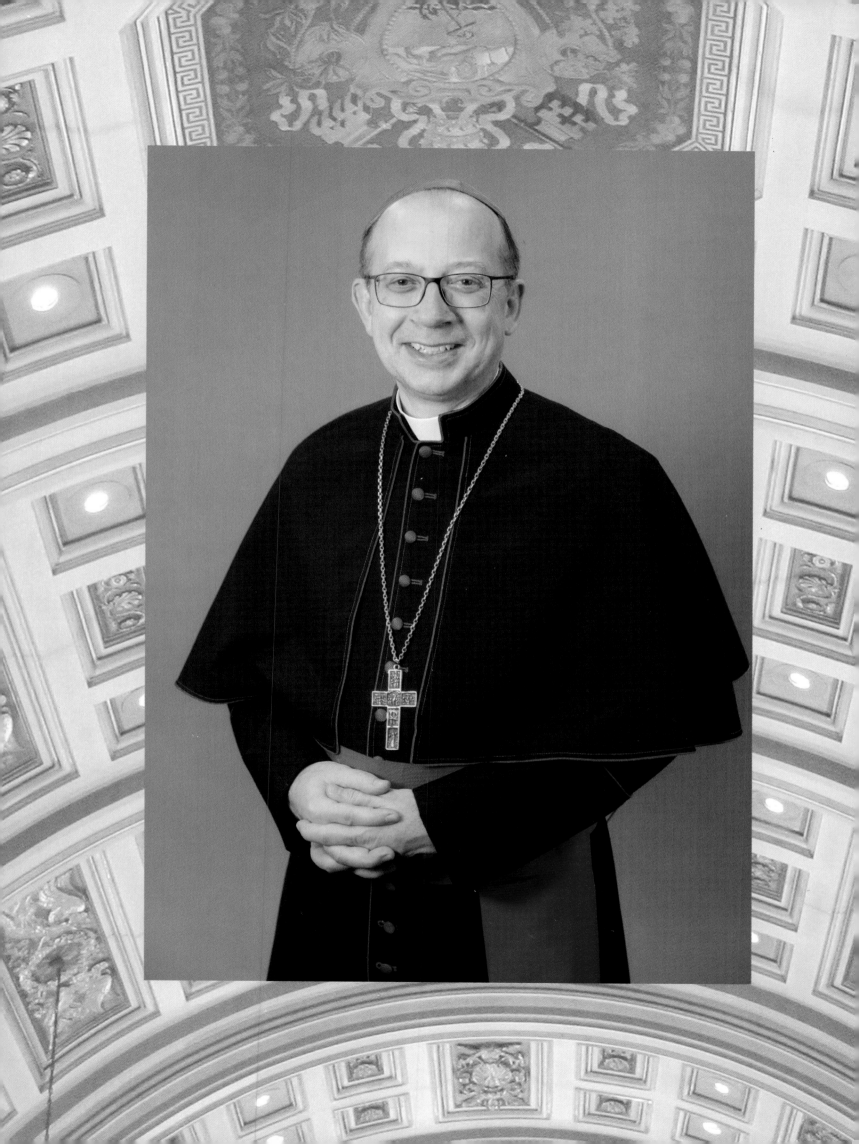

THE CATHOLIC DIOCESE OF
Richmond

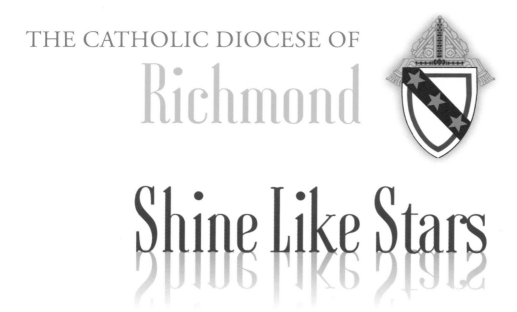

Shine Like Stars

History sections by Anthony E. Marques

Parish sections edited by Anne Edwards & Ann Niermeyer

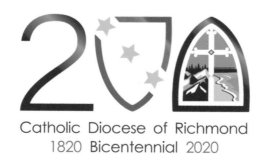

Catholic Diocese of Richmond
1820 Bicentennial 2020

Éditions du Signe
2019

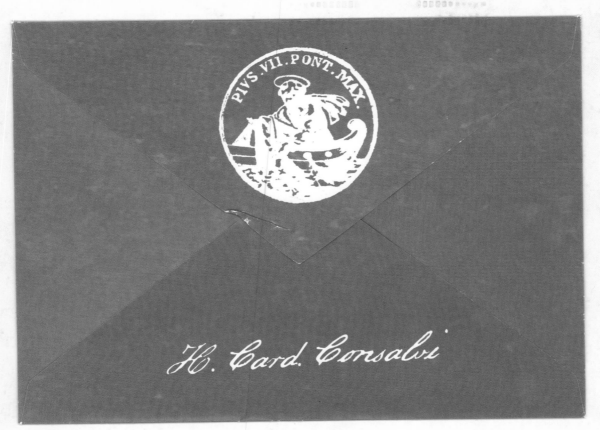

Reproduction of the founding document of the Diocese of Richmond, 1820

Taking Root: A Diocese Established and Suspended (1817-1841)

The establishment of a formal Church structure in Virginia, under the leadership of a bishop, took place while the United States was still a young country and a missionary territory. America had just turned forty-four years old, and James Monroe (1758–1831), the last Founding Father, was president, when Pope Pius VII erected the Diocese of Richmond on July 11, 1820.

Formed from the Archdiocese of Baltimore, which originally had jurisdiction over the entire United States (1789–1808), Richmond was the nation's seventh diocese. (The Diocese of Charleston in South Carolina was created on the same day.) The Richmond Diocese encompassed the Commonwealth of Virginia, which at that time extended from the Atlantic Ocean to the Ohio River. Approximately one thousand Catholics inhabited this massive area.[13] Just two years later, however, Baltimore once more governed Richmond, which remained a separate diocese, albeit without its own bishop, for the next two decades (1822–1841).

Insurrection in Norfolk

In 1817, lay trustees from the Catholic community in Norfolk sent a delegate to Rome to request the establishment of a diocese in Virginia. This maneuver was successful because the trustees' petition deliberately misrepresented the situation in Norfolk, and because Vatican officials were ignorant of American geography. The trustees contended that the distance between Norfolk and Baltimore was so great that their community's pastoral care was being neglected, and that they did not have a priest who could speak English well. They also pressed for the right to appoint their own pastors.[14]

TRANSLATION OF THE APOSTOLIC BRIEF FOUNDING THE DIOCESE OF RICHMOND[1]

To Our Beloved Son Patrick Kelly, Priest of the Diocese of Ossory in Ireland, elected as the New Bishop of Richmond.

Pope Pius VII

Beloved Son, Greeting and Apostolic blessing

Among the multiple and weightiest responsibilities of Our Apostolate, that which concerns the status of Dioceses spread throughout the whole world holds no small part. For indeed it pertains to our supreme power and judgment to regulate them and to set or change their boundaries as We determine leads to the benefit of the faithful, taking into account the times and circumstances. Since now for a long time it has been implored of Us that the State of Virginia in North America, which was enclosed in the Diocese of Baltimore, be erected into a new Diocese separated from it, and since it seems to be very expedient for the extinction of the schisms which have arisen in it that a Bishop of its own be established in it; even more because the State of Maryland, which is subject to the Archbishop of Baltimore and which is filled with a very large number of Catholics, furnishes the same Archbishop with such ample matter for pastoral zeal that he can with difficulty extend his care to other States, We, upon the advice of Our Venerable Brothers the Cardinals of the Holy Roman Church set over the affairs of the Propagation of the Faith, have established and decreed that, after the separation of the said State from the Diocese of Baltimore, a new Episcopal Church, suffragan of Baltimore, should be erected at Richmond, which is the capital city of Virginia, and that it should embrace the whole State of Virginia, not including [the District of] Columbia, as by Apostolic Authority and the tenor of the present decree We separate and erect it as a new Episcopal Church of Richmond, suffragan of Baltimore, with all the rights and prerogatives belonging to these kinds of Churches according to the Sacred Canons.

1 Rev. Msgr. Robert Trisco, professor emeritus of Church history at the Catholic University of America (Washington, DC), made this translation (2018), which is based on the collated transcript that he also prepared.

We also, intending with paternal and solicitous zeal, in which no one besides Ourselves could or can inject himself, to provide quickly and felicitously for the aforesaid new Episcopal Church thus erected, after a diligent and fruitful deliberation that We have had with Our aforesaid Venerable Brothers the Cardinals of the Holy Roman Church in charge of the affairs of the Propagation of the Faith about appointing a person for the same new Church, have directed the eyes of Our mind at last to You, who have been procreated from a legitimate matrimony and are also of legitimate age and of whose purity of life, probity of conduct, as well as piety, assiduity, and learning and zeal for the Christian Religion and the Catholic Faith, and foresight in spiritual matters and caution in temporal matters trustworthy testimonies are furnished, all these things having been considered with due reflection, absolving you and believing that you will be absolved from any sentences of excommunication, suspension, or interdict, and from any other ecclesiastical sentences, censures, and penalties imposed by law, or by man on any occasion, or serially, We provide this same new Episcopal Church of Richmond with your person acceptable to Us and the named Cardinals because of the claim of your merits. And by the advice of the same Brothers, by the afore-mentioned authority and tenor, We set you over it as Bishop and Pastor, fully committing to you the care, government, and administration of the Church of Richmond in spiritual and temporal matters, trusting in Him, who gives grace and bestows gifts, that as the Lord guides your actions the aforesaid Church of Richmond will be beneficially and prosperously directed though your diligence of foresight and zeal and will experience pleasing increases in spiritual and temporal matters. Accepting therefore with ready devotion of spirit the Lord's yoke laid on your shoulders, may you so faithfully and prudently carry out the aforesaid care and administration that the Church of Richmond may rejoice   that it has been committed to a prudent governor and productive administrator. And may you, besides the reward of eternal retribution, more copiously merit to attain therefrom also Our and the Apostolic See's blessing and favor.

Given at Rome at St. Mary Major under the ring of the Fisherman, the Eleventh Day of July in the year 1820, the twenty-first of Our Pontificate.

H. Card. Consalvi[2]

2 - Hercules Cardinalis Consalvi. The name refers to Ercole (Latin: Hercules) Consalvi, a deacon and cardinal of the Church. At the time the Diocese of Richmond was founded, he was the secretary of state (1814–1823), and later became the pro-prefect (1822–1824) and then prefect (1824) of Propaganda Fidei. (Cardinal Francesco Fontana was the prefect of Propaganda Fidei [1818–1822] when the diocese was founded.)

*Archbishop Ambrose Maréchal
of Baltimore, 1764–1828*

Archbishop Ambrose Maréchal of Baltimore (1764–1828) vehemently opposed the creation of a new diocese on several grounds: it was unnecessary because he could feasibly travel by ship between Norfolk and Baltimore; it was unsustainable because the Catholic population in Virginia was small and poor; and it was imprudent because there was already a French émigré priest in Norfolk (who spoke passable English), whom the trustees were seeking to control. Maréchal also warned Vatican officials against setting the precedent of allowing lay Catholics in the United States to appoint their own pastors.[15]

Maréchal was unable to appease the trustees, either by meeting with them (1818) or by assigning a second, Irish priest to the area (1819). Meanwhile, the trustees procured their own priest whom they hoped to make a bishop (1818–1819). This Dominican friar, Father Thomas Carbry, ministered in Norfolk (1819–1821) despite Maréchal's prohibition against him. The dispute over lay trusteeism had now become a schism.[16]

Sacra Congregatio de Propaganda Fide (Sacred Congregation for the Propagation of the Faith), the Vatican department in charge of overseas missions, which included the United States, responded to the crisis by establishing a diocese in Virginia (1819–1820). This decision mostly favored the trustees over the archbishop of Baltimore. *Propaganda Fide* viewed the presence of a bishop in Virginia as the solution to the Norfolk Schism: a new diocese would respond to the trustees' ostensible request for better pastoral care, and a residential bishop would uphold the principle that only a bishop could appoint pastors. Although the schism was based in Norfolk, Richmond was chosen as the headquarters of the new diocese because it was the capital of Virginia.[17]

Map of Virginia around the time the Diocese of Richmond was founded, 1820

Basilica of
Saint Mary of Immaculate Conception

— Norfolk • 1791 —

The Basilica of Saint Mary of the Immaculate Conception is located in downtown Norfolk. It is the oldest parish community in the Catholic Diocese of Richmond and often referred to as "The Mother Church of Tidewater Virginia." It came into existence in 1791 as Saint Patrick Church which was two years before the establishment of the United States hierarchy and twenty-nine years before the institution of the Richmond Diocese. Its first parishioners were French Catholics, compelled to abandon their native land by the French Revolution. In a matter of years, it received some of the earliest Irish Catholic immigrants to the United States.

The original church was built in 1842 but was destroyed by fire in 1856. The present church building was erected in 1858. It was dedicated to Mary of the Immaculate Conception and was the first church to bear the name after the dogma of the Immaculate Conception by Pope Pius IX.

St. Joseph Church

African American Catholics began attending Saint Mary in 1886 where a portion of the choir loft was reserved for them. Subsequently, in 1889 the Josephites began coming from Richmond and by September of that year, Saint Joseph's Black Catholic parish was founded with the Josephites serving as priests; their mission was to serve the spiritual needs of the Black community. Seventy-two years later, 1961, Saint Joseph's was merged with Saint Mary. On November 1, 1989, the newly renovated/restored edifice was rededicated with Archbishop Pio Laghi, Apostolic Pro-Nuncio, serving as the Principal Celebrant of the Rededication Mass. Today Saint Mary is a vibrant, predominately African-American, worship community offering numerous ministries and outreach programs.

On December 8, 1991, the Church of Saint Mary of the Immaculate Conception became a Minor Basilica. The date also marked the 200th Anniversary of the church. The official proclamation was read by Apostolic Pro-Nuncio, Archbishop Agostino Cacciavillan who also served as the Principal Celebrant of the Liturgy. Being named a minor basilica is an honor given by the Pope. It becomes a place of pilgrimage and is an honorary title recognizing the distinguished nature of Saint Mary. There are 33 other minor basilicas in the United States, Saint Mary is the only one in the Commonwealth of Virginia. December 8, the Feast of the Immaculate Conception, is the main celebration at the Basilica.

Saint Paul

Beginning early in the nineteenth century when our republic was still quite young, Father Michael De Lacy accommodated a fledgling Catholic congregation by offering Mass and administering the sacraments in Portsmouth probably about 1804.

The lot on the northeast corner of High Street and Washington Street now occupied by Saint Paul Catholic Church was purchased on March 19, 1810. It became the site on which five successive Catholic Churches dedicated to Saint Paul were constructed over the years. The first church was completed before 1815 with funds bequeathed by Patrick Robertson, a bakehouse owner. A second, larger church was dedicated in July 1831. Between 1839 and 1844, interior walls of the new structure

were frescoed. However, again the congregation outgrew this building, and it was replaced by a larger one. The third church was completed in 1853 at a cost of $18,000 with subsequent improvements raising the sum to $23,000. The first Mass in the third Saint Paul's was offered February 13, 1853. Unfortunately, in April 1859 the church was destroyed by fire, a disaster for the congregation.

Work on the fourth church was begun in 1860 after the marsh west of the site was filled. The foundation was laid fronting Washington Street, but also had an entrance on High Street. During the Civil War, services were held in various locations, as well as in the unfinished structure, and when the war ended, work on this larger,

lovelier edifice was resumed. The new Saint Paul's was dedicated October 4, 1868. Sadly, just as the addition of a rectory, school, convent, and brothers' residence was completed, fire again destroyed Saint Paul's church and rectory on March 29, 1897. Mass was celebrated in Saint Joseph Academy for seven years.

On February 2, 1898 ground was broken for the fifth and present St. Paul's. Larger and more elaborate than the others, it was dedicated on November 12, 1905, by Bishop Augustine Van de Vyver, Sixth Bishop of Richmond. A new rectory was completed in 1914. In 1955, the Golden Jubilee year, rebuilding the organ and repainting the interior were completed.

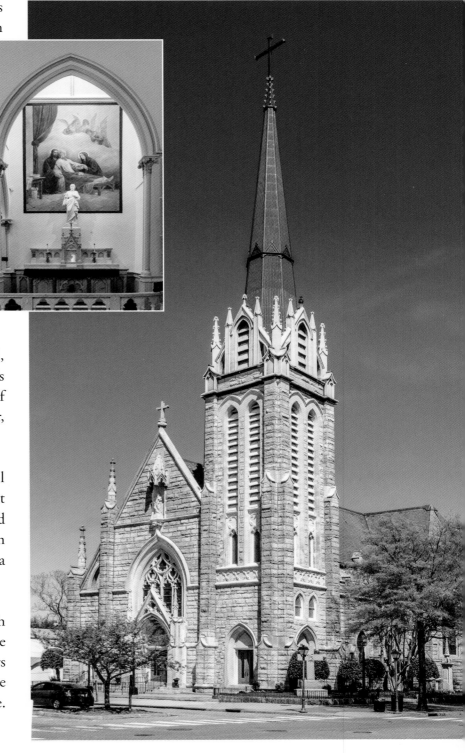

More work included sandblasting the exterior in 1976, installing a new organ in 1983, and restoring the murals in 1988. Recently, the church underwent extensive roof repairs, the restoration of the marble of the high altar, and interior restoration of plaster and painting.

Saint Paul provides parishioners and guests from all over Hampton Roads with a connection to the earliest Catholics in Virginia through its rich history and architecture. In 2002, the current church was placed on the National Register of Historic Places and the Virginia Landmark Register.

In Spring of 2005, Saint Paul was clustered with Church of the Holy Angels in Portsmouth, Church of the Resurrection in Portsmouth, and Saint Mary in Bowers Hill, Chesapeake, and shares priests and staff with the other Cluster Parishes of Portsmouth and Chesapeake.

Bishop Patrick Kelly

Father Patrick Kelly (1779–1829), a priest of the Diocese of Ossory in Kilkenny, Ireland, was appointed the first bishop of Richmond in 1820. He was the president of St. John's Seminary in Birchfield, Ireland at the time.[1] The trustees had asked for an Irish bishop so that he could better minister to the Norfolk Catholic community, which was composed of Irish and French immigrants. Presumably in response to this request, *Propaganda Fidei* recommended to Pope Pius VII that he name Kelly as bishop of Richmond. Kelly was the first in a line of Irish-born clerics to serve the Diocese of Richmond as bishops or priests. Through the years, these men eased the persistent shortage of native priests in the diocese.

Resolving the Norfolk Schism (1820-1822)

After being consecrated bishop in Dublin (1820), Kelly traveled to America. He went first to Baltimore, where a belligerent Archbishop Maréchal used his meeting with the new bishop to condemn the establishment of a diocese in Virginia. Kelly left Baltimore and arrived in Norfolk on January 19, 1821. Once there, he appeared to shift sides in regard to the schism. Eventually the more vocal partisans left Norfolk and the dispute mostly died of its own accord (1821). All the while, Kelly received no income from the Catholic community, and had to resort to teaching in order to support himself.[2]

Propaganda Fide, realizing that Catholics in Virginia could not support their own diocese, had Bishop Kelly transferred to the Diocese of Waterford and Lismore in Ireland. Kelly left Virginia in June or July 1822, having never visited Richmond. He had assigned five priests to lead four main Catholic communities in the diocese: Martinsburg, Richmond, Petersburg, and Norfolk. These congregations were mostly composed of poor, working-class immigrants.[3]

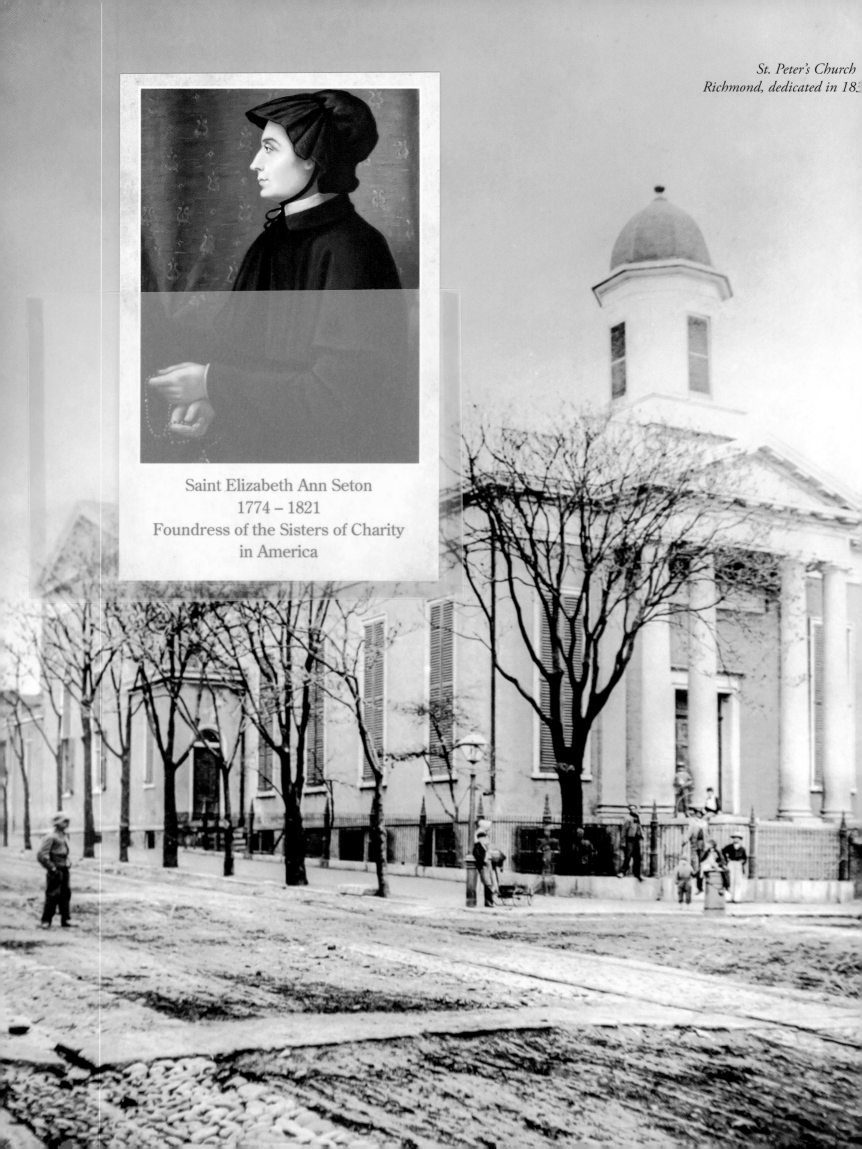

St. Peter's Church
Richmond, dedicated in 183[

Saint Elizabeth Ann Seton
1774 – 1821
Foundress of the Sisters of Charity
in America

Daughters of Charity

*Father Timothy O'Brien
(1791–1855)*

The Diocese Suspended
(1822–1841)

With no residential bishop in place for the Richmond Diocese, the archbishop of Baltimore administered the territory, which continued to be a separate diocese, for the next 19 years (1822–1841). During this period, the bulk of the small Catholic population in Virginia shifted from Norfolk to Richmond.

The construction of St. Peter's Church (1834) in the shadow of the Virginia State Capitol raised the profile of the Catholic community in Richmond. This church eventually became the cathedral of the diocese. Father Timothy O'Brien (1791–1855), a native Irishman and an enterprising priest of the Archdiocese of Baltimore, was responsible for the building feat. But his accomplishment stirred controversy, as O'Brien, who ministered in Richmond for twenty-two years (1832–1850), became embroiled in a financial dispute with future bishops of the diocese over St. Peter's and its property.[4]

A few months after the dedication of St. Peter's, the first religious sisters arrived in the diocese at O'Brien's invitation: the Daughters of Charity (then called the Sisters of Charity

of St. Joseph). This order, based in Emmitsburg, Maryland, was founded by Elizabeth Ann Seton (1774–1821), the first American-born saint to be canonized (1975). The sisters opened St. Joseph's Orphan Asylum and Free School in Richmond (1834), which O'Brien had founded.[5] The contribution of the Sisters of Charity was the first of many that women religious would make to the Diocese of Richmond in the fields of education and healthcare. Over time, the sisters' work helped Catholics, who were often hampered by low socio-economic status and religious bigotry, to enter the middle class and to participate more fully in Virginia society.

Wheat Among Weeds:
Challenges and Changes
(1841–1888)

Pope Gregory XVI restored the Richmond Diocese to independent status in 1841. This decision inaugurated a new era for the Church in Virginia, which included territorial changes and the ravages of the nation's bloodiest war.

Saint Peter

The founding of the first church in Richmond can be traced to when Father Jean DuBois (later the third Bishop of New York) visited Richmond in 1791, carrying letters of introduction from the Marquis de Lafayette to James Monroe, who had just left the Senate to practice law in Virginia's capital. DuBois was graciously received and celebrated Mass in the homes of Richmond's few Catholics.

Mass continued to be celebrated in private homes until 1815, when the Rockett's Chapel, also known as the Sailor's Chapel for its proximity to the James River port facilities, was leased. The Diocese of Richmond was erected in 1820, but its first bishop, Patrick Kelly, found that decision premature and returned to Ireland, leaving the diocese to be administered by the Archbishop of Baltimore. In 1825, a new chapel was constructed at Fourth and I (now Marshall) Streets by Father Thomas Hore, on land bequeathed to the Church by Joseph Gallego, a local merchant.

Father Timothy O'Brien purchased the land at the current location of Eighth and Grace Streets to construct "an ornament to the City." On May 25, 1834, Saint Peter Catholic Church was dedicated, becoming the first Catholic Church in Richmond. After Saint John Episcopal Church on Church Hill, the structure is the second oldest church in the city. The early congregation of Saint Peter consisted mostly of Irish immigrants who worked on the canal. Saint Peter served as the Cathedral of the Catholic Diocese of Richmond until 1906, when the Cathedral of the Sacred Heart was consecrated.

Among the luminaries who worshiped at Saint Peter are John Banister Tabb, the Civil War poet whose thirty-eight books comprised the collection of Richmond's first public library.

President John Tyler's second wife worshiped and was buried at Saint Peter Church, and her daughter was married in the Church. Saint John Neumann ministered to German immigrants in the basement of Saint Peter.

The original structure was enlarged between 1854-1855, adding the front balconies and altar. Portions of the original organ, dating to the 1830s, remain in service today. Paintings purchased by Bishop McGill in Rome, where he was in attendance for Pope Pius IX's papal bull "Ineffabilis Deus," setting forth the doctrine of the Immaculate Conception, still hang in the church today.

Renovations in 1923 added the marble flooring and steps to the Sanctuary and rebuilt the organ. The new stained-glass windows and Stations of the Cross date to 1949. The most recent renovation was coordinated by Father Gino Rossi in 2016. The desk of Richmond's fourth bishop, James Gibbons, who became Cardinal Archbishop of Baltimore, was brought up from the basement offices to the narthex. The church is listed on the National Register of Historic Places and the Virginia Landmarks Register.

The lower level of Saint Peter's has served as the site for innumerable missions. In December 1834, three sisters from Mother Seton's Sisters of Charity of Saint Joseph (which became the Daughters of Charity of Saint Vincent de Paul in 1850) began teaching classes there in what became Virginia's first Catholic school. Another school, this one for boys, operated from the site, except during the Civil War years, until 1873. From 1843 to 1848, following an organizational mission led by Saint John Neumann at Saint Peter's, the German congregation worshiped in the basement. Saint Joseph's on First Street sprang from a community that worshiped here from 1879 to 1885. The pattern repeated in the modern era as a Korean congregation worshiped in the basement from 1983 to 1986, when the parish of Saint Kim Taegon opened in its permanent location.

Saint Peter Church remains active in its downtown neighborhood community, founding the Winter Cots" program, known today as CARITAS (Congregations Around Richmond To Assure Shelter), and providing emergency rent, medication, transportation, and utilities to those in need.

It is as true today as when it was proclaimed by Father Joseph Magri on the 125th anniversary of Saint Peter's founding: "Hallowed by the feet of saintly men and saintly women, Saint Peter is a house of God, a gate of heaven."

CHAPTER III

Bishop Richard V. Whelan

Father Richard V. Whelan (1809–1874) was named Richmond's second bishop in 1841. He was the first of four Baltimore priests to head the diocese. At the time of his appointment, Whelan was an itinerant priest in what was then northern Virginia (the present-day northeast panhandle of West Virginia).

A Missionary Church and the New Diocese of Wheeling (1841-1850)

A connection was forged between two missionary saints and the Diocese of Richmond during Whelan's time as bishop. In 1842, Father John Nepomucene Neumann (1811–1860), a Redemptorist priest from what is today the Czech Republic, preached an eight-day mission to German Catholics in the basement of St. Peter's Cathedral in Richmond.[1] Neumann, a devoted pastor to immigrants, later became the bishop of Philadelphia (1852), a champion of Catholic schools, and the first American bishop to be canonized (1977). The congregation that heard Neumann preach went on to form St. Mary's parish for German Catholics (1848), one of the few ethnic parishes in the Richmond Diocese.

The second missionary saint became the patron of the diocese during Whelan's episcopate: Vincent de Paul (1581–1660).[2] This French priest's care for the poor, which included ministering to galley slaves, co-founding the Daughters of Charity, and establishing the Congregation of the Mission (Vincentians)—a religious order dedicated to evangelizing rural areas—made him an apt saint to intercede for the Church of Richmond. Numerous parishes, schools, and other institutions in the diocese were later named in honor of Vincent de Paul.

One of these institutions was St. Vincent's Seminary and College in Richmond, which Whelan founded soon after

his arrival (1841). On January 6, 1842, Whelan ordained a seminarian of St. Vincent's to the priesthood, making this the first ordination in the diocese. The priest was Father James Hewitt, who died within a year. There were other priest alumni of the seminary, but it closed several years later because of financial difficulties (1846).[3]

The Diocese of Richmond experienced modest growth under Whelan, as advances in transportation during the Industrial Revolution gave rise to communities in central Virginia. St. Francis Xavier parish (1843) in Lynchburg, later renamed Holy Cross, expanded as Irish workers came to build the section of the James River and Kanawha Canal that joined the city to Richmond (1835–1840). (The canal was meant to connect Richmond to the Ohio River at what was then Virginia's western border, but the project was only partially complete when it ended in 1851. It subsequently became a railroad.) Farther north, St. Francis of Assisi parish (1845) in Staunton grew more quickly as the Louisa (later Virginia Central) and Blue Ridge Railroads linked the Shenandoah Valley to Richmond (1850–1858). Priests in central Virginia were circuit riders who covered multiple parishes, continuing the missionary lifestyle that Whelan himself had led earlier in his career.[4]

Father John Lynch

In 1846, Bishop Whelan moved from Richmond to Wheeling, a transportation hub on the route from the East Coast to the Midwest. Seeing many Irish and Italian immigrants come to the region to build the Baltimore and Ohio Railroad (1848–1852), he hoped that Catholics would rapidly populate the area. Whelan subsequently recommended that the large and unwieldy Diocese of Richmond be divided and that he govern the western territory. In 1850, he was named the first bishop of Wheeling, a new diocese comprising the portion of Virginia west of the Allegheny Mountains (present-day southwest Virginia and most of West Virginia).[5]

Holy Cross, Lynchburg

THE JAMES RIVER AND KANAWHA CANAL, RICHMOND, VIRGINIA.—[SKETCHED BY J. R. HAMILTON.]

Saint Joseph

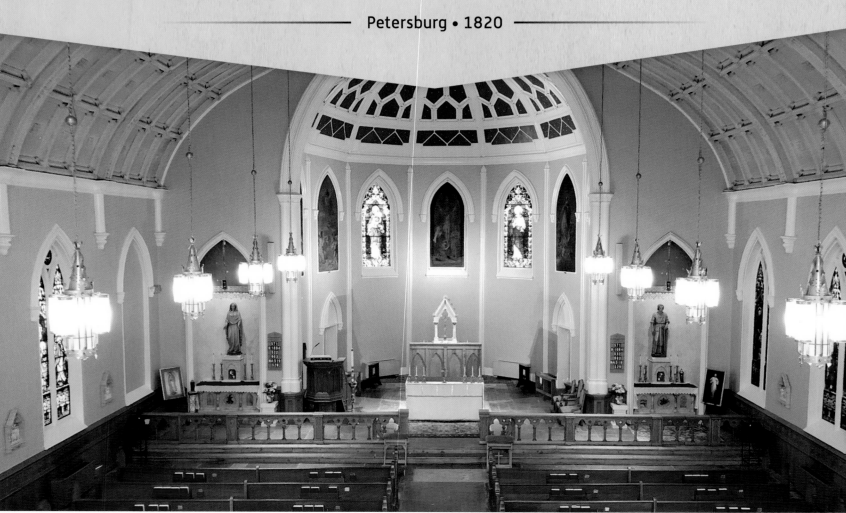

Saint Joseph Parish traces its origin to the year 1820, when Mass was first celebrated in Petersburg in a house at the corner of Short Market and High Streets with approximately 50 people attending. The small Catholic community in Petersburg was a mission of the Baltimore Diocese and had no resident priest.

Land was purchased and the first church was built on the corner of Market and Washington Streets, under the supervision of Reverend Timothy O'Brien, who had also overseen the building of Saint Peter in Richmond in 1834. Saint Joseph was dedicated by Rt. Rev. Richard V. Whelan, Second Bishop of Richmond, on January 23, 1842.

It was not until 1845 that Saint Joseph had its first permanent pastor, Reverend David Whelan, brother of Bishop Whelan. During his pastorate, the rectory (now St. Joseph Parish Center) was built on North Market Street. From 1849-50 there was again no resident priest and Bishop Whelan himself often came, after saying Mass in Richmond. On Sunday mornings, Bishop Whelan, both from a spirit of mortification and a desire to save expenses, would walk all the way to Petersburg, where he would say a second Mass.

In 1856, the beloved Reverend Thomas Mulvey was transferred to Petersburg. A native of Ireland, Reverend Mulvey was one of the heroes of the Siege of Petersburg, during which he fearlessly

ministered to the dying in the city hospitals and on the battlefields. In 1865, he was named to be Vicar General of the Diocese of Richmond, the affairs of which he administered from 1869 – 70, when Bishop McGill was attending the First Vatican Council.

Saint Joseph Catholic Cemetery was purchased, and in 1877 dedicated by Reverend Francis Janssens, Vicar General of the Diocese. On January 17, 1876, Saint Joseph School was opened on Market Street in the charge of the Daughters of Charity of Saint Vincent de Paul.

In September 1885, the Reverend James T. O'Ferrell was assigned pastor of Saint Joseph, where he remained until October 1913, when having been created Vicar General of the Diocese in June, he was made rector of the Cathedral of the Sacred Heart in Richmond. During Reverend O'Ferrell's pastorate, the new Saint Joseph Church was built on the same site at the corner of Washington and Market Streets. Its cornerstone was laid on July 1, 1894, and the completed edifice was dedicated on January 12, 1896, by Bishop Augustine Van de Vyver of Richmond.

Reverend Martin J. Haier, pastor from 1913 to 1934, built Saint Joseph School on Franklin Street to replace the structure on Market Street; it was dedicated in April 1917.

During Reverend Kilgalen's pastorate, a bequest from Richard M. Lavelle made possible the construction of Lavelle Hall. In 1981, Reverend P. Francis Quinn acquired the old A&P grocery store on Washington Street for the use as a parish social hall (later named Quinn Hall).

In 1988, during renovations and remodeling of the church, a Commons area was added to the east side of the church. In March 2011, a fire destroyed Quinn Hall. A new parish hall, relocated behind the Church, was dedicated on August 20, 2017. Efforts were then undertaken to restore the interior of Saint Joseph Church.

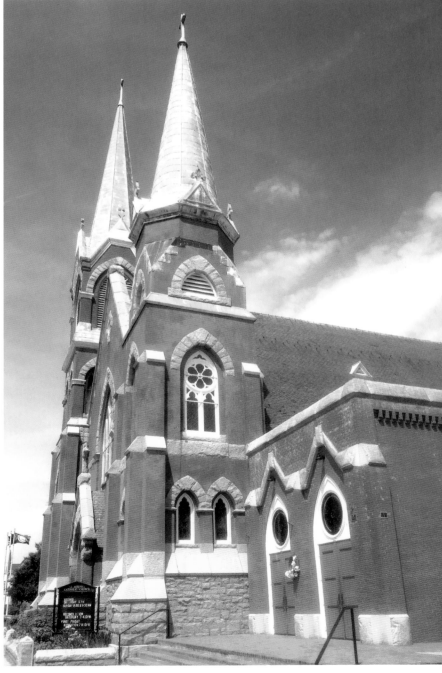

Saint Francis of Assisi

Saint Francis of Assisi Parish began as the Staunton Mission in 1844. It was officially established in 1845 by Reverend Daniel Downey, the first pastor. Church construction was complete in 1851. It was brick, Southern Colonial style with green shutters. The inside was classic revival and was heated by two wood stoves. The church was dedicated in May 1851 by Rt. Rev. John McGill, Third Bishop of Richmond.

Saint Francis School was established by Reverend Downey in 1856. In 1880, a convent was built for the Sisters of Charity, who had been asked to take over teaching duties in 1878. In addition to teaching at the School, the Sisters of Charity would go to Harrisonburg, Waynesboro, and Lexington for Sunday School, as well as Western State to visit patients.

In 1885, plans were drawn up by Reverend John McVerry and the parishioners for a larger church building. The cornerstone was placed on September 10, 1895 and blessed by Bishop Augustine Van de Vyver while the choir sang "Veni Creator Spiritus." The Cornerstone Ceremony concluded with a selection of Mozart's "Twelfth Mass" played by the Stonewall Brigade Band.

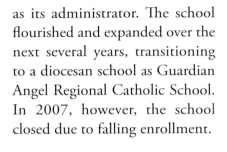

The Gothic revival style church was designed by parishioner Thomas J. Collins and his son, Samuel, and built by a team under the direction of Montague Payne. It was built over the original foundation and was made of green limestone with tan limestone trim and copper finials. The new building was dedicated in 1897, accompanied again by the choir and the Stonewall Brigade Band, which is still in existence today.

The large gilded crucifix hanging above the altar was carved from olivewood in Italy and was commissioned by Monsignor William Meredith in the 1920's. It includes a Latin inscription which translates to "Behold the wood of the Cross on which hung our salvation: Come let us Worship," as well as the traditional symbols of the four Evangelists. The cast-iron bell above the choir door weighs 2500 pounds - so heavy that when a small boy tried to ring it after it was installed, he was lifted off the floor.

Reverend McVerry lived to be the oldest priest in Virginia of his time and one of the oldest in the United States. He died in 1930 at the age of 85. He was interred at Saint Francis in honor of his wishes to be buried "between the church and the school" which he built.

In 1971, Saint Francis School was closed. Several extensive renovations were made to the church. The original slate roofing was replaced with copper roofing, plastering and painting were done inside the church, a heating and cooling system was added, the lighting and sound systems were upgraded, the sanctuary floor was raised, a new altar was installed, and the adoration chapel was restored.

In 1995, Guardian Angel Academy, a private Catholic school, opened for elementary grades through high school with Mrs. Mary Thompson as its administrator. The school flourished and expanded over the next several years, transitioning to a diocesan school as Guardian Angel Regional Catholic School. In 2007, however, the school closed due to falling enrollment.

The parish expanded the buildings and grounds around the church with the addition of the parish social hall, Assisi Hall, in 2004. When it was observed that the green limestone was beginning to crumble, the extensive project of replacing the exterior stone of the church began. Construction was completed in 2016.

Saint Mary Mother of God

— Wytheville • 1845 —

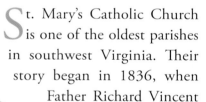

St. Mary's Catholic Church is one of the oldest parishes in southwest Virginia. Their story began in 1836, when Father Richard Vincent Whelan, the pastor of several parishes in the Loudon County area, first visited what was known at the time as "The Wilderness:" the southwestern corner of Virginia and the southern territory of what is now West Virginia. In fact, for a long time, it was the only Catholic parish between Lynchburg, Virginia, and Knoxville, Tennessee. The state of Virginia became a separate diocese in December 1840 and the Rev. R.V. Whelan was named Bishop. He presided over the Diocese from Richmond. His first official act was to appeal to the Church in Europe for aid. He received a good response, and Wytheville was one of the mission churches that benefited. In 1842, Bishop Whelan came to Wytheville for the first time and found 14 Catholics. He founded a mission and baptized several people.

In 1842, Bishop Whelan returned and on August 10, 1842 he blessed the new church, which was dedicated to Mary, Mother of God. The small congregation had built a wooden structure on the cemetery grounds on Peppers Ferry Road. The land for the church had been donated by Capt. John P. Mathews and his wife, Malvina Smith. Shortly after making their donation, they both converted to the Catholic faith. Located on Main Street, the church has been a fixture in the small town of Wytheville for well over one-and-a-half centuries.

Father Edward Fox, who was based in Lynchburg, became the first pastor for the entire region. He made the 200-mile trip to Wytheville on horseback. Father Edward Fox became the first pastor of the church in 1844. In 1846, he was transferred to Lynchburg, but he continued to serve St. Mary's, traveling 150 miles by stagecoach! He served until his death in 1850 bringing many new converts to the church. Rev. Thomas Mulvey replaced Father Fox in Lynchburg and attended to the needs of St. Mary's until 1851.

The church buildings that comprise St. Mary's today are a melding of old and new. The portion that faces East Main Street is referred to as "Old St. Mary's Church" and is comprised of the original church and attached rectory. The buildings were constructed by Father Raymond J. Judge and funded by Mrs. Constance D. Blair in 1935-37 at a cost of approximately $13,000.

In the late 1980s, when Father James Grealish served as pastor, an addition was constructed to the rear of the church. Facing Monroe Street, the addition provided a new worship space, offices and classrooms. The new structure was dedicated by Bishop Walter F. Sullivan on December 15, 1991.

St. Mary the Mother of God isn't the only Catholic institution of historical significance in Wytheville. Villa Maria Academy, a Catholic boarding school that operated from 1902-1944, was also located in the town. In addition to the school, the facility was home to a convent, the Sisters of the Visitation. The Academy survived a devastating fire in 1920 with the help of the people of Wytheville, some of whom offered their homes to the displaced students and nuns. In 1923, classes resumed at Villa Maria, operating until 1944, when the boarding school closed permanently due to a lack of sisters available to teach classes. A grotto of the Virgin Mary and the Baby Jesus belonging to the Academy now stands in St. Mary's Catholic Cemetery, marking the Tomb of the Deceased Nuns of the Visitation of Villa Maria Academy.

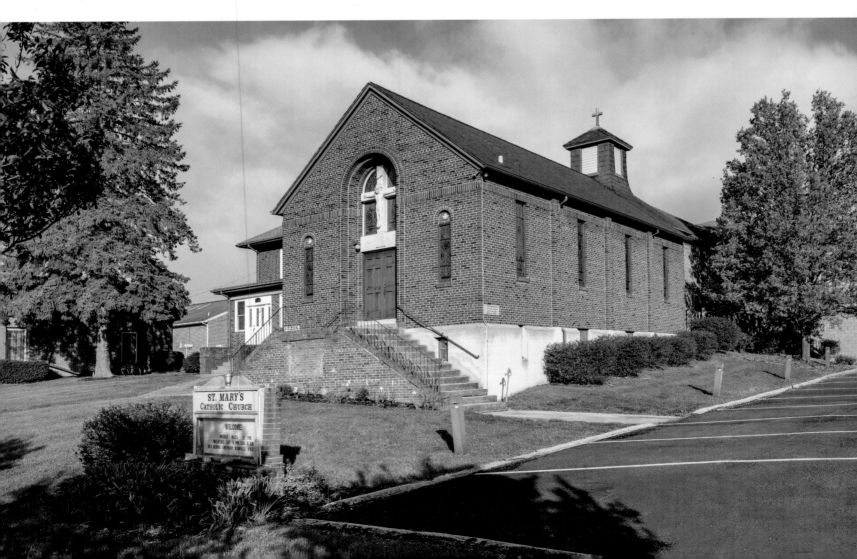

Bishop John McGill

With Whelan's transfer to Wheeling, John McGill (1809–1872) was appointed the third bishop of Richmond in 1850. McGill, who was born in Philadelphia, was a priest of the Diocese of Louisville (formerly Bardstown), Kentucky. In Richmond, he assumed responsibility for a diocese with seven thousand Catholics, ten churches, and eight priests. McGill's long episcopate was filled with adversity: the rise of the anti-Catholic "Know-Nothing" movement, a yellow fever epidemic in Tidewater, and the horrific bloodshed of the Civil War.

"Know-Nothings," Yellow Fever, and the Civil War (1850-1872)

The Know-Nothing party (ca. 1850) took its name from the reply its members were to give when asked about their membership in this quasi-secret organization: "I know nothing." The American Party, as it was formally called later on (1855), spread throughout the United States, and falsely accused Catholic immigrants of seeking to overturn religious liberty. In Virginia, stalled public works—projects that typically employed immigrants—strengthened the movement's influence. Bishop McGill, who was a skilled apologist, vigorously defended the Catholic Church against the Know-Nothings (1854–1855).[1]

While the Know-Nothing controversy was in full swing, an outbreak of yellow fever devastated Norfolk and Portsmouth in the summer of 1855, claiming three thousand lives. Two priests, Father Matthew O'Keefe (1828–1906) in Norfolk and Father Francis Devlin (1813–1855) in Portsmouth, courageously alleviated the sufferings of both Catholic and Protestant victims. O'Keefe was infected twice and survived; Devlin died from the pestilence. In Norfolk, Ann Behan Plume Herron (1802–1855) made her home into a makeshift hospital, where she nursed her slaves. Herron donated her house to the Daughters of Charity before

Priest celebrating Mass during the Civil War. Faith was a motivating force for soldiers during the war.

succumbing to the disease herself. This was the first Catholic hospital in the diocese, which was incorporated as the Hospital of St. Vincent de Paul (today DePaul Medical Center) in 1856. All of these heroic acts of charity lessened anti-Catholic bigotry in the region.[2]

Father Matthew O'Keefe

St. Vincent de Paul Hospital

The Civil War erupted several years later (1861–1865). During this most violent conflict in American history, the territory of the Diocese of Richmond was the heart of the breakaway country. In fact, St. Peter's Cathedral was located just one block from the Capitol of the Confederate States of America. Like most Catholics in the South, Bishop McGill was an ardent supporter of the Southern cause. Few Catholics in Virginia owned slaves but supported others' right to do so. McGill did not regard slavery as a grave sin, and he blamed the abolitionist movement for the breakup of the Union. Numerous popes, beginning in 1435, had condemned racial slavery, or at least some aspects of it, but their pronouncements went unheeded.[3] Leading up to the Civil War, American bishops were divided along regional lines over the issue of slavery.[4]

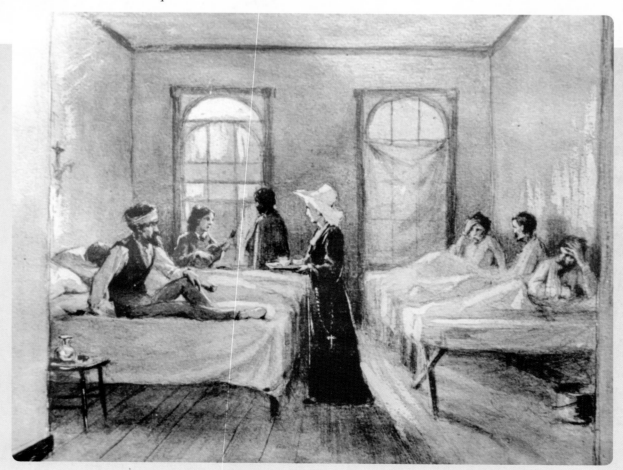

Richmond during the Civil War

Once the Civil War began, McGill was unable to visit or even govern parts of the Diocese of Richmond (1861–1865). Union forces occupied cities such as Martinsburg (1861–1864)—it changed hands thirty-seven times—Norfolk (1862), and Richmond (1865). Consequently, McGill had no communication with his priests who were across battle lines.[5]

Following the Union occupation of Norfolk, Father Matthew O'Keefe suggested to Archbishop Francis Kenrick (1797–1863) of Baltimore that he administer those sections of the Diocese of Richmond that were cut off from McGill (February 1863).[6] The archbishop was already doing so in the case of Fort Monroe in Hampton. O'Keefe, although himself a Confederate loyalist, and Father Michael Ferrin, had braved gunfire to minister at the fort to Union troops who were Catholic.[7] Archbishop Kenrick then asked Redemptorists from Annapolis, Maryland to assume pastoral responsibility for the installation (November 1862).[8] Among these priests who celebrated Mass, heard confessions, and cared for the sick was Father Francis Xavier Seelos (1819–1867). Like his mentor and colleague, St. John Neumann, Seelos was a missionary (from present-day Germany). The "cheerful

St. Mary Star of the Sea, Fort Monroe

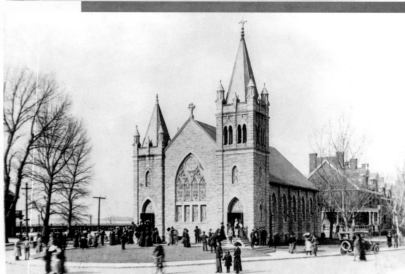

ascetic," as he was known, ministered at Fort Monroe for a brief time beginning in December 1862.[9] Seelos was beatified in 2000.

Even as the war raged and casualties mounted, parishes in the Diocese of Richmond continued normal activities such as celebrating Mass, holding meetings, and providing religious education. Few Catholic churches were damaged during the war, but the conflict still placed a strain on inhabitants of cities occupied by Union forces.[10]

The Civil War also had territorial implications for the diocese. After Virginia seceded and became part of the Confederacy (1861), the northwestern part of the commonwealth formed the new state of West Virginia and joined the Union (1863). As a result, the border of the Dioceses of Richmond and Wheeling crossed state lines (Richmond now included the northeast panhandle of West Virginia, while Wheeling encompassed southwest Virginia). This discrepancy between civil and ecclesiastical boundaries lasted until 1974.

By the end of the war, the South was devastated. Nevertheless, the image of the Church improved in Virginia and throughout the region, owing to the ministry of chaplains, the heroic work of religious sisters in caring

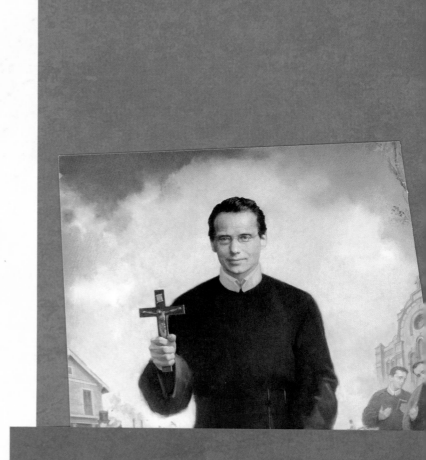

Blessed Francis Xavier Seelos

for wounded soldiers on both sides, and the service of Catholics in the Confederate army.[11]

The formal boundaries of the Richmond Diocese were altered in 1868, when the Eastern Shore of Virginia became part of the newly-created Diocese of Wilmington (which also covered the Eastern Shore of Maryland and the entire state of Delaware). Father Thomas A. Becker (1832–1899), a priest of the Diocese of Richmond, who was an adult convert and a graduate of the University of Virginia, was named Wilmington's first bishop.[12]

Bishop Thomas A. Becker

Across the Atlantic, Pope Pius IX convened the First Vatican Council (1869–1870). This was the first truly "worldwide" (ecumenical) council, in which dozens of American bishops, including John McGill, took part. Significantly, Vatican I proclaimed that the pope's teaching on matters of faith and morals was infallible under certain conditions.[13] McGill, who left the Council early because of health reasons, died in 1872.

Vatican Council I and Pope Pius IX

Holy Cross

Holy Cross Parish can be traced back to 1829, when the first Mass was celebrated in a private home in Lynchburg, and the first baptism was performed in 1841. Over the next decade, the need grew to establish a Catholic Church to minister to the many Irish Catholic immigrants who were working on the James River Kanawah Canal. To answer this need, the chapel of St. Francis Xavier was built in 1843 on Clay Street; this old parish building was converted into Holy Cross Academy in 1879. The Daughters of Charity of St. Vincent de Paul lived in a convent located next door to this building.

Rev. James J. McGurk, appointed pastor in 1869, was responsible for the construction of the present Gothic building. The Lynchburg News dated April 14, 1877, announced: "Ground has been broken for the new Catholic church at the corner of Clay and Seventh Streets. It will be 50 x 120 feet and will be a handsome structure." Thus, began the construction of Holy Cross Catholic Church, where the "blessed ones gave much, and the least ones gave - if only a wisp of hay." The building was designed by architect Colonel Augustus L. Forsberg and was dedicated on September 14, 1879.

Rev. McGurk named the church Holy Cross after the parish of his youth in Ireland. A 2,500-pound bell installed in the steeple on the church roof announced the opening, a separate bell tower was built in 1899. Designed by Edward G. Frye, the construction and design of the campanile is considered an excellent example of Frye's work.

Holy Cross Cemetery was established in 1874 on Bedford Avenue, near Rivermont Avenue, where several of the early parish priests are buried. In 1906, St. Francis de Sales Catholic Church was established to serve the African-Americans in the area.

The magnificent stained-glass windows, original to the church construction, date from 1879. These windows present the richest variegation of colors and are full of appropriate ecclesiastical emblems. The names of some of Lynchburg's first Catholic donors are etched at the bottom of each window. The chapel of the Blessed Sacrament to the rear of the church contains round stained-glass windows depicting the four Evangelists. The ceiling of the church is paneled with decorative stenciling and the Blessed Sacrament chapel features ceiling panels which are painted and stenciled.

Originally, frescoes surrounded the windows and adorned all the walls and ceiling. Over the decades and with various renovations, these frescoes were painted over. With the addition of electricity, all the gas lights were replaced. From 1983 until 1988 the church underwent a major renovation to the interior.

Because of this dramatic reversal, the old entrance in the base of the front tower entrance was closed and the original walnut pews refurbished and arranged in a new configuration. The largest window, previously hidden by the choir loft and organ pipes, now became a striking backdrop to the altar.

The addition of the Commons, built in 1988, has served the community by supporting local agencies with groceries for the hungry, as well as the parishioners using the church as the hub for organization and food distribution.

The Parish Life Center, dedicated in January 1997, has classroom space and office and meeting spaces. Holy Cross is part of the downtown church ministries and all our pastors and staff have been a part of the fabric of interfaith activities for decades. Our daily Mass, religious education programs and expanded faith enrichment services for our youth, serve to continue the spirit of our forefathers.

Saint Patrick

In 1859, Bishop John McGill purchased four lots in the east end of Richmond. On this land, located on 25th Street between Broad (or H Street as it was known then) and Grace Streets, was to be built a new church to serve the growing needs of the Catholics living in Fulton and on Church Hill. The first lots were purchased from the heirs of John Morris, and then "two certain lots or parcels of ground lying and being on Church Hill" adjoining property were purchased from Richard H. Whitlock.

On the Feast of Pentecost, June 12, 1859, Bishop McGill laid the cornerstone. In the cornerstone was placed a Latin inscription on parchment saying: "This cornerstone of Saint Patrick Church was blessed and placed on this 25th of June 1859, by John McGill, Bishop of Richmond, and assisted by Rev. Mgrs. Polk, Brady and Andrews in the presence of a large concourse of people of different denominations."

On November 11, 1860, the new church was dedicated by Bishop McGill. A sermon was preached by the Reverend Mr. Jacobs of the Redemptorist Brothers from the text: "Thou art Peter and upon this rock I will build My Church, and the gates of Hell shall not prevail against it." Saint Patrick was served during the next two years by Father Teeling from Saint Peter Church, the Cathedral.

The organ case in Saint Patrick Church was possibly constructed by Pomplitz in 1867. This may be the oldest extant case in the city. At the close of the Civil War, both Saint Patrick Church and First Baptist Church at Broad and Twelfth Streets purchased identical pipe organs. Years later, New York organ builder, Larry Trupiano, identified the case now in Saint Patrick as being identical to that of an extant Pomplitz organ in Baltimore. A Dispatch report of November 30, 1890, announced that a new organ was being set up in Saint Patrick Church by its builder, Mr. J. Wordsworth of Jersey City. Some records state that the organ was renovated by the French organ builder, Jardin, later. Whether the original organ case by Pomplitz was reused by Wordsworth or Jardin remains a puzzle still unsolved.

Between the years 1885 and 1890, the original wooden steps at the front entrance were replaced by stone steps. The stones came from the quarry across the James River. Each step was cut and placed by men of the parish. They stand as a memorial to people who have always loved their church.

Between the years of 1898 and 1922, several significant additions took place: the main altar was donated by John and Ann McKinley. The Blessed Mother's Altar was given by John R. Bowen and Family. Saint Joseph's Altar (originally Saint Patrick's Altar) was a gift of James and Mary Grant. There was also the gift of the pulpit of rare mahogany and brass by Mr. and Mrs. Phil Bagley, Sr.

Years later, the Sanctuary underwent redecorating to comply with the Vatican Council II. The altar was changed by moving the High Altar to the back of the Sanctuary and the front section was moved forward. The brass altar rails were removed and replaced by green marble rails. The Sanctuary was redecorated again in 1993 and 2008.

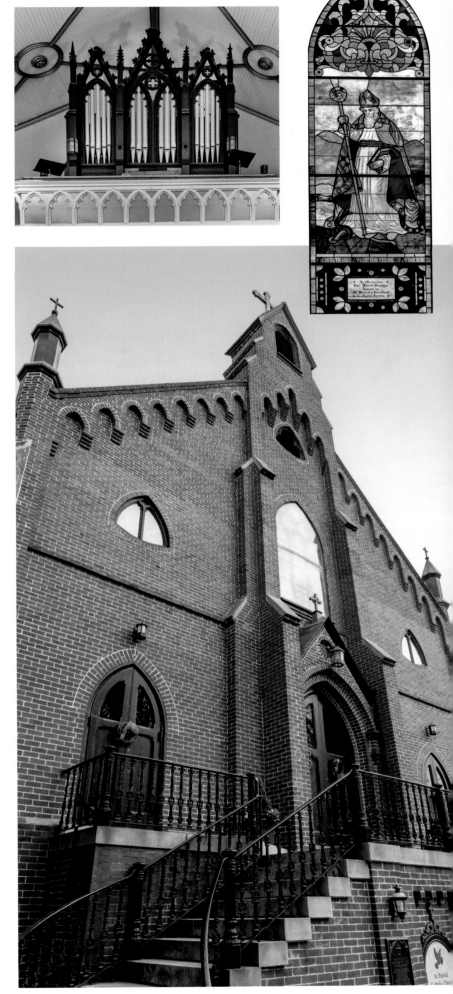

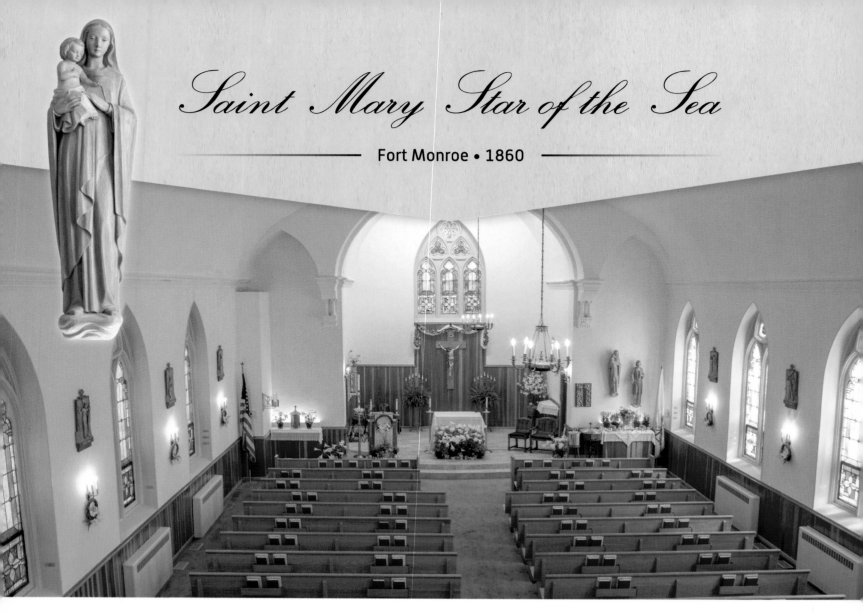

Saint Mary Star of the Sea

Fort Monroe • 1860

Three years after the settlement of Jamestown, a small group of civilians and soldiers moved to the area near Strawberry Banks to avoid the disease and starvation rampant at Jamestown. Fort Algernon (now Fort Monroe) had been fortified in 1609 to guard the narrow point of entrance to Hampton Roads. During the American Revolution, sixty French priests ministered to the French troops in the Battle of Yorktown. After the war ended, Thomas Jefferson wrote in his Act for Established Religious Freedom that Catholics, as well as other religions, were free to worship in Virginia.

In 1823, Rev. Thomas Hore celebrated the first recorded Catholic Mass at Fortress Monroe, though the exact site or date is unknown. By 1825, Fortress Monroe had the largest garrison of any establishment.

The Right Rev. John McGill, Third Bishop of Richmond, and Col. Rene Edward De Russy, representing the U.S. Army Corps of Engineers, signed an agreement, dated June 6, 1860, that, with permission granted by President Abraham Lincoln, authorized the construction of a Catholic church on Fort Monroe. The government would retain ownership of the land but the Diocese would own the church and rectory buildings. Bishop McGill dedicated the chapel on September 9, 1860, and Reverend Joseph Plunkett was the first pastor.

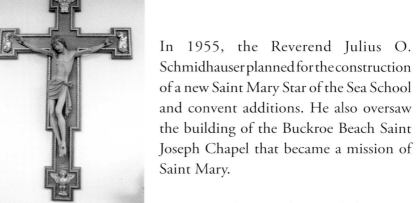

In November 1862, the Redemptorist Fathers of Annapolis, Maryland, were asked by the Archbishop of Baltimore to assume spiritual care of Fort Monroe. The first fulltime resident pastor at Saint Mary was the Reverend John P. Hagan. He arrived in October 1873 and lived in a room off the Sanctuary.

Under the Reverend William A. Fallon's leadership, funds were raised and construction of a new stone church began. The new church building was dedicated on June 9, 1903. Although the interior of the church changed over the years, the exterior appearance remained the same, with the exception of its original cathedral-like spires which had to be removed in 1966 because they were prone to leak.

On January 14, 1933, Reverend Richard B. Washington became the pastor of Saint Mary. He was born in Charles Town, West Virginia, and was a descendant of President George Washington and a convert to the Catholic faith.

In 1955, the Reverend Julius O. Schmidhauser planned for the construction of a new Saint Mary Star of the Sea School and convent additions. He also oversaw the building of the Buckroe Beach Saint Joseph Chapel that became a mission of Saint Mary.

In 1979, the parish raised funds to refurbish the neglected church buildings and remodel the altar to conform to changes in the liturgy under Vatican II. A new 1,300 square foot parish hall, attached to the original historic rectory, was completed in 1989. Because the rectory is considered an historic building, the project needed approval from the National Register of Historic Places.

In 2011, the parish saw the decommissioning of Fort Monroe and the parish was joined with Saint Joseph and Saint Vincent de Paul to form the Peninsula Cluster of Catholic Parishes with Rev. Msgr. Walter Barrett, Jr., as pastor.

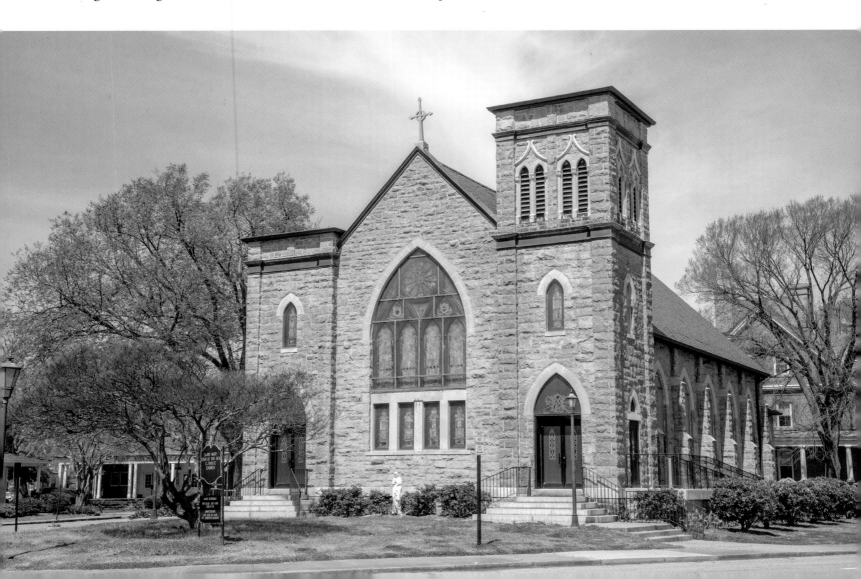

Bishop James Gibbons

James Gibbons (1834–1921) succeeded John McGill as the fourth bishop of Richmond in 1872. He was from Baltimore, ordained a priest of that archdiocese, and was then appointed the first vicar apostolic (missionary bishop) of North Carolina (1868) at age thirty-three, earning him the nickname "The Boy Bishop." During his time in Richmond, Gibbons retained pastoral responsibility for North Carolina (an arrangement that continued until 1882).

Reconstruction and a Rise to Prominence (1872-1877)

Gibbons's transfer to Richmond took place during the era of Reconstruction (1865–1877), when the Catholic Church in the South began to evangelize freed slaves. American bishops gathered at the Second Plenary Council of Baltimore (1866) had urged this course of action.[1] (This assembly manifested a spirit of collegiality that characterized the American hierarchy from its inception until the early 1900s, a period during which the Vatican considered the United States to be a missionary territory. The periodic gatherings of American bishops were the forerunners of what became the United States Conference of Catholic Bishops [USCCB].)

In regard to evangelizing African Americans, the few Catholic slave owners in Virginia always had their slaves baptized. Later, during his episcopate in Richmond, James Gibbons took tentative steps in the direction proposed by the Second Plenary Council of Baltimore. Yet the results were meager, statistically speaking: for example, there were only a hundred black Catholics out of a total black population of twenty-five thousand in the city of Richmond at that time.[2]

Gibbons was far more successful in the realm of apologetics. There he earned national renown during his tenure in Richmond by writing an influential treatise

In a spirit of collegiality, the American bishops gathered for nine plenary councils.
This is the gathering of the Third Plenary Council of Baltimore, 1884.

on Catholicism: *Faith of Our Fathers* (1876). A priest of the diocese and poet, Father John Banister Tabb (1845–1909), made stylistic contributions to the book. *Faith of Our Fathers* presented the Catholic faith positively, a unique approach for the time that reflected a historical reality in the Diocese of Richmond and Gibbons's own experience: Virginia's Catholics were a religious minority striving for acceptance. Parish missions, which spread throughout the diocese, used Gibbons's approach. Often led by religious orders, these missions prompted many people to return to the sacraments.[3]

Gibbons left Richmond after just five years to become the archbishop of Baltimore (1877). (He was appointed coadjutor, meaning that he would automatically succeed the sitting archbishop, who died before Gibbons even departed Richmond.) Gibbons later became America's second cardinal (1886).

Father John Banister Tabb

THE

FAITH OF OUR FATHERS:

BEING A

PLAIN EXPOSITION AND VINDICATION

OF

The Church Founded by Our Lord Jesus Christ

BY

JAMES CARDINAL GIBBONS,

Archbishop of Baltimore.

Forty-Seventh Carefully Revised and Enlarged Edition.

BALTIMORE:
JOHN MURPHY & COMPANY.

LONDON: R. WASHBOURNE.
1895.

Bishop James Gibbons

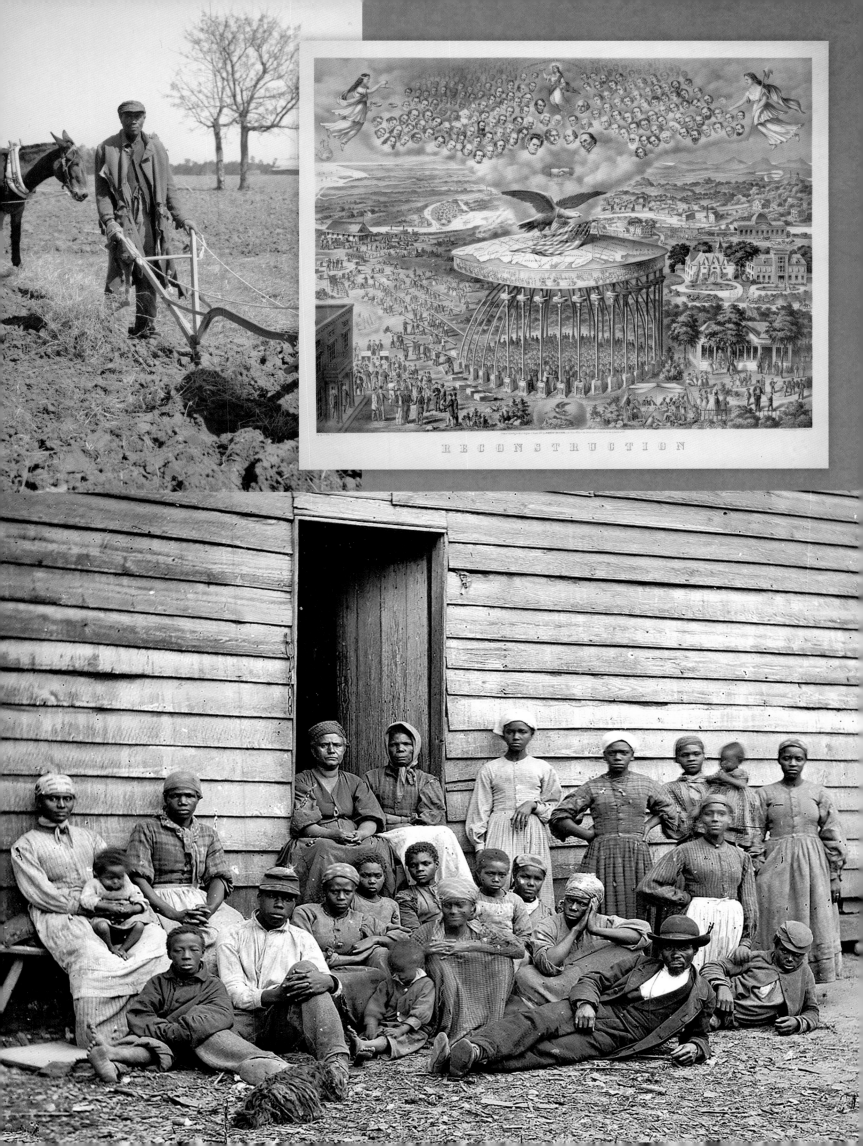

RECONSTRUCTION

Saint Patrick

Eight years after the close of the Civil War, which had taken a terrific toll of men and money, the cornerstone of the original Saint Patrick Church, on Henry Street, was laid in 1873. What indomitable courage it took in those days with finances at a low ebb to undertake the building of a church. Records of Rockbridge County show the cost of the church to have been just under $3,000. The entry is dated August 12, 1874 and shows G. W. Shields as the contractor. Rt. Rev. James Gibbons, the Fourth Bishop of Richmond dedicated the new church on July 19, 1874.

For many years, Lexington was a mission of Lynchburg, or Clifton Forge, or Staunton.

Priests came by train and were met by parishioners in a horse and buggy, and later by automobile, from Staunton to celebrate Mass. Finally, after World War II, Bishop Peter Ireton of Richmond asked the Provincial of the Precious Blood Society for a priest to take over the pastoral duties and establish a permanent parish in Lexington.

In 1948, the parish acquired the Gassman property on West Nelson Street as a building site. The 19th-century Gassman House with its intricate vergeboards serves today as the Parish House. The Philadelphia architectural firm of Mulrooney and Gleason was chosen to design the Church. The design is very similar to the Huntington Court Methodist Church in Roanoke, which is cited in the architects' specifications as the model

for Saint Patrick's stonework. Ground was broken on April 27, 1952, with the dedication on October 11, 1953, by Bishop Peter Ireton on the eightieth anniversary of the founding of Saint Patrick Catholic Church.

The stained-glass windows, fabricated by the Lynchburg Stained Glass Company, were added in 1987 as part of a renovation by Lexington architects Roberts & Kirchner. Saint Patrick's understated Gothic Revival exterior is faced in light-hued Catawba sandstone. The steep slate-singled gable roof, the buttresses that flank the segmental-arched front entry and line the sides, and narrow lancet-arched windows recall the medieval parish church architecture of the British Isles. Inside, laminated Douglas fir trusses in the form of lancet arches span the simply appointed nave and focus the eye on the chancel and its rose window glazed in shades of blue, gray, and red. Bishop Walter Sullivan was the principal celebrant of the rededication liturgy on October 22, 1987.

The Parish now offers a preschool program for children 2 ½ to 5 years of age. In addition to our local community efforts, our parish is fortunate to celebrate over a decade of twinning with our twin parish in Fond Pierre, Haiti. During this time, we have completed the parish house, a new school, a new church, and a clinic with and for the Rockbridge-Haiti Medical Alliance. We have provided new benches for parishioners of Saint Peter's and completed the cafeteria for the children. The Parish also offers Catholic Campus Ministry to the nearby Virginia Military Institute, Washington and Lee University and Southern Seminary students.

Through the grace of God, we, the members of Saint Patrick's Parish, accept the task of proclaiming the Gospel, seeking the Kingdom of God, and building our community on the foundation of Jesus Christ.

Holy Name of Mary

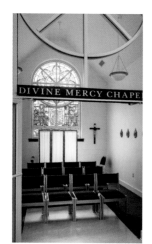

The construction of the Kanawha canal in the early 1840s brought Irish Catholic laborers to the Lynchburg area. Many stayed in the area and spread into the fertile farm areas of Bedford County and the Town of Liberty. Father Edward Fox, a zealous and talented preacher, traveled to Liberty to teach and preach to the faithful. Unfortunately, his death brought an end to all such contact with the Catholic Church for over a decade.

The Civil War brought upheaval to the area, but railroads brought an influx of more Catholics. In the spring of 1874, Father James McGurk, a young priest assigned to Holy Cross in Lynchburg, felt empathy for the Catholics in Liberty and took up the mantle of Father Fox, celebrating Mass in the courthouse basement or in the homes of Catholics. Within a year, church construction was started on a donated lot in downtown Liberty. On August 29, 1875, the first Mass was celebrated by Cardinal Gibbons for 50 Catholics of the fledgling parish.

Liberty grew and became the town, and then the city, of Bedford. The little parish of St. Mary grew, too. It was noted in the Bedford newspaper in 1937 that while St. Mary's was relatively small,

they had an unusually well-attended Sunday school, attesting to their fervor for the faith.

In the early 1950s, the parish had outgrown their little brick church downtown and a new church was built not far from where the new city hospital was being built. The Parish was renamed Holy Name of Mary. The newly renamed Parish of 150 families continued to be an active, joyful place. As a founding member of the Bedford Christian Ministries Association, the Parish united with all Christian churches in the area to meet the needs of the less fortunate.

As the Parish entered the 21st century, it continued to grow in numbers and spirituality with almost 400 families registered. Continuing in their passion for their faith and love of the sacraments, weekly Adoration and Benediction is faithfully attended and there is usually a line for Reconciliation. With the canonization

of St. Faustina and the promotion of the Divine Mercy, a Divine Mercy Cenacle was formed.

Adult Faith formation classes on a variety of topics are offered at various times to accommodate busy lives. Children's faith formation and sacramental preparation boast over 120 students. Each summer, Vacation Bible School builds the faith of both young and old through faith-themed fun. The youth attend retreats, conferences, and service work camps.

It is the parishioners fervent hope, that filled with the Spirit and the Love of God, they will continue to pass on the Faith to the young, care for the needy both within the parish and in their community and live as examples of the Catholic faith to all they encounter.

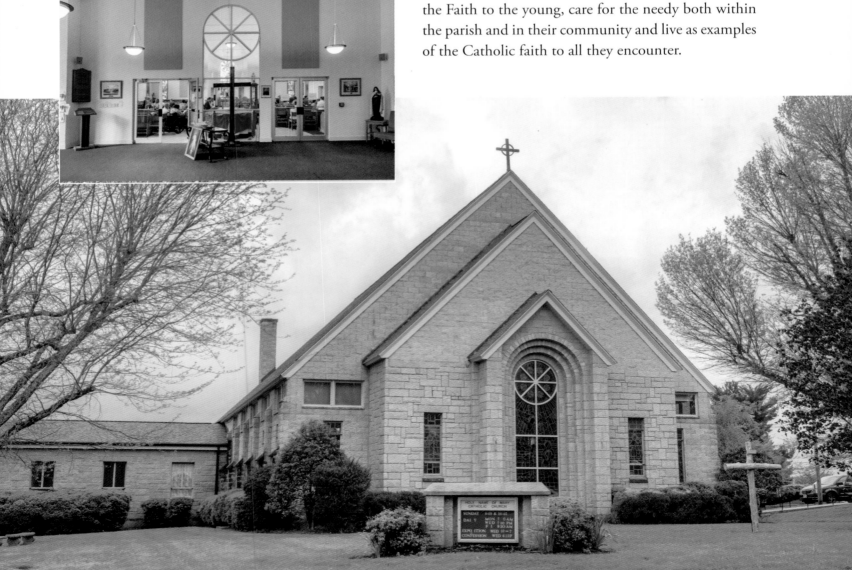

Immaculate Conception

— Buckner • 1876 —

Immaculate Conception Church is one of the oldest continuously operating churches in the Diocese of Richmond.

Around 1868, a small group of families, mostly farmers of German and Irish descent moved to the Buckner area of eastern Louisa County from Carrolltown, Pennsylvania. Benedictine priests came out from Richmond one Sunday a month to hold Mass for these families in a room graciously set aside as a chapel. On July 31, 1875, Mr. and Mrs. Alexander Hay of Philadelphia donated land for the establishment of a Catholic Church.

Construction was completed in 1876, and the church was dedicated by the Rt. Rev. James Gibbons, Fourth Bishop of Richmond, in honor of Saint Boniface on June 25, 1877. The name was changed several years later in honor of the Immaculate Conception.

The church at Buckner was a mission to the old Saint Mary's church in downtown Richmond and was well-shepherded by priests of the Order of Saint Benedict. For the first fifty years, Benedictine priests from Saint Mary's Parish in Richmond, traveled out to Buckner on the Sunday morning train.

One Saturday every spring, the parishioners of Saint Mary's and several other Catholic churches in Richmond sponsored an all-day event at "Plain View Farm," where food was sold, games were played, and people danced on a wooden platform. All proceeds were for the benefit of Immaculate Conception Church.

In 1905, the bell tower and bell were added, and have been calling God's people to worship ever since. In the early 1920's, the parishioners donated an automobile to the priest, and this event marked a major improvement for the Catholic families in Buckner. The priests arranged for nuns to come out from Richmond to instruct the children and for the Bishop to visit for Confirmation.

During the years of 1945 to 1955, the head of the Diocesan Missionary Fathers served Buckner. He conducted night services from a Mission Trailer Chapel which he and his associates brought to Buckner for a week each summer, holding discussions and showing films on the Catholic faith. During this week, the priests would visit and share meals with the local parishioners. In 1956, the church became a mission of Saint Ann Church in Ashland. Then, on December 10, 1974, Bishop Walter F. Sullivan established Immaculate

Conception as a Mission under the newly dedicated Saint Jude Parish Church in Mineral.

The Parish Hall was built in 1986, to hold religious education programs and to bring community members together.

Immaculate Conception has been serving the needs of the Catholic Community in Louisa County continuously for more than 141 years. Because of the love of the parishioners and the dedication of the religious, this small, historic rural church is ready to support everyone who comes to worship for the next 100 years and on.

Bishop John J. Keane

The Diocese of Richmond, which expanded in northern Virginia during Gibbons's episcopate, began to grow in the western region (Roanoke Valley) during the tenure of its next bishop, John J. Keane (1839–1918). Born in Ireland and a priest of the Archdiocese of Baltimore, Keane was serving as a pastor in Washington, DC when he was appointed to Richmond in 1878. Like his predecessor, Keane was simultaneously bishop of Richmond and vicar apostolic of North Carolina (until 1882). The Richmond Diocese realized three pastoral gains during Keane's tenure: the evangelization of African Americans, the development of parochial schools, and the promotion of lay spirituality.

Evangelization of African Americans, Development of Schools, and Lay Spirituality (1878-1888)

Bishop Keane himself initiated the evangelization campaign by conducting prayer services for African Americans and instructing them in the basement of St. Peter's Cathedral (1879). After stressing the importance of this ministry to his priests, Keane raised funds for additional missionary outreach to African Americans. This effort led to the founding of the diocese's first black church (St. Joseph's in Richmond, 1885), along with missions and schools. Priests of the Society of St. Joseph for Foreign Missions or Josephites (beginning in 1883), and the Franciscan Sisters of St. Mary (beginning in 1885), were largely responsible for these accomplishments. Both orders had been founded at St. Joseph's Missionary College in Mill Hill (London), England.[1]

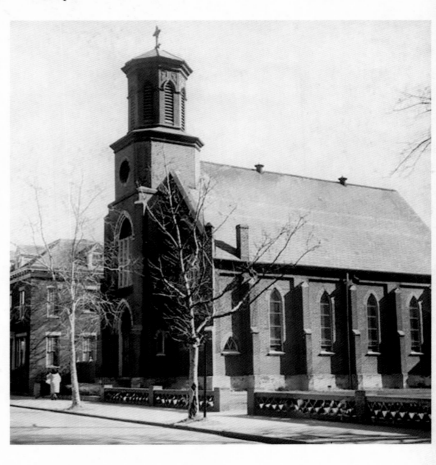

Father John R. Slattery

The first Josephite priest in Richmond and the founder of St. Joseph's Church, Father John R. Slattery of New York, became the superior of the Josephites when the American mission separated from Mill Hill (1893). Slattery later aroused controversy when he accused the Church of condoning racism. He then left the priesthood and renounced the Catholic faith (1906).[2]

Several parochial schools for white children, also operated by religious orders, were founded during this period. Notably, Bishop Keane improved the quality of Catholic education by creating a board to evaluate student learning and the academic qualifications of lay teachers (1887). He also bolstered the spiritual life of lay people by promoting regular parish missions and devotion to the Holy Spirit. Keane resigned as bishop of Richmond in 1888 to focus exclusively on his position as the first rector of the Catholic University of America in Washington, DC (1886–1897). He was later appointed the archbishop of Dubuque, Iowa (1900).

St. Joseph's Church, Richmond

Yielding Fruit:
A Centennial Diocese (1888-1934)

There were signs of growth and maturity as the diocese reached its centenary (1920): immigrants arrived from Europe and Lebanon (Maronites), expanding the Catholic population in Virginia; evangelization of African Americans continued; a diocesan seminarian, Frank Parater (1897–1920), bequeathed a legacy of holiness; and the entry of the United States into World War I (1917), coupled with advances in transportation, brought development to some regions of the commonwealth.

Switching passenger cars, Roanoke Station, 1895

Hampton Roads shipyard, 1912

*American Locomotive Works
Richmond, 1911*

Spooners and doffers in cotton mill, Danville

Dear Old Scouts:

You may never see this letter, but if you do, it is to tell you that God has granted me the greatest desire of my life — to die for love of Him and of my fellow man. Never fear death — it is the most beautiful thing in life, for it is the great portal to the real life. Ever since I was a little fellow I have wanted to be like the martyrs of old, and give my life to God.

I have loved each of you. … Now that God has called me to Himself, don't think that I shall forget you; nor shall I leave you – but will be much nearer to you than I could ever be in this life.

And now, old Scouts, I must say "so long for a time." But occasionally think of your old friend and camp director, and when the time comes for you to hit the trail for home, I'll promise to be near and to welcome you to the campfire of eternal life. God's blessing be with you all.

Sincerely,

Your friend,

Francis Parater

Frank Parater, 1897–1920

Sacred Heart

Danville, Virginia, is often referred to as the "City of Churches" because it has more churches per square mile than any other city in Virginia. Father J.J. McGurk, a priest from Lynchburg, visited Danville and celebrated the first Mass in 1875 in a small tailor shop. During his short visit, Father McGurk selected a site and solicited the funds needed to establish the town's first Catholic church. With a total of $800, a little white Victorian church was built at the convergence of Ross Street and South Holbrook Street. The parish was canonically established in 1878 under Father Augustine Habets, the first pastor of Sacred Heart Parish.

In 1886, Father Francis McCarthy became the first resident priest. For several years, Sacred Heart was a mission of Lynchburg and Martinsville at different times. As a result, the strength of the Catholic community began to waver. According to the annals of the parish, "A resident priest is needed here to hold the newcomers, for good Catholics do not desire to remain in a place where they are deprived so often of Sunday Mass."

On March 17, 1915, Father Augustus J. Halbleib, the seventh and longest tenured pastor in the church's history, took on the task of restoring stability within the church. His determination increased the membership from 95 to 172 during his first eight years. On May 21, 1939, Coadjutor Bishop Peter Ireton consecrated the new Sacred Heart Church on West Main Street.

Sacred Heart Catholic School opened its doors on September 13, 1953, at 344 West Main Street for 67 students in grades one through eight. The school was staffed by four Sisters of Mercy from Merion, Pennsylvania. In the 1960's under Father Charles Ferry, Sacred Heart became the first school in Danville to achieve integration. In 1966, Sacred Heart School relocated to its current site on Central Boulevard and in 1972 enlarged the school to include grades kindergarten through nine. By July 1980, the Franciscan Sisters of Baltimore became the new staff.

In 1995, Father David McGuire spearheaded the plan to build a bigger church next to the school. Father McGuire wrote, "If we are to respond to our mission – to heed the urgent call of Jesus in our times – it is our turn to build for tomorrow's community." Sacred Heart Church relocated to its third and current site on Central Boulevard and was dedicated on September 23, 2001.

The church saw significant growth in the Hispanic community. From 2002 to 2007, Sacred Heart welcomed over 300 families, with the majority speaking

The second Church

Spanish as their first language. Currently, comprehensive ministry is provided in both English and Spanish.

Sacred Heart prides itself on being the only Catholic church and school in Danville. It brings together over 800 families of different cultures across southside Virginia and North Carolina. In the 2002 parish directory, the pastor shared these encouraging words, "Let us look in the direction we want to go – forward into a future in which our parish becomes more and more a community of believers, with a shared spirit of faith, hope and love of God and all God's creatures."

The original Church

Holy Comforter

— Charlottesville • 1880 —

The first Catholic Church in Charlottesville, the Church of the Paraclete, was erected in 1880. Initially, priests came from Staunton by train, once or twice a month, to say Mass in the Charlottesville church before traveling on to Gordonsville, Culpeper, and Orange. The first resident pastor, the Reverend John Massey, was appointed in 1896.

Early in the 20th century, the church became Holy Comforter Catholic Church. The original building as renovated and enlarged, and a rectory, adjacent to the church, was added. A 1906 article in the local newspaper, describes Holy Comforter as "an ornament to the city."

In 1919, Mr. and Mrs. Thomas Fortune Ryan, of New York City and Oak Ridge in Nelson County, donated funds to enlarge and modernize the church and provide a more suitable rectory. The old edifice was demolished in 1924, and construction began on its replacement. The architect for the new building, S. J. Makielski, AIA, was an assistant professor of art and architecture at the University of Virginia. His brother, M. A. Makielski, created the oil painting of the Risen Christ which adorns the Sanctuary today. A building just west of the church was purchased in 1925 to serve as a rectory, and the new church was dedicated the following year. Not long after that, in 1932, the Austin organ, which is still in use, was installed.

A Newman Club was founded at the University of Virginia in 1947, under the direction of the Reverend Francis J. Blakely, pastor of Holy Comforter. This club evolved into the Catholic Center for the University in 1959. The ultimate outgrowth of these early groups led to the establishment of Saint Thomas Aquinas Church in 1963.

Formal Catholic education at Holy Comforter began in 1951, under the direction of the pastor, the Reverend J. Bernard Moore. A kindergarten, staffed by Adrian Dominican sisters, was opened on Park Street. In 1953, a school was established in what is now the Berkley subdivision. The following year, the church purchased Branchlands, an estate on Route 29 North, and classes were held there in the "big white house." A campaign to reduce Holy Comforter's debt was so successful that, in 1960, Holy Comforter School and Holy Comforter Chapel were both established at

Branchlands. The chapel and the original downtown church both grew, and in 1976, the "Branchlands Catholic Community," now the Church of the Incarnation, came into being.

In 1980, Holy Comforter celebrated its centennial by adopting a mission statement that emphasized its social outreach and soup kitchen programs and its plans to renovate and enlarge existing facilities. The rectory was demolished and an addition to the church was constructed in its place. A new residence on Evergreen Street was purchased for the pastor. In 2006 the rectory was sold and replaced by a smaller condominium.

While physical space may be restricted by the church's urban location, its mission remains boundless: to worship, formation, service and evangelization, in service to others within the local and global communities.

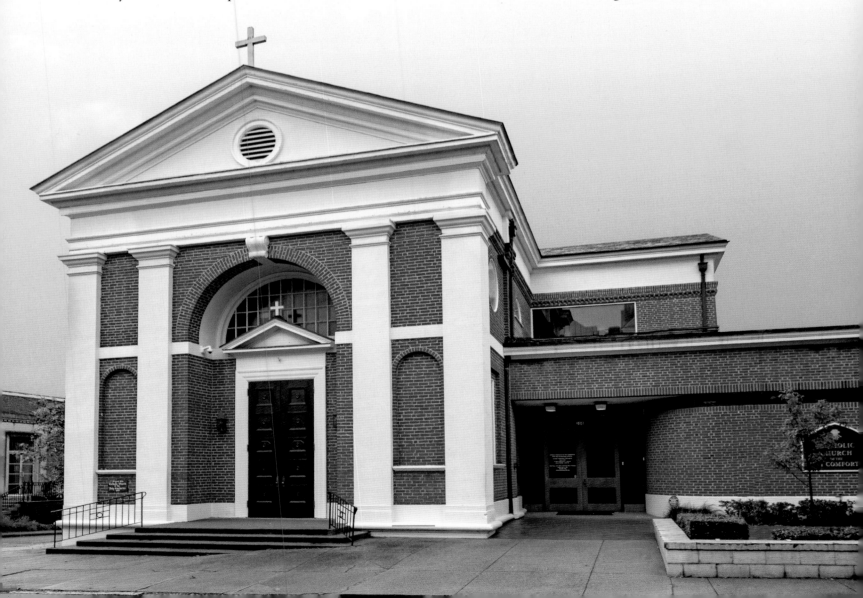

Saint Vincent de Paul

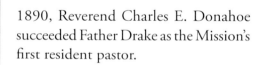

In 1881, Mr. and Mrs. Charles W. Lohmann, Sr., along with thirty other Catholics who gathered for worship in their home at 201 23rd Street, established the Parish of Saint Vincent de Paul as a Mission of Saint Mary, Fort Monroe (the first Catholic parish on the Peninsula). On March 30, 1890, parishioners petitioned Bishop Van de Vyver for a priest, and in April 1890, Reverend Richard A. Drake was assigned to the Mission. He would travel from Richmond, saying Mass first at Johnson's Hall and later in the original Baptist chapel which stood at the northwest corner of Washington Avenue and 30th Street. In November 1890, Reverend Charles E. Donahoe succeeded Father Drake as the Mission's first resident pastor.

Construction of the first church began on Washington Avenue near 34th Street in February 1891. The first Mass was celebrated on Sunday, April 5, 1891, and the church was officially dedicated on July 19, 1891. The congregation increased so rapidly there was a need for a new church in 10 years.

In May 1916, ground was broken for the new church on 33rd Street in Newport News. The church and rectory were completed in 1917 and the first Mass was offered on Sunday, May 27, 1917. The church building was formally dedicated to God on June 3, 1917. Father David Coleman celebrated the first Mass in the new

church building and served the parish for fifteen years. Father Coleman died on December 16, 1932, and he was buried alongside the rectory where a statue of the Sacred Heart now stands.

In the Fall of 1970, Saint Alphonsus Mission merged with Saint Vincent; Saint Alphonsus had been established in 1944 as an Apostolate to African American families. The merging of Saint Alphonsus with Saint Vincent proved to be a happy union for both parishes. The new Parish's Social Action Center was partially funded by the sale of Saint Alphonsus property and was established to provide assistance to the disadvantaged in the local area. This assistance came in the form of youth counseling, summer programs for inner city children, mental health assistance, food assistance for families in need, and programs for shut-ins and the elderly.

The Parish of Saint Vincent de Paul continues to minister to those in need in the area through both its Social Action Center and its "Back Door" hot lunch ministry. The Back Door ministry has been feeding a hot lunch to people every Monday through Friday since 1976.

Reverend Lloyd Stephenson, a native son, was assigned to Saint Vincent de Paul in 1997. He was known for his lively homilies and his passion for the Back Door ministry. In 2011, the Diocese of Richmond joined Saint Vincent de Paul, Newport News, Saint Joseph, Hampton, and Saint Mary Star of the Sea, Fort Monroe into the Peninsula Cluster of Catholic Parishes. Monsignor Walter Barrett was assigned as the Pastor of the Peninsula Cluster Parish. Father John Bosco Walugembe is the current Pastor of Saint Vincent de Paul.

Saint Charles Borromeo

Father Edward E. Mickle, a priest of the Diocese of Wilmington (the Diocese in which Cape Charles was situated), was the founder of Saint Charles Borromeo Catholic Church in Cape Charles. He was twenty-nine years old and had been recently ordained in Rome on May 29, 1889. Saint Charles became his first and, as he chose, only parish.

Father Mickle lived in the church sacristy until the rectory was completed in 1894. He was a missionary at heart, visiting every household to introduce himself and to share his faith and devotion. The parish grew, and he became known as the Apostle of the Eastern Shore.

The Holy Family Convent and School building was finished in 1898. The school was taught by four Sisters of Saint Francis. The Mother House and the school closed in 1934-35.

In 1916, Father Mickle was appointed Vicar General of the Diocese of Wilmington, Delaware, and on September 29, 1927, Father Mickle was named Domestic Prelate with the title of Monsignor. He died on August 16, 1930. He had requested in his will to be buried in the "shadow of my church." The town granted an exception, and he was buried within the town limits in a favorite place between the church and the rectory where he sat

in the afternoons to read his breviary.

In June of 1941, Rev. Henry A. Miller became the fifth pastor. During his time the parish once again thrived and experienced a period of growth and community spirit. He visited every parishioner in their home once a year. He celebrated Mass and was pastor to the soldiers stationed at nearby Fort John Custis, an Army Base. He counseled the men held at the German Prisoner of War Camp in the area. His unscripted sermons were acclaimed for being timely and heartfelt. Father Miller's Christmas Eve Mass crowds were so large the people overflowed out the doors and onto the church steps and sidewalks.

In 1974, the parish was transferred by Pope Paul VI from the Diocese of Wilmington to the Diocese of Richmond. While Northampton and Accomack Counties originally belonged to the Diocese of Richmond, with the establishment of the Diocese of Wilmington in March 1868 by Pope Pius IX, the Peninsula section of Virginia was transferred to the Wilmington Diocese.

Rev. J. Michael Breslin became the sixteenth pastor in 1995. During his tenure, the parish has grown spiritually as well as in enrollment. The Pastoral Council, Knights of Columbus, and other volunteers have been generous with time, abilities, monetary contributions, and resources. Hispanic, Migrant, and Helping Hands Social Ministries are a benefit throughout the community. We have religious education for the youth and a Centering Group for quiet reflection. Father Breslin has emulated Monsignor Mickle in requesting to remain with his people. He has been our spiritual leader for over twenty years. In 2015, the parishioners formally renamed the Holy Family School the Breslin Center to honor his devotion to the parish of Saint Charles Borromeo.

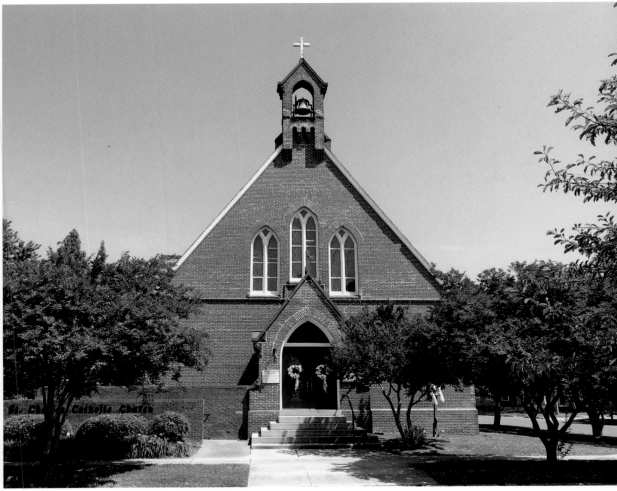

Bishop Augustine van de Vyver

Augustine van de Vyver (1844–1911) succeeded John J. Keane as the sixth bishop of Richmond in 1889. He was born in Belgium and was educated at the American College in Louvain, a seminary that trained numerous priests for service in the Richmond Diocese. After his ordination, Van de Vyver came to America and worked in the western reaches of Virginia. He later became vicar general and then diocesan administrator. Two notable benefactions were made to the diocese during Van de Vyver's time as bishop.

Outreach to African Americans and a New Cathedral (1889-1911)

First, St. Katharine Drexel (1858–1955) of Philadelphia, and her half-sister, Louise Morrell, opened two schools in Rock Castle (Powhatan County) for black youth: St. Emma's Industrial and Agricultural College for boys (1895), and St. Francis de Sales School for girls (1899).

Then-Father Augustine van de Vyver with his friend, and fellow future bishop, Father Francis Janssens

St. Katharine Drexel

Mother Katharine Drexel and Louise Morrell

Mother Katharine Drexel and Louise Morrell

The Drexels used the fortune they inherited to fund charitable causes; in Katharine's case, this included the work of the religious order she founded to care for African Americans and Indians (Sisters of the Blessed Sacrament). Mother Drexel herself visited the schools in Rock Castle (1900), which provided vocational training, secondary education, and religious instruction to generations of African Americans.[1] Katharine Drexel was the second native-born American to be canonized (2000).

St. Emma's Industrial and Agricultural College

St. Francis de Sales School

St. Katharine Drexel at graduation for St. Emma's, 1923

79

A second philanthropic gift received during Van de Vyver's episcopate became a monument to the Catholic presence in Virginia: a new cathedral in Richmond. Thomas Fortune Ryan (1851–1928) and his wife, Ida Mary Barry (1854–1917), financed the construction of the edifice. It was said that Ryan, who was from Nelson County, decided to become a Catholic after a long discussion with a conductor on a train ride to Baltimore. True to his middle name, Ryan subsequently made his fortune in tobacco, insurance, and transportation. He gave generously to the Catholic Church, both in New York and in Virginia. The papal representative to the American hierarchy, Archbishop Diomede Falconio, dedicated the Cathedral of the Sacred Heart on Thanksgiving Day, 1906. This event recognized the growth of the Church in Virginia and symbolized the compatibility of the Catholic faith and American society.[2]

Overall, Van de Vyver's tenure witnessed steady growth in the diocese. By the end of his episcopate, the Catholic population numbered thirty thousand, and there were sixty priests (diocesan and religious), thirty-five parishes with a resident priest, forty-eight missions, and forty schools. There was also a concerted effort to reach out to African Americans, not only by the sisters associated with Katharine Drexel, but also by other religious orders working in new parishes and schools located in cities. Van de Vyver twice sought to resign, but partly at the urging of his priests, he remained in office until he died (1911).[3]

Exterior of the Cathedral of the Sacred Heart, 1906

Thomas Fortune Ryan,
1851-1928

Ida Mary Barry Ryan,
1854-1917

Procession in front of the Cathedral of the Sacred Heart, from the Cook Collection, VALM

Saint Joseph

— Clifton, Forge • 1889 —

Saint Joseph Catholic Church, located in the town of Clifton Forge, Alleghany County in the Highlands of Southwestern Virginia, is about 24 miles from the West Virginia border, approximately 30 miles west of Lexington and 50 miles northwest of Roanoke.

Saint Joseph Church has deep historical roots in Alleghany County. In the late 19th century the area was the center of a large ore mining industry and the regional headquarters of the Chesapeake and Ohio Railroad. This resulted in a large influx of Irish Catholic immigrants to work in the ore mines and on the railroad. They formed the nucleus of the Catholic community in Alleghany County. Due to the mountainous terrain and the lack of major highways in the area at the time, it was imperative that a Catholic Church be established in the county to meet the spiritual needs of the immigrant Catholic population. Mt. Carmel Church in Low Moor was established in 1882 and Father John Lynch, pastor of Saint Patrick Church in Lexington, built the church and served as its pastor. In 1889, Saint Joseph Church was established and Father Lawrence Kelly, pastor of Saint Patrick and Mt. Carmel, became the first pastor. Father Kelly moved to Clifton Forge from Lexington in 1892 to supervise the building of the church and rectory. In 1894, Sacred Heart Church in Covington was established, and these three churches served the Catholic population in Alleghany County until

the late 1950's when Mt. Carmel Church was severely damaged in a wind storm and was demolished.

Saint Joseph's original rectory next to the church later became the education building and currently serves as an administrative building. The house adjacent to the former rectory, purchased in the 1950's, was used as a convent for a short period of time and now serves

a close family environment. Most of its parishioners are older, with very few young, married couples with children. Descendants of the first parishioners of the parish remain a significant part of its present community. The weekend Mass attendance averages around 50, which includes a 5:00 pm Saturday Vigil Mass and 9:00 am Sunday Mass. Saint Joseph also receives visitors at Mass from nearby Douthat State Park during the summer as well as other visitors attracted to the beauty, character, and outdoor activities of the Alleghany Highlands. Today, Saint Joseph and its sister parish, Sacred Heart, provide the Catholic presence in the Alleghany Highlands.

as a rectory. Asttached to the church are the parish hall and kitchen, which are used for various church gatherings, meetings, and social events. Saint Joseph also maintains Mt. Carmel Cemetery. Because of several legacies, the cemetery remains financially independent and provides perpetual care for the grave sites.

Saint Joseph is a welcoming parish, and due to its small congregation, it has always maintained

Saint Andrew

St. Andrew's history began on November 19, 1882. A small group of Catholics gathered for Mass presided over by Father John W. Lynch. Land had been donated for the construction of a church, but construction

had not yet begun. Father Lynch arrived in Roanoke on Saturday, November 18, only to find the building where he was to celebrate Mass no longer available. Mr. William Brophy, an officer with the Shenandoah railroad, offered the use of a railroad car. Thus, the very first Mass to be celebrated in Roanoke was in Shenandoah Valley Railroad Passenger Car #6.

Over the next few months, Father Lynch continued to travel from Lexington to Roanoke for Mass. Finally, on September 23, 1883, the small

congregation gathered for Mass in the first Saint Andrew Church. At the time, Saint Andrew was a mission of Saint Patrick Church in Lexington. As the congregation grew, they asked for a resident pastor. The Diocese had a shortage of priests and the Rt. Rev. John J. Keane, Fifth Bishop of Richmond, was unable to grant their request.

It wasn't until November 19, 1889, seven years to the date of that first Mass, that Father John Lynch was installed as resident pastor and Saint Andrew became an independent parish.

The congregation of Saint Andrew continued to grow, and the church became inadequate. The only solution was to build a new church.

In 1899, Father Lynch launched a fundraising campaign. Construction on the new building began in September 1900 and was completed in 1902. On November 30, 1902, the Feast of Saint Andrew, the second Saint Andrew Church was officially dedicated.

In 1995, a fundraising campaign was started to add a much-needed social center, classroom space, chapel, and music room. At the same time, Roanoke Catholic School was expanding and with these two construction projects, we saw the demise of some of our historic buildings. The Ryan Building was the first building to be torn down, followed by the convent. Saint Vincent Orphanage was occupied by the Achievement Center and remained until the Achievement Center moved to a new location. The building was demolished and much needed parking space was added. A memorial to Saint Vincent's was

erected in 2011 and has a prominent place on the property.

In 2013, we received news that our historic steeples were in dangerous condition. Other projects that we had hoped to begin were superseded by the necessity to repair the steeples. Official construction began in May of 2014, and the steeples were completed in October 2014.

From the construction of that very first Saint Andrew's to the reconstruction of the steeples on the second Saint Andrew's, our parishioners have proven themselves to be wholly dedicated to their Church. They have shown time and again that this House of God, which began as a small brick building in 1883, will withstand the test of time and continue to be a beacon of light and hope in the Roanoke Valley.

Saint Ann

— Ashland • 1892 —

The Bishop of Richmond established Saint Augustine Chapel in a former schoolhouse on Railroad Avenue in the village of Ashland. Before that, Ashland Catholics took the train to Saint Peter Catholic Church in Richmond. From time to time, a visiting priest or the bishop would celebrate Mass in the home of Henry and Caroline Scott or Louis and Adele Delarue.

A church was built on England Street through a gift from Andrew and Ann Pizzini and named after Mrs. Pizzini's patron, Saint Ann. Bishop Augustine Van de Vyver donated the gothic-style altar. Still, Mass was celebrated only monthly by a visiting priest.

Under Father Walter J. Nott and architect L.P Hartsook, the congregation transformed the building from a simple clapboard church to Tudor-style with the addition of a bell tower, choir balcony, and sacristy. Father John Fayhe and Father Francis Byrne, who followed Father Nott, were assigned two additional mission churches in Caroline County, Saint Mary and Saint Cyril & Methodius.

Recognizing the need for assistance, the Bishop contracted with the Oblates of Mary Immaculate, a mission order from Massachusetts, to staff Saint Ann Parish. Establishing a parsonage at 307 College Avenue, OMI priests served the parish for 45 years. Under Father Joseph Curtin, the parish bought a school bus to transport Catholic children to the Catholic school at Saint Joseph Villa in Richmond. During this time, the parish raised funds for a new parish hall by selling spaghetti suppers and by staffing the Saint Ann food tent at the State Fair every year.

The Oblates returned the Parish to the Richmond Diocese, and diocesan priests served the Parish. The parishioners outgrew the small church on England Street and sold the building to Randolph-Macon College. They began using the Curtain Center as a temporary worship space until they could raise enough funds for a new church. For years, Thursday nights were given to bingo at Curtin Center, and Saturday and Sunday nights to worship there.

In 1996, under the leadership of Monsignor William Sullivan and numerous parish committees, the cornerstone for the new Saint Ann Church building was laid. Wishing to preserve its history, the parishioners decided to place the 1892 altar in the new chapel.

In 2005, Father Christian J. Haydinger was appointed pastor when there were 511 registered families. Today, Saint Ann Parish has grown substantially to 855 families.

Saint Ann Parish has a twin parish in Dubisson, Haiti, that they help to fund their church and school. Along with other Ashland churches, Saint Ann's assists the Ashland Christian Emergency Services, Prison Ministry, and CARITAS for the homeless. The former Curtain Center serves as the Saint Ann Sunday School and Parish Hall.

The Catholic community of Sacred Heart Church began in 1894. Sacred Heart is the second enclave in Norfolk, Virginia, growing out of Saint Mary of the Immaculate Conception. Father Francis X. McCarthy was the founding pastor. The chapel of Sacred Heart was located on the corner of York and Dunmore Street in what is now downtown Norfolk, and it served the parish community until 1924 when building on the new site off Princess Anne Road

and Stockley Gardens was started. The new church, designed in the Florentine Renaissance style, was dedicated on Sunday, November 1, 1925, by Bishop William Hafey of Raleigh, North Carolina. Bishop Denis J. O'Connell was the Bishop of Richmond at the time.

Sacred Heart Parish also had a parochial school. The first school opened in 1920 at Princess Anne Road and Colonial Avenue with about 180 students. In 1953, a

new school was built under the direction of the pastor, Father Thomas Walsh, and dedicated by Most Reverend Joseph H. Hodges, Auxiliary Bishop of Richmond. The school was located on Stockley Gardens and remained open for nearly 25 years, staffed by the Daughters of Charity.

During the years following the Second Vatican Council, parish priests stressed the importance of education and ecumenism. Due to the ever-increasing demand for space, Sacred Heart Church has undergone major renovations throughout its history. Parishioners of Sacred Heart Parish are commended for the painstaking preservation of the notable Florentine renaissance style, the Travertine floor, three Italian marble altars, the classic columns and arches, the open woodwork in the ceiling, rose window, and other features, that are the hallmarks of this beautiful structure.

Saint Elizabeth

The beginnings of the Catholic Church in Pocahontas started in the late 1800s, almost 10 years prior to the arrival of the first Catholics in the area as the Southwest Virginia Improvement Company was formed, paving the way for settlers in search of jobs to move to the area. In January 1890, property was deeded from the Southwest Virginia Improvement Company to the Wheeling Diocese to provide the site for what is now known as St. Elizabeth's Catholic Church.

The early church population was predominantly newly arrived Hungarian immigrants, recruited to work at the Southwest Virginia Improvement Company in Pocahontas. The church construction was completed in 1896 under the leadership of

Father Emil Olivier, who also served as its first pastor. The church was named St. Elizabeth after the patron saint of Hungary. At the time the church was built, there was no rectory or resident priest and Fr. Olivier traveled by horseback from Bluefield one Sunday each month to say Mass.

The lack of a rectory to house a priest was seen as the primary impediment to being able to keep a priest in residence at the Pocahontas church. In 1906, through the generosity of Pocahontas Collieries, successor to The Southwest Virginia Improvement Company, land adjacent to the church on which to build a rectory was deeded to the church.

One year later in 1907, the new rectory was completed, and two Benedictine priests came to take care of the coalfield area, traveling from Pocahontas in Virginia to Welch in West Virginia. Father Anthony Hoch arrived in 1906 and became the first resident pastor when the rectory was completed and held that position for 26 years. In the years that followed, there were as many as four Benedictine priests ministering to the area -- all living in the Pocahontas rectory.

In 1919, Theodore Brasch, from Cincinnati, Ohio painted ten life-size murals which still grace the church today. In the main body of the church, there are six murals on the ceiling and the remaining four are in the sanctuary. Included in the murals is one of St. Elizabeth, for whom the church is named.

During the Depression years, the Benedictines retired to their Monastery and St. Elizabeth was once again a mission church. Several priests came to serve the parish for a year or two. The Oblates of Mary Immaculate served on a limited basis. Priests from Powhatan, West Virginia, continued to serve even after St. Elizabeth's was transferred from the Diocese of Wheeling to the Diocese of Richmond in August 1974.

The physical church building has changed little since its original construction, with the exception of the church steeple which was lowered after the church sustained repeated lightning strikes. A metal roof was installed, and a wheelchair ramp was added to make the church more accessible. Stained glass windows were refurbished and general maintenance on the more than 120-year-old church has maintained its character and the beauty and craftsmanship of the original church building throughout its long and storied history.

Sacred Heart

In 1876, Bishop James Gibbons, Fourth Bishop of Richmond, purchased a tract of land at 14th and Perry Streets in Manchester, but it was not until 1901 that Sacred Heart Church was built and dedicated. A generous gift was given from Mrs. Ida Barry Ryan, who along with her husband, Thomas Fortune Ryan, also provided the funds for construction of the Cathedral of the Sacred Heart. Two years later, the current rectory was built next to the church that had been the site of the Manchester Catholic School. That building was moved to a spot behind the church, later called the White House and more recently, The Hall of Nations.

In 1931, a one-story brick building across the street from the church was built as Sacred Heart School. Benedictine sisters who staffed the school lived in a wooden convent next door. In 1951, a second story was added to the school giving the building its current look. In 1959, Saint Edward the Confessor Parish was established from territory that had been in Sacred Heart Parish. In 1973, territory for Saint Augustine Parish was also carved out of former Sacred Heart Parish territory.

In the late 1960s, in an effort to integrate African American and Caucasian Catholics, two African American parishes were closed, Saint Gerard on Clopton Street not far from Sacred Heart (1967) and Saint Joseph in Jackson Ward (1969). Members of both parishes joined the Sacred Heart family.

Sacred Heart School closed in 1987 due to declining enrollment. In 1990, Jesuits from the Maryland Province of the Society of Jesus were appointed to run the parish and opened Sacred Heart Center in the former school building. Sacred Heart Center was conceived to be a neighborhood resource to empower residents of the Bainbridge-Blackwell area and offered programs among area residents, from child care to youth activities and adult education.

Beginning in 1992, a weekly Mass in Spanish was held at Sacred Heart under the auspices of the "Centro Católico Guadalupe" (the Guadalupe Catholic Center). In 1999, members of this group became members of Sacred Heart and Saint Augustine Parishes. Our Spanish-speaking parishioners come predominantly from Mexico, Guatemala, El Salvador, and the Caribbean, along with others from the rest of the Spanish-speaking world. Asians and English and French speaking Africans also call Sacred Heart home. Growth in our church community has resulted in a parish of more than 1,000 families.

In 2011, Sacred Heart Center refocused its outreach to the region's Latino communities. Sacred Heart Church, born of a dream to give greater access to the Sacraments for Catholics living south of the James River continues to do so today and dreams of being "sacrament" –a channel of God's grace—to all we serve.

Sacred Heart

While the history of the Catholic faith in Stonega can be traced back to the 1840s, when priests would travel to the mountains to provide for local miners, the first records of a parish in the area begins in 1902. That year, the Bishop of Wheeling assigned the Benedictine Fathers of Cullman, Alabama, to minister to Catholic communities and coalmining areas in southwest Virginia and northeast Tennessee. This action led to the creation of Sacred Heart Catholic Church shortly after. The church building was built and owned by the Stonega Coal and Coke Company in order to care for the spiritual wellbeing of its workers. The priests serving Sacred Heart Church would frequently act as mediators between the workers in their parish and the company.

In the 1930s, Sacred Heart Church began to move from its first home in Stonega to Appalachia. The new church building was designed by Father Peter Aarts and dedicated by Bishop Swint on August 28, 1938. In 1945, Glenmary Priests, from Cincinnati came to Appalachia and provided spiritual and financial support for local parishes, including Sacred Heart, and would remain active in the area until the 1980s. Glenmary Priests would also help establish St. Mary's Hospital, first named Norton Clinic, when they asked Bishop Swint to invite the religious sisters, the Poor Servants of the Mother of God, into the area to establish a Catholic hospital.

In the mid-1960s, the decision was made to move Sacred Heart, this time to the current location in Big Stone Gap; Father John Otterbacher oversaw the move and even personally worked on the construction of the new worship space. The new church began operation in 1966, and Mass was said in the basement of the new building while the upper levels were still under construction.

In 1984, the Glenmary Priests began to leave southwest Virginia, and priests from the Diocese of Richmond began to care for Sacred Heart Parish. At the same time, the laity sought and gained approval from Bishop Sullivan of Richmond to construct a new sanctuary, although it would not finish construction until 1990. This building is the current worship space for Sacred Heart Church. The old building was renamed Glenmary Hall after the move, to honor the Glenmary Priests who served Sacred Heart since the 1940s. In 2015, Sacred Heart joyously celebrated its 25th anniversary of this new worship space as well as the 113th anniversary of Sacred Heart Catholic Church.

Saint Anne

— Bristol • 1903 —

In 1860, a group of Irish immigrants were involved in building a railroad line from Richmond to Bristol, Virginia. During the year, the group reached Wallace, Virginia, and requested a Catholic church be built in which they could worship. Since this part of the state was then part of the Diocese of Wheeling in West Virginia, Bishop Whelan directed that the Church of Saint Joseph be built to serve the needs of the railroad workers.

By 1868, the railroad had wound its way into Goodson-Bristol, Virginia and Tennessee, and most of the railway workers settled there. A group of Protestant and Catholic men gathered together and pledged money to Father Michael Duggan for "building a Catholic church in the city of Goodson, Virginia (later named Bristol)." Property on Spencer Street was donated by Colonel Sam Goodson, and the church was completed in 1888 at a cost of $3,000.

In the early 1900's, Benedictine Father Theodosius Osterieder, became the first resident Pastor. In 1926, the church of Saint Joseph in Wallace was closed and the faithful joined with the parish of Saint Ann in Bristol. Benedictine priests served the parish until 1928 when the Benedictine Order withdrew from the area. Priests from the Diocese

of Wheeling were assigned and faced many challenges during the Great Depression. In 1936, the Bishop of Wheeling realized the congregation had outgrown the church on Spencer Street and the new church on Euclid Avenue was completed in 1936. When Saint Ann's moved to Euclid Avenue, the old church building on Spencer Street became Saint Augustine Church and was the place of worship for black Catholics until the late 1950's when parishes were integrated, and everyone attended the new church on Euclid Avenue.

In 1949, a parish school was established and has expanded several times throughout its history. It still actively serves the community today. A convent was also built to house the Sisters of Saint Joseph, who were the original teachers in the school.

In 1974, the parish was transferred from the Diocese of Wheeling to the Diocese of Richmond. Although not documented, it was at this time Saint Ann became identified as Saint Anne. Bishop Walter Sullivan sent diocesan priests who worked tirelessly to smooth the waters of change during the transition and to unite the parishioners.

A new worship space was built, and the church offices and the new rectory were completed, in 1984. The history of Saint Anne Catholic Church continues, combining the skills of each pastor with the gifts of the faithful to form a parish that advances the mission of the Catholic Church in Southwest Virginia and Upper East Tennessee.

Blessed Sacrament

Harrisonburg • 1906

The early Catholic community in Harrisonburg was first served by priests from Saint Francis of Assisi in Staunton. It was not until 1871, when Father John McVerry acquired a former Methodist Church, that Blessed Sacrament community had its first church building. The church was located on West Market Street and was used by the congregation until it was destroyed by a fire in April 1905.

The need for a new church was recognized by Mrs. Ida Barry Ryan. She and her husband, Thomas Fortune Ryan, a native of Nelson County, Virginia, had already contributed the funds to build the Cathedral of the Sacred Heart in Richmond. She donated funds for the construction of the church on the east side of North Main Street.

On November 28, 1907, the new church was dedicated as Blessed Sacrament Catholic Church and it was not until later in 1919 that Blessed Sacrament received her first resident pastor, Fr. Joseph J. DeGryse. Soon after his arrival the church was beautifully embellished and programs like the Parish Social Club, and Ladies Auxiliary were created.

On Sunday, March 24, 1957, the parish celebrated its 50th anniversary at which Bishop Peter Ireton, Ninth Bishop of Richmond, presided.

The parish saw great expansion in 1958 due to James Madison University and many industries moving into Harrisonburg. Soon it was decided that Blessed Sacrament needed new facilities to maintain the growing population. The old rectory and parish hall were demolished and a new rectory, parish offices, multi-purpose building with classrooms, a community room, and kitchen were added on.

In the early 1970's, parish growth and the need for extra staffing was recognized. Religious Sisters of several communities were recruited to help with religious education programs, and to assist with the pastoral ministries of the parish. The

Catholic Student population at JMU was again growing rapidly and in 1976 the Diocese purchased a house for the students to gather for Mass and other actives. It was named, Emmaus House.

A parish Soup Kitchen, begun by volunteers, quickly grew along with those who came to the church for financial aid. In the last several years, projects to repair and preserve the building, stained-glass windows, purchase of the current CCM house, a new rectory, and rebuilding the church organ were undertaken. Ministry for Hispanic Catholics began, and a Spanish Mass is celebrated every Sunday. Bishop Walter Sullivan dedicated the new Sanctuary in June 1995. In the early 2000's many new programs like RCIA and spiritual retreats for the Spanish community where created. We thank all our parishioners for their hard work and dedication to our parish.

Cathedral of the Sacred Heart

— Richmond • 1906 —

The Cathedral of the Sacred Heart in Richmond, is the Mother Church of the Diocese of Richmond. Planning for the Cathedral began in the mid-19th century. Bishop John McGill recognized that Saint Peter Cathedral, the Diocese's first Cathedral located near the State Capitol, could not accommodate a growing Catholic presence in Richmond.

He purchased the land for the new Cathedral shortly after the end of the Civil War. Richmond's growth in the late 1880s propelled the city's population westward. Additional land was purchased near Monroe Park in 1884 to accommodate the new Cathedral, a rectory, and a bishop's residence.

The Cathedral of the Sacred Heart was built through the generosity of one family. Thomas Fortune Ryan

and his wife, Ida Barry Ryan, donated $500,000 in 1901 to build and furnish a new Cathedral for the Ryan's home diocese. A native of Nelson County, Ryan moved to New York City to make his fortune in tobacco, coal, banking, railways, and insurance.

New York architect Joseph H. McGuire designed the Cathedral. One of the few examples of Italian Renaissance Revival in Virginia, the Cathedral is listed on the National Register of Historic Places, a Virginia Historic Landmark, and earned Historic Richmond Foundation's 1992 Award of Achievement for its restoration.

Built of Indiana limestone and Virginia granite, the Cathedral was consecrated on Thanksgiving Day, November 29, 1906. "With all the solemn pomp and ceremony of the ancient faith, in the presence of thousands of every creed and condition and beneath the full beauty of a perfect autumnal sky, the massive doors were thrown wide yesterday," reported the Nov. 30, 1906 (Richmond) Times-Dispatch, "admitting to the sanctuary the most notable gathering of high dignitaries ever assembled upon Southern soil."

From its earliest days, the Cathedral has been a natural gathering place for people of all faiths to commemorate important events in the Church, in Virginia, and in our country and the Universal Church. Grateful prayers were offered in the shadows of its graceful arches at the close of World War II. Hundreds streamed into the Cathedral after a 1969 peace protest in Monroe Park to attend Mass and pray for an end to the Vietnam War. The Cathedral hosted ecumenical prayer services shortly after the terrorist attacks of Sept. 11, 2001, and following the April 16, 2007, shooting at Virginia Tech. The death of Saint John Paul II in 2005 also was commemorated with a prayer service attended by many throughout Richmond who admired the pope.

The generous support of parishioners allows the Cathedral to carry out its many ministries. A major renovation and preservation project were completed during the Cathedral's 50th Anniversary in 1956 and again for its 100th Anniversary in 2006.

The parish hosts its temporarily homeless brothers and sisters through CARITAS – Congregations Around Richmond Involved to Assure Shelter.

Parishioners frequently visit the people of Carissade, Haiti. They have supported, and helped build a church,

a school, a corn mill, two wells and a cafeteria serving over 500 children, teachers' salaries, and the school's clinic for many years.

Given its location on the campus of the ever-growing Virginia Commonwealth University, Catholic Campus Ministry is an important part of parish life. Parishioners and Cathedral staff members strive to ensure that no matter what brings someone through the doors of the Cathedral – an event, a liturgy, or the need for a place to pray – it is a moment of evangelization. All those who do cross the granite threshold into the magnificent space, are welcome.

Church of the Sacred Heart

Prince George • 1906

Located at 9300 Community Lane in Prince George County, Church of the Sacred Heart Parish was founded in 1906. After the Civil War, cities, towns, and rural districts experienced increasing migration from Europe. New cultures and farming techniques in Virginia created a semblance of Eastern Europe in the small community of Estes (originally called Wells Station) in Prince George County, where a small group of Czech and Slovak immigrants resettled in a new land, the first of whom was Joseph Machat in 1887.

Settlers came from the Province of Bohemia (now a part of the Czech Republic) and were predominately Catholic. They hoped to form a Church community with a Czech-speaking priest. In 1905, Father Jon Konicek was sent to pastor the growing community.

The first church building was constructed on 11 acres of land acquired from Marie Hanzlik, whose son married the daughter of Joseph Machat. The land was deeded to the Diocese of Richmond and on September 28, 1906, (the feast of Saint Wenceslaus, patron saint of the Czechs), the church was dedicated and became the first Czech Catholic Church in the Commonwealth of Virginia.

The church was built by the Czechs with lumber cut and milled from their wooded farmlands. A rectory was constructed adjacent to the church in the same manner. A parish cemetery was established with its first recorded interment in 1908. At least fifteen of the first Czech families are buried here, and many of their descendants are members of Sacred Heart Parish.
It was a time when the railroad assigned

the names to the villages along its routes. Since the stores and farms in and around Estes were owned and operated almost totally by Czechs from the area of Bohemia, in 1911 residents of Estes met with the president of Norfolk and Western Railroad to request that the name of Estes change to "Bohemia." The president suggested, "New Bohemia," and the community retains that name to this date.

Over the years with the growth surrounding New Bohemia, the original wooden church needed repairs and expansion, and it was replaced in 1951. The present church was dedicated on the Feast of the Sacred Heart of Jesus, June 25, 2006, (the 100th anniversary of the parish). It is the nature of the Czech people to save and reuse as many things as possible; the preservation and re-use of furnishings was evident in the transition from 1951 to 2006.

Because of its significance in the acculturation of the Czech-Slovak immigrants into American, Church of the Sacred Heart Parish, buildings, grounds and cemetery, were entered into the Virginia Landmarks Registry and the National Register of Historic Places, National Park Service on February 8, 2012.

Just as our founders did, we still roll up our sleeves and volunteer; for stronger than church buildings or material things, the people are the Church. We worship, follow Christ's teachings and carry them beyond the church doors. Whether cleaning the church or grounds, celebrating Eucharist, teaching our children, or being part of the many other ministries at Sacred Heart, we reach out to those in need – a legacy our founding families would be proud we are continuing.

Saint John Nepomucene

—— Dinwiddie • 1907 ——

Established in the late 1800's and early 1900's and known as the Sacred Heart of Mary, this small Catholic community consisted of fifteen to eighteen families gathering in homes and celebrating Mass led by Monsignor O'Farrell, Pastor of Saint Joseph in Petersburg.

The dream of having their own church became a reality in 1906 by using donated materials and building a modest wooden church on three acres of land provided by the Piecek and Blaha families. This new church was named Saint John Nepomucene and was dedicated on May 16, 1907.

Saint John was a mission of Sacred Heart Church in New Bohemia. The church was served by resident Pastors for the Czech communities in the Petersburg area. The church also has a cemetery, believed to have been established in 1910, and remains to this day.

In 1931, the wooden church was replaced with a larger, brick structure, built by parishioners, with seating capacity of 130. It stands today as it was built in 1931. In 1948, plans for a parish hall began. Completed in 1954, the hall was built of sturdy cinder block construction, with a large kitchen, a raised stage, and an expansive dance

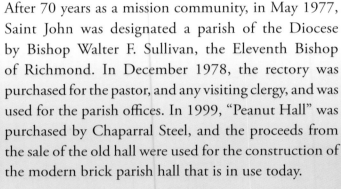

and social hall. The building was well known in the area as "Peanut Hall" with lively square dancing, the sounds of polka and big band music resounding on Saturday nights. Large crowds were drawn from near and far. With the funds raised from these public dances, the building debts were quickly paid off, and the building was further redesigned to establish classrooms for religious education.

After 70 years as a mission community, in May 1977, Saint John was designated a parish of the Diocese by Bishop Walter F. Sullivan, the Eleventh Bishop of Richmond. In December 1978, the rectory was purchased for the pastor, and any visiting clergy, and was used for the parish offices. In 1999, "Peanut Hall" was purchased by Chaparral Steel, and the proceeds from the sale of the old hall were used for the construction of the modern brick parish hall that is in use today.

In August 2014, we joined Church of the Sacred Heart in Prince George County, and Saint James in Hopewell, and became part of the Cluster Parishes sharing a pastor and staff.

Saint Benedict

Saint Benedict Parish was founded in 1911 to minister to Catholics of German ancestry. They were originally parishioners of Saint Mary in downtown Richmond and began migrating to the West End of Richmond. According to an agreement reached by Bishop Augustine Van de Vyver, the Sixth Bishop of Richmond, and Bishop Leo Haid, OSB, of Belmont Abbey and Vicar Apostolic and territorial Abbot of North Carolina, the Benedictine monks would open a high school for boys and oversee the parish in what is now "The Museum District" in Richmond.

After the parish and high school, Benedictine, were established, a parish elementary school was built in 1919. A high school for girls, Saint Gertrude, was built in 1922. With the parish and schools nearby, the Benedictine Monks and Religious Sisters forged a nexus that would educate generations of young people in Richmond.

The parish church was dedicated on August 28, 1929, with Bishop Andrew J. Brennan, the Eighth Bishop of Richmond, presiding. The church building was considered among the most beautiful in the Diocese, with the

classical shape of a Roman basilica, it included Byzantine and Gothic ornamentation. From its beginning through the 1960s, Saint Benedict Parish, together with its associated schools, grew in proportion to the West End of Richmond. Many Catholics moved into the area around the parish, making it a neighborhood community.

The identity of the parish shifted during the 1970s and 1980s. There was confusion and debate at Saint Benedict about how to implement the reforms of the Second Vatican Council. The parish adopted a contemporary liturgical style and music, which encountered both support and resistance, even as the parish remained active in other ministries.

In 1989, the Monks of Saint Benedict Priory formed an independent community apart from Belmont Abbey, with its own Abbey named Mary, Mother of the Church and moved to their new monastery in Goochland County in 1994. During the same period, Saint Benedict Parish was becoming less of a neighborhood parish, with more of its members coming from outside the parish boundaries. In 1999, Monks turned the care of the parish over to the Diocese.

In the new era, Saint Benedict emerged as a more traditional parish. Today, people from within the Museum District and beyond worship here. The parish is best known for its majestic building and reverent worship. Notable, too, is the annual Oktoberfest, a three-day festival that pays tribute to the parish's German roots, gathering 40,000 people and raising tens of thousands of dollars for Catholic education each year. Saint Benedict School provides a strong Catholic identity in the city and beyond.

For more than a century, the Benedictine motto has guided the work of the Parish: *ut in omnibus glorificetur Deus,* "that in all things God may be glorified." (1 Peter 4:11)

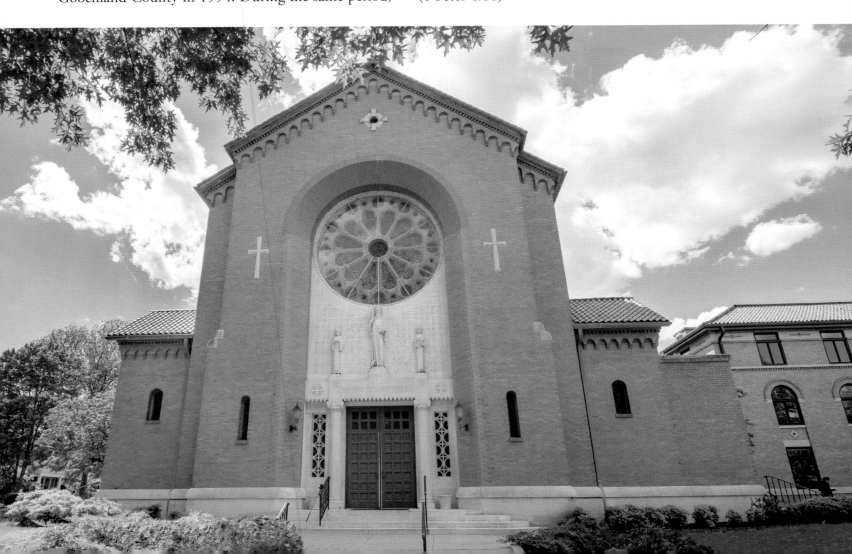

Bishop Denis J. O'Connell

Denis J. O'Connell (1849–1927) was the third native Irishman and the second of three Richmond priests to become diocesan bishop. He returned to the diocese after thirty years away. O'Connell's tenure marked a turning point in the history of the diocese, as Tidewater and northern Virginia experienced their first stage of rapid growth.

Americanism, World War I, and Postwar Growth (1912-1926)

Diocesan Union Holy Name Society Convention, St. Andrew's, Roanoke,
Denis J. O'Connell, seventh bishop of Richmond

O'Connell was a significant figure in the American Church prior to becoming bishop of Richmond. Earlier in his career, he had played a leading role in the "Americanism" controversy (1895–1899) that dealt with the question of the Church's identity in the United States. Significantly, the historical experience of the Diocese of Richmond became a point of reference in this dispute.

Americanism sought to adapt Catholicism to the American way of life. Its leaders included James Gibbons and John J. Keane, both former bishops of Richmond, and O'Connell, who was the movement's intellectual architect. O'Connell was a close aide to Gibbons, his mentor and patron, going back to Gibbons's time in North Carolina and Virginia (1868–1877). O'Connell had also been the rector of the North American College seminary in Rome (1885–1895), where he functioned as a liaison between US bishops and the Vatican.

Americanist bishops held that constitutional norms such as religious freedom and the separation of Church and state were beneficial to the Catholic Church. They also saw the value of ecumenical collaboration in overcoming ignorance of Catholicism and in reducing anti-Catholic bigotry. Opponents argued that this program risked obscuring Catholicism's status as the true faith, and that the spirit of American independence would weaken the

Church's unity. The Americanist perspective was based on the experience of bishops like Keane and Gibbons as leaders of a religious minority in the Diocese of Richmond. When Pope Leo XIII condemned some aspects of Americanism (1899), Gibbons denied having ever held such views.[1] The Americanist position on religious liberty was eventually vindicated at Vatican Council II, which declared the freedom of religion to be a human right (1965).[2]

While O'Connell was bishop of Richmond, the death of a seminarian in Rome inscribed a witness of heroic sacrifice in the annals of the diocese. Francis (Frank) J. Parater (b. 1897), a Richmonder and student at the North American College, died unexpectedly at the age of twenty-two (1920). He courageously offered his life and sufferings "for the spread and success of the Catholic Church in Virginia."[3] The cause for Frank Parater's canonization was introduced in 2001.

At the time of Parater's death, the Richmond Diocese was in the midst of a growth spurt. It began when the United States entered World War I (1917). Catholics, as they had done during the Civil War for either the Union or Confederacy, once more demonstrated their patriotism, this time by supporting the national war effort. In the meantime, a naval base opened in Norfolk that quickly brought thousands of people to the area.[4]

After the war (1918), even as the military demobilized, Norfolk, Hampton Roads, and Virginia Beach continued to grow. The invention of the trolley, as well as the construction of new rail lines, fueled this expansion. Farther north, the opening of the Key Bridge (1923) enabled trolley cars to cross the Potomac River, a

The Women's Land Army of America trained women in agriculture, replacing men who served in the military during World War I

pivotal development that made northern Virginia a suburb of Washington, DC. New parishes were opened to accommodate the growing Catholic population in northern Virginia and Tidewater. In several cases, lay persons took the lead in developing existing missions into these new parishes.[5]

O'Connell's tenure also included the founding of a bureau of Catholic Charities in Richmond (1922), one of the first in the country. This new institution evolved from a long tradition of charitable work done by religious sisters and parishes, especially the St. Vincent de Paul Society and the St. Vincent de Paul Auxiliary. By employing professional social workers, Catholic Charities enabled the Richmond Diocese to provide more systematic assistance to the poor for housing, placement in orphanages, and legal matters.[6]

Bishop O'Connell resigned at the end of 1925 due to illness. He was then named administrator of the diocese and an honorary archbishop (1926), one year before his death (1927).

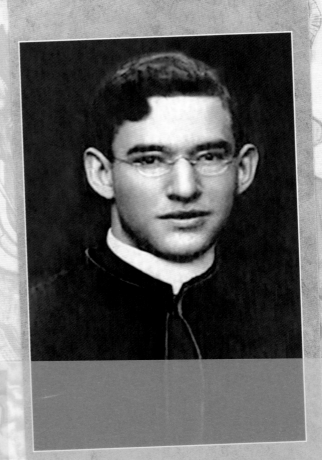

Frank Parater

Sacred Heart

The congregation came into existence in 1897 when a group of German immigrants settled in Lunenburg County and they met in private homes. The first Mass was celebrated by Father Welibard, a Benedictine priest from Richmond. Mass was celebrated every three months and Father would be there to hear confessions and perform whatever sacraments were needed at that time. His visit was always a time for great rejoicing, and the congregation would make the day of it, preparing food for the social time to be enjoyed after Mass was celebrated.

In 1913, Mr. Fred Herzig, a non-Catholic, donated an acre of land to the congregation for a church to be erected. On September 26, 1914, the Church was canonically erected. It was in the spring of 1914 that a class of five made their first Holy Communion, and in the fall of that year, Bishop O'Connell confirmed a large group.

The priests that served this small community would travel to Lunenburg County via railroad, spend the night, and in the morning celebrate Mass. Later in the day the train would be flagged down, Father would board and return to Richmond.

In 1939, Sacred Heart became a mission of St. John's Catholic Church in Crewe. It was at this time that the Precious Blood Fathers began their ministry, which would last until 1978. It was during Father Fortman's time the Mass schedule increased to twice a month at Sacred Heart, and in 1948 Mass was celebrated every Sunday and Holy Days of Obligation.

During Fr. McCarthy's pastorate St. Theresa Parish in Farmville and Immaculate Heart of Mary in Blackstone were built. The cluster of parishes consisted of Sacred Heart, St. Theresa, St. John, and Immaculate Heart of Mary. Mass was also celebrated in Amelia and Victoria. During WWII, the parish priests served the soldiers at Fort Pickett. In 1965, the Parish was divided, St. Theresa and Sacred Heart making one parish.

In 1984, construction began on the pavilion which contains a stage, picnic tables, restrooms, and storage room. In 2003, through the generosity of many parishioners, a new organ was purchased. Linda Shook Jenkins, the organist at the time, pre-recorded many of the hymns which are still in use today. Linda passed away a few years later, but her music continues to resonate in the Parish.

A new altar and ambo, and a new roof for the Community Hall were added as part of our 100th anniversary celebration.

Our mission statement, "We, the parishioners of Sacred Heart Catholic Church, are called by Baptism to be faithful witnesses to the Good News of Jesus Christ and are committed to building the Kingdom of God while serving the needs of others," will continue to inspire us for generations to come.

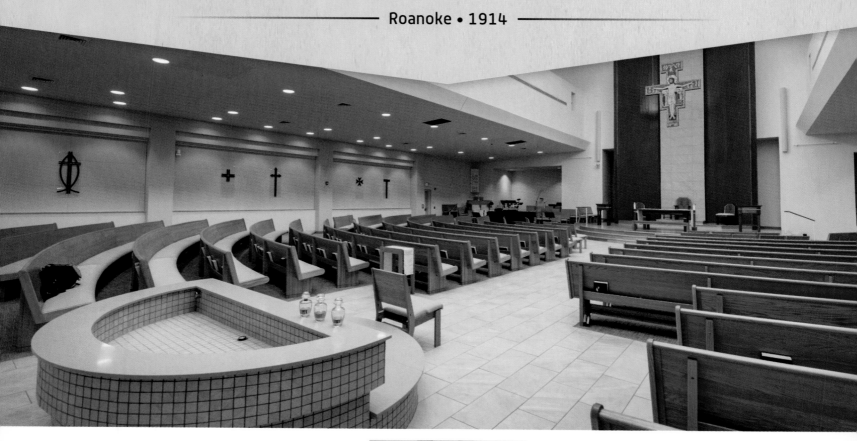

In 1914, Irish-born Father James Gilsenan was sent by the Bishop of Richmond to the 30-year-old City of Roanoke to assistant at Saint Andrew, the large, Gothic-style church on the hill downtown. Because of the growing Catholic population, particularly in the southwest part of this young city in the Blue Ridge Mountains, Father Gilsenan was asked to establish a new parish. Our Lady of Nazareth Catholic Church, a large, modern, brick building now located in southwest Roanoke County, began as a small, wooden hall on Campbell Avenue in downtown Roanoke.

Father Gilsenan bought property on Campbell Avenue on the other side of the railroad lines so that children walking to school would not need to cross the tracks. The purchase included a large brick building that became the convent for the Sisters of Charity of Nazareth and a two-story frame building that the sisters would run as a school. In 1916, the school opened with eight grades; eventually it grew to include a high school. Over the next 56 years, the school would educate more than 11,000 students. In 1950, the high school joined with St. Andrew's to form Roanoke Catholic High School, and in 1973, the lower grades consolidated with St. Andrew's to form Roanoke Catholic Elementary School.

Father Gilsenan began construction on a parish hall in 1918. The lumber came from the razing of the old wooden school just below the Saint Andrew's hill. On the Sunday before Christmas 1918, a public Mass was celebrated at the new facility for the first time. When Bishop Denis O'Connell visited on February 16, 1919, he announced that the new parish would be named Our Lady of Nazareth, a name held by no other U.S. church at that time.

A new building was completed and dedicated by Father Gilsenan in 1926. Named Monsignor in 1940, Father Gilsenan passed away on September 12, 1953. He was succeeded by Father Robert Beattie, who made improvements to the Campbell Avenue property and bought the land for a new church farther out in the county. On the morning of July 9, 1978, the last Mass was celebrated at the old church, followed by the dedication of the new church on Electric Road (Route 419) by Bishop Walter Sullivan that afternoon.

The original rectory is now home to Commonwealth Catholic Charities, the former convent is used by Madonna House. Roanoke Area Ministries occupies the former church building.

The new building on Electric Road was built with the help of a legacy from Miss Anita Obermeyer in the amount of $450,000. On June 25, 1989, the Christian Life Center was dedicated in memory of Miss Anna Louise Haley.

In 2017, the church building underwent major renovations to provide more natural light, upgrade the heating and cooling system, to widen the visibility of the altar, to improve accessibility for the handicapped, and to accommodate the large parish family.

In addition to the church's vibrant ministries the parish also has: a twin relationship with *L'École Normale* in Hinche, Haiti, service projects for migrant workers on the Eastern Shore of Virginia; a Creation Care committee that follows Pope Francis' environmental care suggestions in *Laudato Si*; weekly donations to Saint Francis House food pantry; and a partnership with Family Promise of Greater Roanoke.

The church property also includes a swimming pool, which was purchased in 1988. The pool has a competitive swim team as well. The parish also is the birthplace of Logos Theatricus (Theatre of the Word), a theatre company formed in 2003. Proceeds from community performances are donated to local charities.

The church's covenant states that members of Our Lady of Nazareth parish family are "united by our commitment of service to others as living witnesses of the life, death and resurrection of Christ as taught by the Scriptures and His example."

Saint Mary of the Annunciation

At the turn of the century, a small group of Slovak immigrants established the community of Saint Mary of the Annunciation, Mother of Our Savior. A priest from Fredericksburg traveled by train to Caroline County to celebrate Mass in homes on a periodic basis. In 1914, by the work of their own hands, they built a small wooden church. This building had no running water or electricity but did have two outhouses. Father Delaunay wrote to the Bishop of Richmond in March 1914, "Never have I experienced a Mass so devoutly celebrated than by the people of Woodford." Later in 1937, Rt. Rev. Msgr. Francis J. Byrne wrote the Bishop, "The people of Woodford are among the best Catholics in the Diocese."

The founders of Saint Mary of the Annunciation left a rich legacy. Originally, the parish was entitled Saint Mary of the Annunciation,

Mother of our Savior Parish, a daughter parish of Saint Mary's in Fredericksburg. For some years the Oblates of Mary (OMI) provided pastoral leadership for Saint Ann in Ashland and for the mission of Saint Mary of the Annunciation. In 1992, Bishop Walter F. Sullivan purchased 23 acres central to the parish population.

The parish numbered 88 families when the new church was dedicated on October 16, 1996. On that occasion the pastor, Father James F. Kauffmann, remarked "Tonight our Liturgy of Dedication gives witness to the truth that our future lies in the power of God and not on human calculation. Thus, we receive this new church as a gift come down from heaven as a sign that we can embrace the future with confidence and hope. God has gathered us under one roof to be one people united at one Holy Table where all are welcome."

During the Great Jubilee of the year 2000, Saint Mary of the Annunciation Parish was privileged to be designated a pilgrimage site for gaining the Jubilee Indulgence by Bishop Walter F. Sullivan. The Parish of Saint Mary comprises only 1/2 of one percent of the population of Caroline County.

The present facility was designed by Wisniewski, Blair and Associates of Alexandria, Virginia, and constructed in 1996. The church is a simple wooden structure whose form echoes a medieval, wooden, Slovak Church. It seats 200-250 people. The generous use of windows floods the worship space with natural light. This openness also allows the community to enjoy its rural, woodland setting. The church complex also includes a small office, nursery/conference room and large narthex with breakfast bar, used for social gatherings and religious education. The master plan of the facility allows for future expansion of the worship space and a social/education facility with additional office possibilities. The church recently hosted a concert series and the members of the Richmond Symphony remarked about the excellent acoustical quality of the church for music production. Tyra Sexton, a landscape designer from Fredericksburg, designed the gardens that surround the church.

The garden in front of the church is dedicated to Saint Mary of the Annunciation and the garden behind the church is dedicated to Mary, Mother of Our Savior. Statues of Our Lady will be placed in each of the gardens.

Saint Mary

— Chesapeake • 1915 —

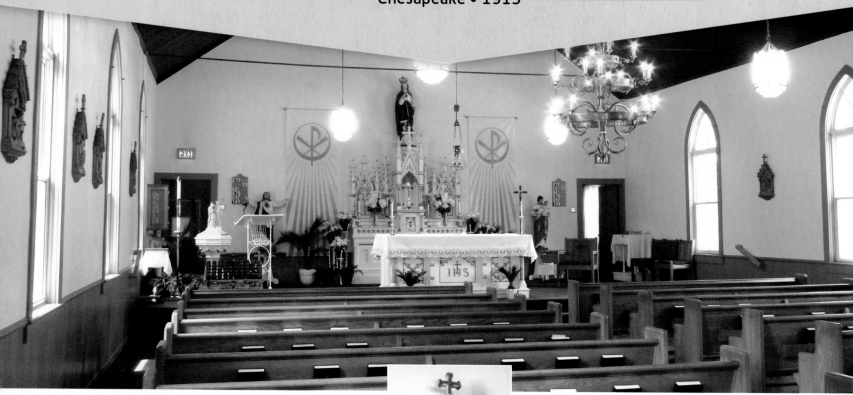

Between 1908 and 1912, a small group of Polish families answered a newspaper advertisement to settle in the Bowers Hill area of Norfolk County. The land had recently been cut for timber by the Franklin Land and Lumber Company. Mr. Joseph Janusz, a Polish immigrant who envisioned the possibilities of a settlement with his fellow countrymen, convinced the company to sell the land to immigrant farmers. Instead of the pristine farmland advertised, the men and women found what could best be described as swamps, rocks and tree stumps. The first settlers in the Sunray community worked to push back the Great Dismal Swamp and to finish clearing the land.

Being Catholic, the community would gather each Sunday in the house of Jan Zawada. Finally, in 1912, a mission priest, Reverend W. A. Gill, appeared in Sunray. A small one-room cottage was converted for the celebration of Mass. An altar was crafted by the men and hidden behind a curtain during the week when the building served as a school.

In January 1912, Isadore Herz, a major stockholder in the Franklin Land and Lumber Company, generously donated six and a half acres of land to the church. On July 6, 1915, the deed was recorded at the Norfolk County Courthouse at a cost $1.64 (fourteen cents of which was tax).

Ground was broken for the church on November 2, 1915. With Mr. Grant Revell to supervise and with the men of the parish each donating at least two-days labor, the church was completed and dedicated during the first Mass on February 16, 1916, just 15 weeks later.

ST. MARY CATHOLIC CHURCH 1916 — 2016

Father Wawrzyniec Bundy, our first pastor, arrived in 1918. Soon after, the parish noticed a need for a parish hall. Again, each man in the parish donated his time for the construction of the building. The first floor of

the building was used as a public school, leased by the Norfolk County school system. The second floor was used as the parish social hall. In 1922, Norfolk County erected a new school building north of the church. The first floor was then converted into a rectory. The present parish hall was completed in 1922.

In the 60s, a large-scale renovation of the church facilities was begun to include the changes mandated by the Second Vatican Council. These included: the altar rail being removed, the platform being modified, new carpeting and a new modern altar built.

On December 9, 1970, fire blazed in the church and did considerable damage to the Sacristy and the rooms behind the Tabernacle. For several months during the repair work on the church, Mass was held in the social hall.

In 1974, Father Richard Kirch removed the altar built in 1966 and returned the original altar. From 1997 to 2002, major renovations occurred to the church and the social hall.

In 2005, Bishop Francis DiLorenzo formed the Cluster Parishes of Portsmouth and Chesapeake. Together with Saint Paul, Holy Angels, and Resurrection (all of Portsmouth), the four parishes were assigned two priests to oversee the everyday activities and responsibilities of the cluster.

In 2012, the parish organized the first annual Polish Fest and continues each year to celebrate our Polish heritage through Polish food, music, dance, and Mass celebrated in Polish. In April 2016, the parish celebrated its Centennial Jubilee.

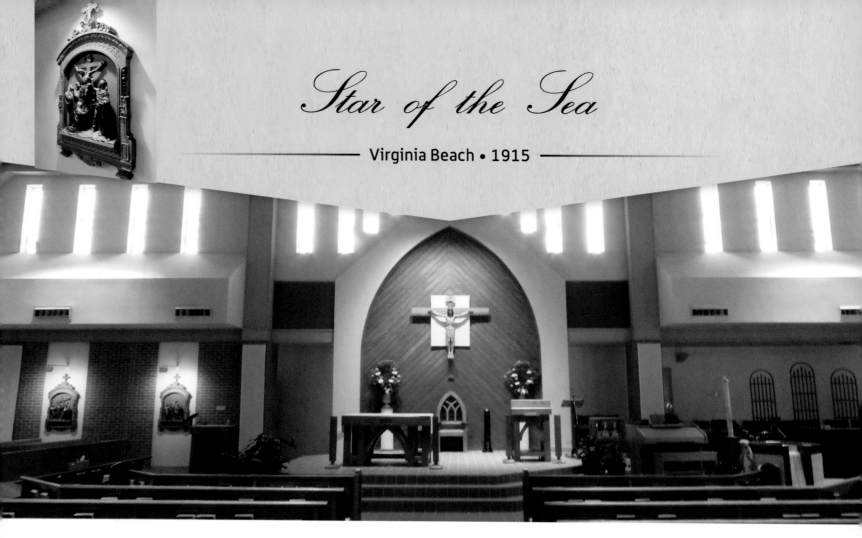

Star of the Sea

Star of the Sea originated with Bishop Denis J. O'Connell, the seventh Bishop of Richmond, and Father John Doherty, then pastor of St. Mary in Norfolk, who met with laity from Norfolk and Virginia Beach. They began with plans for a small chapel beside Lake Holly on land obtained from Mr. James S. Groves of Virginia Beach Development Company. On June 4, 1915, Father Philip P. Brennan, the first pastor, laid the cornerstone for the oldest parish in Virginia Beach, one block from the Oceanfront.

John Kevan Peebles, a leading architect and a native of Petersburg, designed the structure. Peebles had gained recognition for designing Saint Paul Catholic Church in Portsmouth and had recently completed a renovation of the State Capitol in Richmond.

Completed in only two months under the supervision of Mr. R.E. Johnson, the new chapel was a small red brick structure with a green slate roof and seated 200 worshippers. The interior was constructed of a lighter brick, framed by wooden rafters, crossbeams and unique corbels. There was a marble altar against the back wall with the entire structure less than 1,800 square feet.

The first regular Mass in the new church was one week later, August 15, 1915, a Holy Day in honor of the Assumption of the Blessed Virgin Mary.

Over the next four decades, rapid growth of the parish placed demands on the small chapel. Upon his arrival as pastor in 1950, Father Nicholas Habets began further expansion of the south wing, doubling the seating capacity of the church. It was during the tenure of Father Habets that Star of the Sea School was established. Star of the Sea Catholic School opened in 1958 and was staffed by sisters, servants of the Immaculate Heart of Mary, IHM. At that time there were eight classrooms; grades one through eight.

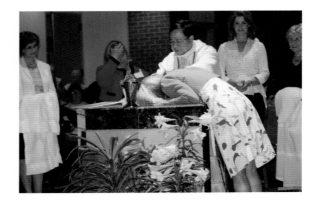

Through the 1990's and into the 21ˢᵗ Century, the parish community continued to grow, beginning with several strategic land acquisitions by Father James Dorson. Later, construction plans for an 18,700 square foot Parish Hall was initiated by Father Kevin O'Brien and brought to realization by the current pastor, Father Esteban "Steve" DeLeon. To make room for the newest addition, the former Rectory and a Winter Chapel, built in the 1950's were razed. The Parish Hall, named Crawford Hall in honor of Father Robert Crawford, C.M., was equipped with a partitioned dining area and a full commercial kitchen on the first floor and meeting rooms on the second floor. It has been a blessing to the Parish. Father Steve's 25ᵗʰ Anniversary of Ordination and many other special events were celebrated in Crawford Hall without the parish needing to rent outside space as it had in the past.

Star of the Sea in 2015 is truly blessed to have an inviting sense of family and warmth. Whether vacationing in Virginia Beach for the first time, just moving to the area or having been here for 20 years, you absolutely know you are welcomed! The parishioners, the staff,

the ministries, and the location provide a rewarding, spiritual and familial experience. Visitors to the parish always say they feel welcomed, and they always return when they are in town.

In addition to being welcoming, Star of the Sea is diverse. We are a family of multiple age-groups, ethnicities and socio-economic classes. The faith, kindness, and spirit of the people make us more than just bricks and mortar. Today, Star of the Sea Parish is a thriving Catholic community of over 1,400 families looking forward to another century of service to the community and praise to the Holy Trinity and "Mama" Mary, our Patroness.

Church of the Holy Angels

At the end of World War I, one hundred Catholics living in the U.S. Housing Corporation project known as Cradock felt the need for a church of their own. In October 1919, Bishop Denis Joseph O'Connell approved the plan and the official name, "Church of the Holy Angels," Cradock. It is said that this name was selected because of the proximity of Paradise Creek to the site where the church was to be located.

On Columbus Day, October 12, 1919, Father Magri blessed the new church and celebrated Mass for the first time. On December 18, 1922, a block of land on Afton Parkway was purchased as a future site for the church. Two years later, on February 6,

1924, a major storm came through and lifted the church building from its foundations and deposited it on the ground some feet to the East. The parishioners decided to remove the partially damaged church to the property which had been acquired on Afton Parkway.

In 1933, the members of Holy Angels Mission requested that Bishop Brennan establish the mission as an independent parish, with a resident pastor. In October 1933, Fr. Philip C. Blackburn became the first permanent pastor. In 1939, a new building plan for a larger church, parish hall, and rectory were created. The new buildings were erected in 1950.

Children from Church of the Holy Angels had attended Saint Paul Parochial School since 1919, but due to the increasing number of students,

Saint Paul's could no longer absorb the student load from outside. A tract of land, part of a former old farm, and the massive residence thereon, located near Brentwood, was purchased in the Fall of 1953. In 1954, the parish had plans drawn for a new parochial school and by 1955 the school was completed. It was a 10-classroom building dedicated by Bishop Hodges in October 1955. In September 1956, five sisters of the Daughters of Wisdom Order arrived to teach at the school. By 1958, over 300 students attended the school.

In February of 1970 the decision was made to consolidate and centralize all Catholic elementary schools in the Portsmouth and Chesapeake areas.

Saint Paul's School, Little Flower, and Holy Angels School merged to form the present Portsmouth Catholic Regional School. The school was staffed by The Daughters of Charity and lay teachers through 2000. Due to a shortage of Sisters, the Daughters were unable to return to teach at the school. Presently Portsmouth Catholic is staffed by a lay staff.

In the Spring of 2005, Bishop Francis DiLorenzo created the Cluster Parishes of Portsmouth and Chesapeake: Church of the Holy Angels, Saint Paul, and Church of the Resurrection in Portsmouth and Saint Mary in Chesapeake. Father Anthony Morris is the current Pastor of all four Parishes.

Our Lady of the Blessed Sacrament

West Point • 1918

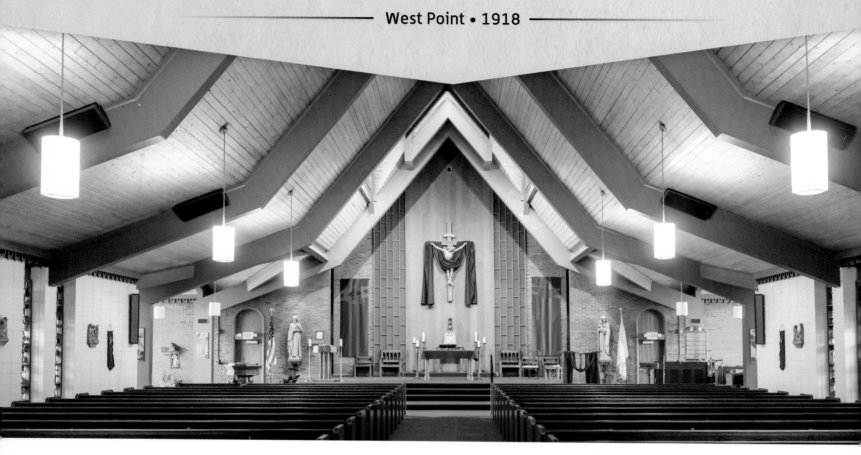

Prior to the establishment of Our Lady of the Blessed Sacrament Parish in 1918, a few Catholic families residing in the West Point area were privileged to attend Mass only once a month, in the residence of the Pumphrey family by a priest from Richmond.

Several prominent Catholic men, Mr. James B. O'Connor, Colonel William Burleigh and Captain Frank Rogers, realizing the need for a permanent church, combined their resources and constructed Saint Theresa Church on 13th Street. It was dedicated in 1906.

Polish families settled here in the early 1900's for the ship building and paper making trade. With the influx of many Catholic families, the need for the establishment of a Parish was finally realized in August 1918. The original frame building at a site in the Port Richmond area was constructed in 1925.

The first priest assigned as Pastor of the newly organized parish was the Reverend Ceslaus Jakubowski. "Father Jack" labored ardently and served well his parish and the community for forty years until his death July 20, 1961.

In 1931, the needs of the Catholic children were recognized, and a Parochial School and Convent were constructed. The Sisters of Mercy, of Baltimore Diocese, taught the ninety students until June 1968 when the closing of the school was necessary because of the lack of teaching sisters.

In 1965, the Reverend Henry van den Boogaard, M.S.F., was assigned as Pastor by Bishop John J. Russell. Upon his arrival, he realized the need for a new rectory. It was soon completed and dedicated in August 1965. He then began the design for a new church. Much of the work was done by parishioners, including the creation of the stained-glass windows. Construction was begun in November 1967 and the dedication was in 1968 on the 50ᵗʰ anniversary of the parish.

The roof of the main body of the church is shaped like an arrowhead, pointing toward Heaven. The statues were purchased by Mr. Karl Rudolph, the chief benefactor of the new building. He was a personal friend of the wood carvers, Oscar Lang and John Lang, who both played the part of Christ in the famous pageant at Oberammergau, Germany, where these statues were hand carved. The statue on the left as you enter the church is Saint Anthony, requested by Mr. Rudolph.

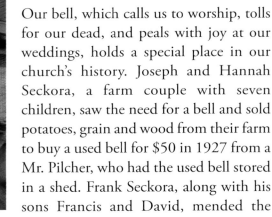

Under the direction of Father van den Boogaard, approximately 30 people fashioned the stained-glass windows. Working three or four evenings a week, the installation took approximately eight months. The lead strips were made by the workers, as well as the kiln in which the windows were baked. Notice the names of the individuals baked into the glass throughout the 12 windows, each of which represents an event of the New Testament.

Our bell, which calls us to worship, tolls for our dead, and peals with joy at our weddings, holds a special place in our church's history. Joseph and Hannah Seckora, a farm couple with seven children, saw the need for a bell and sold potatoes, grain and wood from their farm to buy a used bell for $50 in 1927 from a Mr. Pilcher, who had the used bell stored in a shed. Frank Seckora, along with his sons Francis and David, mended the bronze bell in 1987.

The parish oversees two Catholic cemeteries, the parish cemetery adjoining the town's cemetery and Saint John Kanti Cemetery, a Polish cemetery adjacent to a former church site in New Kent County.

In 2002, the parish undertook a major renovation of the parish hall interior, updated rectory heating/cooling systems, and completed reroofing of church portico.

Saint James

On July 7, 1887, Rt. Rev. John J. Keane, Fifth Bishop of Richmond, purchased a lot from the Eppes family for the site of a Catholic Church and by 1888 a Chapel was built. At that time, the parishioners at the Chapel were the seamen and their families who were based in Hopewell. It became a mission church of Saint Joseph in Petersburg and was served by Father James T. O'Farrell, pastor of Saint Joseph. Mass was given every Sunday until 1903 when the United States Navy withdrew the fleet, discontinued the use of City Point as a base, and many of the Catholic population left. Due to the small Catholic population left, the Chapel was sold. The Chapel located 609 Brown Avenue in City Point is presently owned by the Historic Hopewell Foundation.

Father Martin J. Haier from Saint Joseph and other priests would come for Sunday Masses. In 1914, the European War broke out and the E.I. Du Point de Nomours & Co. opened a guncotton plant. Hopewell's population quickly grew with the need of factory workers. Father Haier saw the need for a Catholic Church and a small chapel was set up on Broadway, once again becoming a mission of Petersburg.

The corner lot of City Point Road and Sixth Avenue was purchased in 1916 for a new church. The cornerstone was laid that July and the church was officially named Saint James Catholic Church and dedicated on October 15, 1916. The two-story, red brick building had a basement, parish hall, and a Sanctuary with two sacristies. In 1918, Saint James became a parish and the first appointed resident pastor was Father John J. Massey.

On December 22, 1927, Father James P. Gacquin joined Saint James. While at Saint James, Father Gacquin organized the Holy Name Society, and the Sodality of the Blessed Virgin Mary. He also established Saint James School, built the convent, painted and renovated the church. Saint James celebrated its Silver Jubilee on October 10, 1941.

In 1950, a new church was needed because the original Church suffered structural damage in a storm. While the new church was under construction, Masses were said at the Beacon Theater. On March 1, 1951, the new Saint James was opened.

In 1970, major renovations were undertaken at the church, rectory, convent, and school hall.

With the church community continuing to grow, it was decided in 1980 that renovations were needed again. The church continued to serve the community and celebrated 100 years of service to the people of Hopewell on October 22, 2016.

In 2016, the main Sanctuary was remodeled and positioned back to its original location with a center aisle. The crucifix and statues were refurbished. The first Mass in the newly renovated space was celebrated by Father Chris Hess on Easter Sunday, April 16, 2017.

Blessed Sacrament

— Norfolk • 1921 —

In 1905, Catholics of Lamberts Point, Park Place, Colonial Place, and Edgewater in Norfolk assembled to worship at Saint Francis de Sales, a small mission of Sacred Heart Church located at the corner of Bluestone Avenue and 39th Street. By the end of World War I, the congregation had outgrown the mission and built a church at 37th Street and Colley Avenue on a plot of land given by Mr. and Mrs. John Clark. The Right Rev. Dennis J. O'Connell, seventh Bishop of Richmond, dedicated the church to the Blessed Sacrament on February 20, 1921; Father Leo J. Ryan was the first pastor.

In 1940, Father Joseph F. Govaert, succeeding Father Ryan, did much to build up the young parish and beautify the church. Father Joseph V. Brennan became pastor in 1942 until his death on December 19, 1951. Father Brennan promoted participation by the youth in parish life. The Newman Club at the Division of the College of William and Mary in Norfolk (presently Old Dominion University) was organized under his direction. Father Francis J. Blakely became pastor in July of 1952. Under his leadership, Blessed Sacrament School and Convent were built and the Sisters of Notre Dame de Namur came to teach the children in 1953. The school closed in 1988.

In 1963, the decision was made to build a larger church to accommodate the growing congregation. The new Blessed Sacrament Church was built at the corner of Newport Avenue and Painter Street, adjacent to Norfolk Catholic High School and DePaul Hospital, it was dedicated on April 10, 1965. The old church on Colley Avenue became known as the Chapel and served as a place of worship for the parish school and the parish community until 1989. The convent building now houses Madonna Home, a communal home for the elderly. The rectory on 37th Street is now the Dwelling Place, an ecumenical shelter for homeless families.

The Most Reverend J. Louis Flaherty, the auxiliary to the Bishop of Richmond, returned as pastor and Dean of the Tidewater Deanery in December 1971. Blessed Sacrament had been Bishop Flaherty's home parish as a youth.

In 2001, the parish began a renovation of the 1965 worship space. The parish continued expansion efforts to accommodate the growing parish needs for worship space, meeting rooms, k-12 and adult education classrooms, and hospitality and outreach efforts. Blessed Sacrament parish continues to grow as a faith-filled community, witnessing the Gospel, nurturing family life, and making the teachings of Jesus central to its parishioners.

Holy Trinity

Holy Trinity started as a mission of Saint Mary Church in Downtown Norfolk. In 1918, His Excellency, Bishop O'Connell announced the founding of Holy Trinity Parish.

This same year the Reverend Robert B. Kealey, who was assistant at Saint Mary, was appointed the first pastor. Coming

into the new parish, Father Kealey found it necessary to reside in a private home until adequate quarters could be built. Then there was the need for a church. On August 28, 1919, the first Mass was celebrated in a movie house. Later, a room adjoining the Ocean View Bank was used for services. In 1920, property was purchased on the northeast corner of First View Street and Government Avenue. Construction on both the church and the rectory started on Saint Patrick's Day, 1920. On Trinity Sunday of this same year, Mass was offered for the first time in the uncompleted Church.

Bishop O'Connell dedicated the church on June 5, 1921.

The year 1924 saw the completion of an eight-room school. The first registration of 103 pupils was under the guidance of four Sisters of the Holy Cross. Holy Trinity School was the third parochial school in Norfolk. High school classes were instructed in the school from 1927 until 1950. The Sisters lived in what is now the parish house until the present convent was completed in October 1928. Three additions have since been added to the school, and the auditorium and gym were built in 1940.

On December 13, 1953, the present church and rectory were blessed and dedicated by Fr. Martin J. Harrison. In 1958, other additions were made to the school.

In 2007, our parish entered into a shared ministry experience with Saint Pius X Parish in Norfolk for one year. During that time, our parish was served by Father Venancio Balarote, Jr., and Father Dan Beeman. In June 2008, Father Beeman was assigned as pastor of Holy Trinity.

Saint Paul

Before July 4, 1920, a Catholic parish for Northside Richmond was a dream. That dream, the longing for a neighborhood church and school, became a reality when Barton Heights parish was established.

Prior to the establishment of Barton Heights Catholic Church, Northside Catholics had worshiped at other parishes in the city. In 1915, Barton Heights Catholic Church (the orginal name of Saint Paul) acquired a small frame building on Fendall Avenue for services of their own. The group was served by a visiting priest and by the Sisters of Charity. With the establishment of

a Northside parish, the little building on Fendall Avenue became Barton Heights Catholic Church and the visiting priest, Reverend Edwin P. Shaughnessy, became the parish's first pastor. Father Shaughnessy got right to work renovatioing the first floor of the church and started organizations like the Ladies' Tabernacle & Aid Society, Men's Holy Name Society, League of the Sacred Heart, League of the Holy Souls, Altar and Sanctuary Soceity, and Soceity of the Blessed Virgin Mary.

As Barton Heights Catholic Church flourished, the desire for a parish school increased and the need for a larger building became apparent. On August 6, 1922, Bishop Denis O'Connell,

136

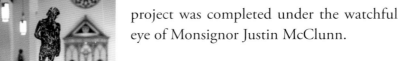

dedicated the new church building on North Avenue. Bishop O'Connell advised that since the church was being changed from being used by the Medodists to that of Catholics, it was fitting that the proper name for the parish should be Saint Paul, instead of Barton Heights parish. In the following September, Saint Paul School opened its doors.

For 28 years, Saint Paul remained on North Avenue. During that time, Saint Paul School expanded and in 1926 the school moved to a building on Fendall Avenue. By the early 1940's, Saint Paul was outgrowing the North Avenue loaction. Under the guidenace of Monsignor Thomas O'Connell, a series of fundraising drives began and in 1950, Saint Paul's present church building on Chamberlayne Avenue was constructed and dedicated. In September of 1967, Saint Paul School relocated to a new building on Noble Avenue. This

project was completed under the watchful eye of Monsignor Justin McClunn.

On Sunday March 26, 2000, the parish broke ground for a new Parish Center. With the dedication of the new Parish Center by Bishop Walter Sullivan on Sunday, October 14, 2001, the congreation gained an inviting space to gather before and after the Liturgies. Additional meeting space, kitchen, and restrooms provide for the needs of a growing parish community.

During the years 2002 and 2003, a Columbarium, located under the stained-glass windows on the south wall of the church, was added to the courtyard. The Church underwent an interior renovation and was rededicated by Bishop DiLorenzo on February 26, 2017.

The diversity of Saint Paul's parishioners has helped it grow and prosper through the years. The parishioners' devotion to God, their hard work and financial support have made Saint Paul's the outstanding parish we all cherish so very much. As we look ahead to the future, may we continue to rejoice in the gifts we have as a parish family.

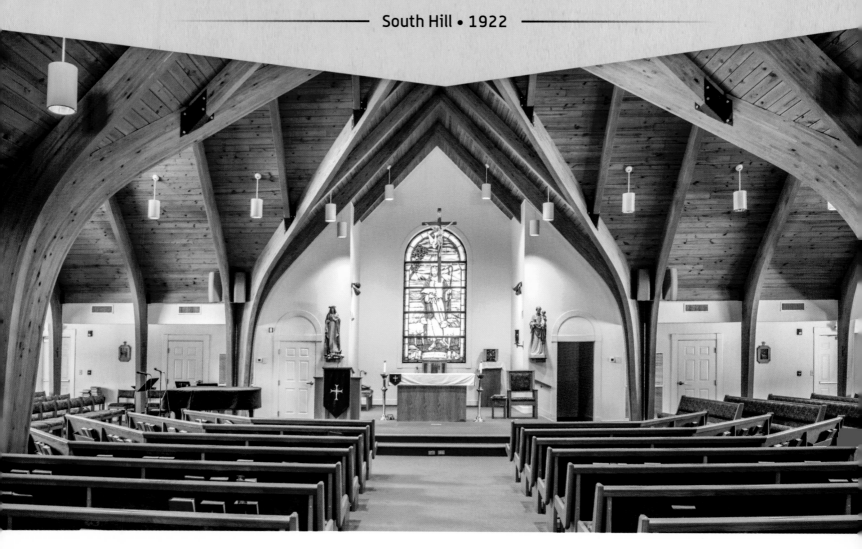

Good Shepherd

In 1922, Good Shepherd was established just two miles from where the present Church stands today. Liturgy was celebrated several times a year in the first Church by a priest from Danville. Bishop Peter Ireton saw a need for more priests in the area and asked the Franciscan Fathers of New York to assist him in the work in southside Virginia. After their arrival, regular church services began in South Hill by 1943.

The Franciscans ministered in South Hill and the surrounding area from 1941 until 1977 when the Diocese of Richmond took over. The original church for Church of the Good Shepherd in South Hill was constructed in the early 1950's and dedicated on February 7, 1954. The new church is 7,491 square feet and was dedicated on September 15, 2006, by Bishop Francis X. DiLorenzo. The capacity of this church is 300 people. The parish is currently home to 230 members from 78 registered

families. Our parish members are from all walks of life and nationalities. The parish in rural southside Virginia serves the counties of Mecklenburg, Brunswick, and Lunenburg, and the main industries are agriculture, manufacturing, and recreation or tourism.

As the church has grown over the years, we have added many ministries: Liturgy, Christian Formation, Knights of Columbus, Justice and Peace, Pastoral Council, Parish Community Life, Youth, Prison, Hispanic, and Migrant Ministries.

We have a bilingual Mass every Saturday and an English Mass each Sunday morning. The parish supports daily prayer and other devotions. We have a weekly weekday Mass on Wednesday followed by Holy Hour. Good Shepherd has parishioners who actively reach out to those who are sick and homebound. Lectors enhance our worship of God by the way they deliver the Gospel message during liturgy, while other parishioners usher,

serve as a choir member, or as sacristans. The parish participates in interfaith programs such as the hosting of the Ash Wednesday service, and luncheon each year for the South Hill community. We have a Fiesta and Our Lady of Guadalupe celebration each year for the Hispanic community, which the whole parish attends. Good Shepherd also has had a twinning project with our brothers and sisters at Saint Joseph Busibo Church in the Diocese of Masaka, Uganda, Africa. Good Shepherd provides a food bank service to the needy in our community.

The relatively new Tri-Pastoral Council includes three members from each parish – Good Shepherd, Saint Paschal Baylon and Saint Catherine of Siena – to assist the pastor. Sharing experiences and formulating combined vision and mission statements for our communities will serve to strengthen our faith. We are truly blessed to have parishioners and members of our community who devote so much of their time and energy to help the church.

Shrine of the Sacred Heart

— Hot Springs • 1922 —

The Shrine of the Sacred Heart Catholic Church was built in 1894 to welcome visitors to the Alleghany Mountains. It is in beautiful Hot Springs, Virginia, and currently has just a few dozen parishioners in the counties of Highland and Bath. The small, faithful group of registered parishioners are often outnumbered by visitors who own vacation homes in the area or who are staying at the nearby Omni Homestead Resort. Also, two state parks draw year-round visitors to the area. As a mission parish within walking distance of a luxury resort, the Shrine is unique in its remote location. Although Covington is fewer than 20 miles away, the drive is a perilous 30-to 40-minute drive through the Allegheny Mountains, complete with hairpin turns and switchbacks. Parishioners and visitors are committed to supporting the Shrine so there is a place to worship in this scenic, but isolated community.

Over many years, the renovation of the Church and rectory has been ongoing. The parish has replaced the electrical wiring, the HVAC system, the roof and siding, installed a ramp to facilitate entrance for visitors and parishioners needing a wheelchair. One of the most well-known such visitors was His Eminence, Cardinal Hickey who offered daily Mass at the Shrine when he would come for treatment at The Spa.

The Shrine continues to welcome people from all over the country to worship in the scenic mountain location. Father John McGinnity, a priest of the Diocese of Wheeling-Charleston, West Virginia, served as pastor for 15 years before retiring. Father Augustine Kalule Lukenge from the Diocese of Kiyinda-Mityana, Uganda, is the current administrator.

Saint Elizabeth

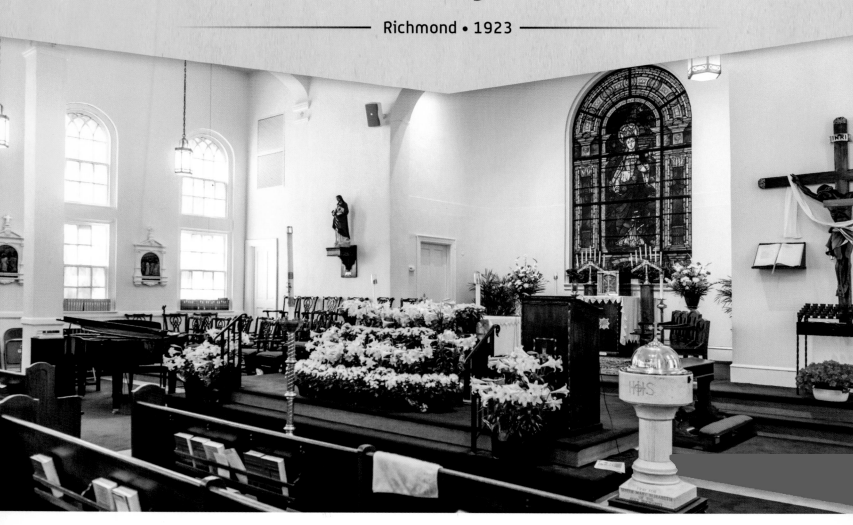

Mr. Fritz Sitterding donated the lot at the southwest corner of Second Avenue and Fourqurean Lane for the future church building. In early 1925, the cornerstone of the church was laid. The building was designed by William H. Rhodes, a parishioner, and by the architectural firm who employed him. The stained-glass window of Saint Elizabeth of Hungary was donated by Joseph Heye, an architect with the same firm. The first Mass in the new church was celebrated on Christmas Day, 1925 by our first pastor, Reverend Louis A. Rowen.

The year 1930 saw the establishment of the first school, located at 925 Fourqurean Lane, which was staffed by three Daughters of Charity of Saint Vincent de Paul. In 1936, during the Depression, the school was closed, and the children were transferred to Saint Paul School that was located not far away in Barton Heights. The elementary school was re-established after a 12-year closure and was staffed by the Sisters of Mercy of Merion, Pennsylvania. The rectory, at that time located on Fourqurean Lane, was given to the sisters as a convent. The present rectory was purchased in 1949. Ground was broken for the much-needed school in May of 1950 and classes began in the new building on January 2, 1951.

During the late 1950's and early 1960's, the church was renovated, redecorated, and modernized with air-conditioning and new lighting. During 1978, the interiors of the church sanctuary and parish were renovated per the liturgical restoration called for by Vatican II and because of growing parish ministries. The result expressed the needs of a racially and economically diverse Catholic Community in an urban neighborhood.

In 1982, the school was closed, and the students moved to classes in the newly named All Saints School, formerly Saint Paul School. The convent was destroyed by fire in September of 1983 and a year later the school building was sold.

In 2006 - 2007, the church had major renovation and restoration, and again in 2012, major renovations and restorations have been made to the rectory and the parish hall.

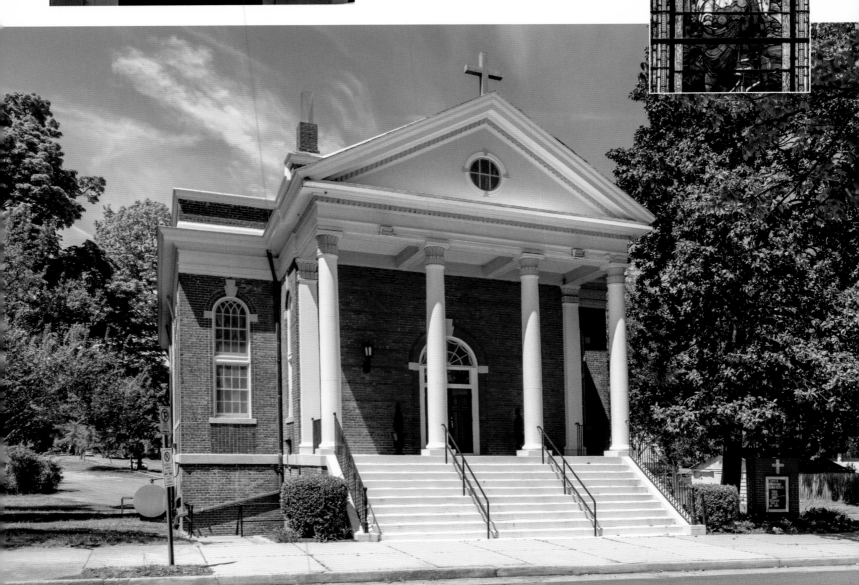

Sacred Heart

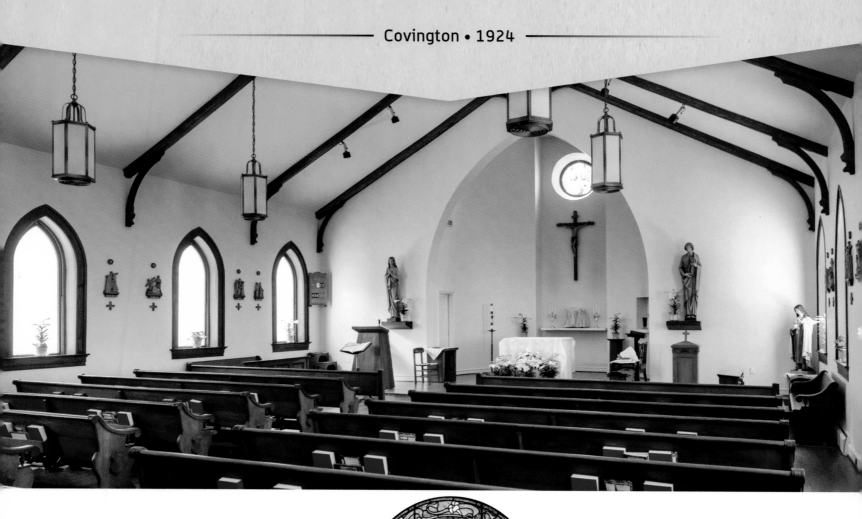

Under the pastorate of Father Kelly of Saint Joseph Church in Clifton Forge, and the guidance of Bishop Augustine Van de Vyver, the first Catholic Church in Covington, Sacred Heart, was erected in 1894 on the corner of Oak and Monroe Streets. On August 19, 1894, Sacred Heart was dedicated by Bishop Van de Vyver.

In 1907, the present church was purchased from the Methodist Episcopal Church for a total of $3,000. After the purchase, the church was renovated and the altars and statues from the first church were transferred to the new building.

Reverend William Gaston Payne of Saint Joseph in Clifton Forge was named Sacred Heart's first parish priest in the newly renovated church on Main Street in 1908. He also served the churches in Alleghany, and Bath Counties, and in Lexington. Sacred Heart was a mission of Saint Joseph in Clifton Forge until 1924, when Sacred Heart became a parish.

Reverend Joseph Jurgens came to Sacred Heart from 1939-1968. While he was at Sacred Heart,

the present parish hall was built, the debt for the Sunday school rooms was paid off, Sacred Heart purchased the current rectory from the Hammond family, and Father Jurgens supplied part payment for the second renovation of our Sacred Heart Church in 1976.

In 1981, the church again went through renovations. This time the building was enlarged to add more seating, a vestibule, reconciliation room, the church was sandblasted to return to the original brick color, a new organ was installed, and a new baptismal fountain was added.

Saint Matthew

— Virginia Beach • 1924 —

Saint Matthew started when a group of determined Catholics initiated plans to build a new church. With much hard work and an inheritance from the estate of Mr. Matthew Duggan, a chapel was built in 1907 on Hardy Avenue, Berkley Section, in Norfolk, and named Saint Matthew. A new chapel was dedicated by Bishop Denis O'Connell in 1908. At that time, there were 45 families.

Saint Matthew was a mission of Saint Mary in Norfolk from 1908 to 1924. Priests who served in the mission suffered much hardship. Parishioners would relate how the priests would row themselves across the icy waters of the Elizabeth River when the ferry wasn't available. Father Michael J. Hartigan became the first resident pastor in 1924. During this period, Saint Matthew suffered its first fire.

Father Thomas Healy was sent to Saint Matthew in 1949 and Saint Matthew suffered a second fire in 1950, so Father Healy began looking for a new location for his overcrowded parish. In 1958, Healy purchased thirteen and a half acres in Sherry Park and was making plans for a building program when he died unexpectedly. In 1959, Father Harris Findlay was appointed pastor. It was under his leadership that Saint Matthew went on to build a church, school, convent, and rectory.

In September of 1962, Bishop John J. Russell dedicated classrooms, a new convent and a parish office building. The new Saint Matthew School opened in September 1963, and was staffed by the Felician Sisters of Lodi, New Jersey.

completed three new additional classrooms, a library, and a tele-conference center.

In telling the story of this parish, words cannot relate the sacrifice, loyalty, and hard work of the many who served for the love of the Church for more than half a century. It is their legacy that we look to for inspiration as we face the future. It is in their spirit of devoted giving of self and substance that we pray we can pass on…as we work to make our own history.

In May of 1967, a cafeteria wing was added. During the tenure of pastor Father Timothy A. Drake, the new church was dedicated by Bishop Walter F. Sullivan in May of 1991; the school gymnasium in 1994, and the middle school wing in 1996. The building for the pre-school was complete in the fall of 1999.

The Marion Powers Fletcher Annex which includes a bride's room and two new restrooms was dedicated in June 2003. In May 2008, Saint Matthew School

Saint Ann

At the beginning of the 20th century, nine Catholic families of Czechoslovak nationality settled in Chesterfield County near Petersburg. To attend Mass, they had to travel distances of 10 to 15 miles by horse and buggy to Sacred Heart in New Bohemia or Saint Mary in Dinwiddie County. Father John Konicek, a Czech priest, preached to the families in their native language. He was later succeeded by Father Leopold Stefl.

Father Stefl, realizing the difficulties experienced by these families, arranged to travel from New Bohemia on First Fridays and some Sunday afternoons to say Mass in private homes. These services were usually held in the homes of Frank Berberich or Vaclav Kuzelka.

In January of 1924, this small group of Catholic families decided to build a chapel in which they could hold their own services. The land was donated by Mr. Vaclav Kuzelka. The Catholic Church Extension Society contributed $1000 towards the building of the chapel. Most of the work was done by the people with the supervision of the pastor. The glazed brick and frame church was built on Beechwood Avenue not far from the Richmond/Petersburg Pike. The lumber was from the old barracks at Camp Lee. The cornerstone was laid in 1927. On June 6, 1927, a cross was blessed and placed on the steeple of the Chapel. The same cross now stands atop Condon Hall. This Chapel was named Saint Ann and was used until July 26, 1955.

As was the tradition of early churches, a cemetery was started behind Saint Ann on Beechwood Avenue with the first interment in 1929. Through 1955, fifty-two burials were recorded, the majority being the Czech immigrants who began Saint Ann Chapel. The cemetery has now expanded, and a Columbarium was added in 2001.

During the early years, funds were raised by hosting dinners and dances in Sacred Heart's and Saint John's Halls. A parish family held dances in their basement. Each year a picnic was held during July 26th weekend (Saint Ann's Feast Day), in parishioner's yards, then on Moorman's Swift Creek grounds and finally on Elko's Farm.

As the number of parishioners increased, a new church was built on the Richmond/ Petersburg Pike, a location accessible to tourists who traveled the "Pike." Six lots were purchased, and the contract to build the new church was awarded to Mr. John W. Elko and his son George. The groundbreaking took place on September 19, 1954. Saint Ann was still considered a mission church at the time, under Sacred Heart in New Bohemia. Saint Ann was established as a parish in 1961.

The property on Jefferson Davis Highway where Saint Ann was built was the site of a motel with tourist cabins. The Confraternity of Christian Doctrine (CCD) classes were held in those cabins. The nuns from Claremont, Virginia, traveled to Saint Ann to teach Saturday classes. It was under Father Michael McDermott's tenure that the school was built and the Catholic Youth Organization (CYO) was formed.

As Saint Ann continued to grow, the parish developed a master plan for expansion and conducted a fund drive. In 1988, they went forward with the building of a new church. Groundbreaking for the third and present Saint Ann Church took place on June 24, 1990, and it was dedicated June 16, 1991. The old (second) church space was converted into a parish hall, named and dedicated as Condon Hall.

Bishop Andrew J. Brennan

Andrew J. Brennan (1877–1956) of Towanda, Pennsylvania, a priest and auxiliary bishop of Scranton, followed O'Connell as the eighth bishop of Richmond in 1926. Under Brennan's leadership, the diocese launched the *Catholic Virginian* newspaper (1931). The presidential campaign of 1928 was the impetus behind the diocesan newspaper, when Governor Alfred E. Smith of New York became the first Catholic nominee for president. Some opposition to Smith was based on his stance against Prohibition (1920–1933). Smith also became a target of anti-Catholic bigotry, facing charges that, as a Catholic, he was not a Christian, and that, as president, he would allow the pope to interfere in public policy. In order to dispel such prejudice, Bishop Brennan decided that the diocese should have its own periodical to espouse its views. So the Richmond Diocese purchased the *Virginia Knight*, which the Knights of Columbus had published since 1925, and renamed it the *Catholic Virginian*.[1]

Social Ministry,
the Great Depression, and Personal Misfortune
(1926-1935)

St. Joseph's Villa, Richmond

The opening of two schools for children in need were additional accomplishments of Brennan's tenure. The first was St. Joseph's Villa in Richmond (1931), which replaced St. Joseph's Orphan Asylum and Free School (1834). As they had at the previous location, the Daughters of Charity provided housing and education for girls. The second institution was the James Barry Robinson Home and School for Boys in Norfolk (1934), run by Benedictines from Latrobe, Pennsylvania.[2]

James Dooley

James Dooley (1841–1922), a Confederate veteran who became a prominent member of Richmond society while serving in the Virginia General Assembly, and then as a lawyer and businessman, donated the funds for St. Joseph's Villa. Dooley came from a family of distinguished Catholics. He inherited the title of "Major" from his father, John Dooley, an Irish immigrant who ran a successful hat and fur business in Richmond.

During the Civil War, John Dooley had helped command a Confederate regiment that was composed of Irish Catholics from Richmond, including two of his sons. He was also an influential figure at St. Peter's Church. Another of John Dooley's sons, John Jr., was also a Confederate veteran and a Jesuit novice, who died before being ordained a priest.[3]

Not long after the dedication of St. Joseph's Villa, the Great Depression (1929–1939) struck Virginia (1932) and left many people destitute. Parishes struggled to meet expenses; building and expansion within the diocese were curtailed. When President Franklin D. Roosevelt established the Civilian Conservation Corps (1932–1942) to employ young men for infrastructure projects, priests in the diocese ministered to the estimated 1,400 Catholics who were distributed among 61 camps in Virginia.[4]

Brennan experienced his own calamity in the form of a stroke in 1934. The resulting limitations prevented him from carrying out his duties, although he officially remained the bishop of Richmond for another decade (until 1945).

Branching Out Toward Modernity: World War II, Vatican II, and Beyond

The Diocese of Richmond changed significantly as a result of World War II (1939–1945). In Virginia, as throughout the country, there was a population explosion followed by social upheavals as the "baby boomer" generation came of age. Around the same time, a momentous event brought change within the Church: the Second Vatican Council (1962–1965). The implementation of Vatican II took place amid the convulsion of Western society, and became intertwined with the sense of optimism, the eagerness to break with the past, and the realization of personal autonomy that characterized a stormy decade (ca. 1963–ca. 1974). A key result of these trends was that the Catholic Church in Richmond, as in the rest of the United States, faced an increasingly secular culture in the second half of the twentieth century. At the beginning of the new millennium, a crisis emerged: the scandal of clerical abuse (2002–2019).

Saint Mary of the Presentation

— Suffolk • 1927 —

It is fitting that a church dedicated to our Blessed Mother has its roots in the faith of three devout women. The first of these, Mrs. Katherine Woodley Holland, brought Catholicism to Suffolk in 1836. She imbued her daughter, Elfrida, with a devout and tenacious faith, and in turn, Elfrida's daughter Katie inherited her mother's and grandmother's evangelistic spirit. These three women – Katherine Woodley Holland, Elfrida Holland Lewis, and Katherine "Katie" Lewis Crowder – played key roles in building up Saint Mary's Parish in Suffolk.

The first recorded Mass was celebrated in Elfrida's farmhouse in 1873 by Father Thomas Brady of Saint Paul's in Portsmouth. Priests from Saint Paul's ministered to Catholics in Suffolk for

nearly 100 years. For 30 years, in three different residences, Elfrida opened her home for Easter Sunday Mass. Katie wrote in her dairy that Confession was heard in one room, with the priest sitting in a chair and the penitents kneeling on the floor, and Mass was celebrated in the living room where white cloths were draped over a bureau to serve as the altar. It was in Elfrida's last residence that Father Brady celebrated the first Baptism in Suffolk in 1902.

In 1903, priests from Portsmouth began to travel to Suffolk every three months to say Mass for approximately 25 Catholics. In 1908, Elfrida's daughter, Katie organized the Ladies Aid Society and went door to door asking for donations to build a church for the growing congregation of

20 families. The lot and the building cost $1,700, and the new church seated 100 people. When it was dedicated on November 21, 1909, Catholics in Suffolk had increased to 40.

Father Joseph Brennan was appointed first resident pastor of Saint Mary's in 1927. Under his tenure, a rectory was purchased and Saint Mary's established missions in Courtland, Sebrell, Franklin, and Smithfield. During the next 25 years, pastors from Saint Mary's oversaw the building of Saint Jude Church in Franklin and the Shrine of the Infant Jesus of Prague in Wakefield.

In 1954, the original white wooden church, built as a mission of Saint Paul's, was moved around the corner where it was used for a social and education building. The new church seated 240 people. In 1975, a new two-story education building replaced the old mission church that had inspired so many faith-filled sacrifices.

Saint Mary's Italian mosaic of the Crucifixion is formed by more than 50,000 half-inch squares of colored glass. It hangs behind the high altar at 11 feet tall by 9.5 feet wide. Three other mosaics Our Lady of Fatima, Our Lady of Perpetual Help, and the Lamb of God mounted on the high altar, the French stained-glass windows, and the Italian carved Stations of the Cross, are features that set this church apart.

Almost 200 years ago, grace began to flow through three generations of faithful women. It coursed down through the decades inspiring many loving sacrifices and giving Saint Mary's much for which to thank God.

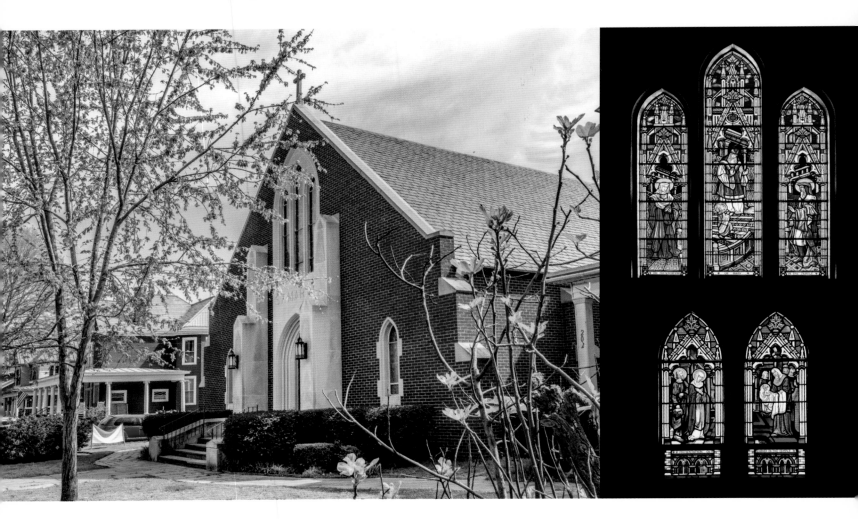

Saint John

THE WORD BECAME FLESH AND ... MADE HIS DWELLING AMO...

Saint John was originally a Mission of Saint Patrick Church, Richmond with Father Hugh J. McKeefry the pastor in 1913. During the Civil War, a Chapel was built near the battle grounds of Highland Springs - a Military Chapel to serve as a perpetual monument for all soldiers who died. Saint John Mission Chapel was dedicated on September 27, 1917. As the number of Catholics grew in the area, Saint John Mission was raised to the status of a Parish in 1929, with Father Michael D. Godfrey assigned as pastor. A Social Hall was added to the Church in 1950 and named McKeefry Hall, providing a place to host many dinners and receptions for Saint John's

parishioners. A school building was constructed in 1964 through the efforts of Father Donfred H. Stockert, but never opened as a school because of the lack of nuns to staff the school. The school building with eight classrooms, then as now, serves as the religious education building.

The military style Chapel and Hall were demolished in 1975 to build a spacious new worship center, that was dedicated in 1976. A new "Commons Area" with offices and meeting rooms, was added to the Church and a social hall was added to the religious education building in 1993.

In 1915, six women from Saint John Mission formed the Society of Saint Elizabeth to assist the pastor with the spiritual and material welfare of the children for Sunday school. In 1929, the Society of Saint Elizabeth became the Sodality of the Blessed Virgin Mary. Around 1960, the Sodality's name was changed to Saint John Guild. In November of 1979, the name was changed again to Saint John's Council of Women. Over the past hundred years, the name has changed, but their goals have never changed - to assist the pastor with fundraisers and the needs of the parish.

The men's organization from the 1920s to the late 1970s was the Holy Name Society. A Knights of Columbus Council was formed on May 22, 1977, and it was named the Father James J. Scanlon Council. The Council is still active today with its members participating in and supporting all the activities of Saint John Parish.

The Hispanic community was growing and in 2005 a Spanish Mass was added. The Hispanic community has many younger families with lots of children. Saint John has an active catechetical program for children and adults. Over 100 children are educated yearly in the religious education program with about 90% of Hispanic ancestry. An adult education program, under the patronage of Saint Andrew and organized by lay leaders in the Hispanic community, is dedicated to the efforts of evangelization within the Hispanic community. It has resulted in adult education for over 100 Hispanic members each year. A Hispanic Charismatic Group meets weekly for prayer and adoration. We have a strong RCIA program for both English and Hispanic communities. Parishioners in both communities are dedicated to their parish. The ethnic makeup of the parish changed over the past hundred years to become a multi-cultural Catholic community.

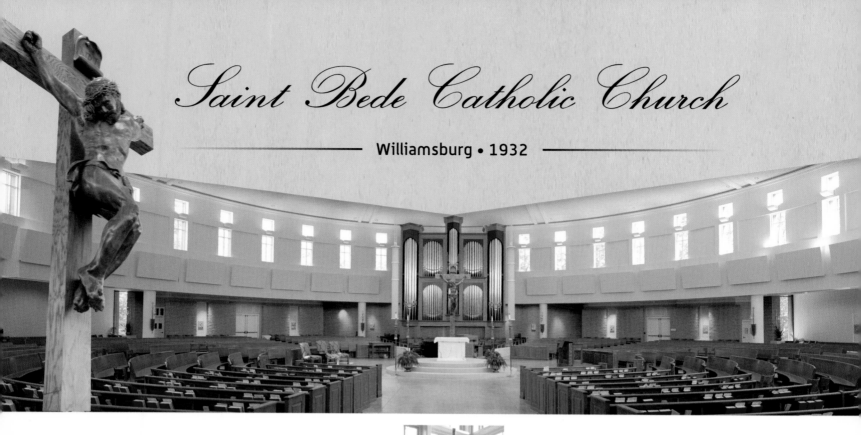

Saint Bede Catholic Church

——— Williamsburg • 1932 ———

In the early 1900s, there were few Catholics in Williamsburg, however the few Catholic families, most notably the Hanrahan's, the Wright's and the Gilliam's, were keenly interested in creating a permanent Catholic presence. On May 30, 1905, Father L .F. Kelly, a priest from Saint Vincent de Paul Church in Newport News, traveled to Williamsburg by horse and buggy to baptize children, perform marriages, and celebrate Mass in an outdoor area at Eastern State Hospital Grounds where the DeWitt Wallace Museum stands today. By 1908, Father Joseph Fioli said Mass monthly at Cameron Hall on the grounds of Eastern State Hospital. After Mass, the women of the community sold baked goods and hand-made items to raise money to build a Catholic Church. The small amount of money that they raised was held by Richard Gilliam, who was a Justice of the Peace.

The parish began with a small nucleus of Catholic students at The College of William & Mary. In December 1923, twenty-three students formed the Gibbons Club with the purpose of obtaining a priest to celebrate weekly Mass at the College. A professor of Spanish at the College, Carlos Eduardo Castañeda, was the Club's advisor. Their petition bore fruit by 1926 when the Bishop in Richmond appointed the Reverend Leonard J. Koster as the Catholic Chaplain at the College.

By October 1928, Reverend Gregory Eichenlaub, O.S.B., of the Monastery of Saint Benedict in Richmond, celebrated weekly Sunday Masses in Rogers 101, a room in the Chemistry lab which the College made available. Catholics in Williamsburg attended Mass and formed part of this new congregation.

In the same year, John D. Rockefeller established the Williamsburg Restoration Foundation. The builders and crafts--men who the Foundation brought to Williamsburg swelled the ranks of Catholics in the area and provided the men and women who would ultimately build Saint Bede Catholic Church.

A bequest to the Diocese by Miss Margaret Burns provided Bishop Andrew Brennan of Richmond with funds to build a Catholic Chapel at the College which he consecrated in October 1932. The Burns bequest of $25,000 was augmented by the monies raised by the community and conserved by Justice of the Peace Gilliam for nearly thirty years. The Chapel was dedicated as a memorial chapel to the Venerable Saint Bede (673-735 AD), an English Benedictine monk, scholar, and doctor of the Church. Built on the supposed spot of the Spanish Chapel of Saint Michael, it was consecrated as holy ground eighty-one years before the English settled at Jamestown.

The Bishop officially formed Saint Bede Catholic Church as a parish of the Diocese of Richmond with Father Thomas J. Walsh as its first resident pastor in 1939. On Father Walsh's inspiration, the College Chapel was dedicated as a National American Shrine to Our Lady of Walsingham on February 1, 1942; this designation was confirmed by the United States Conference of Catholic Bishops in a letter to Bishop Francis X. DiLorenzo dated March 30, 2016.

The parish of Saint Bede grew rapidly, and the College Chapel built in 1923 was thrice enlarged. From its root grew the parish churches of Saint Joan of Arc in Yorktown and Saint Olaf in Norge and, in 1947, the Walsingham Academy

which is operated by the Sisters of Mercy. By the mid-1990s, the College Chapel had become too small for the growing Catholic population in Williamsburg.

In 2000, construction began on a new church built on 43 acres of land donated by Mary Dick and John Digges on Ironbound Road in Williamsburg. The "New" Saint Bede was dedicated on May 31, 2003, by Bishop Walter Sullivan and Monsignor William Carr.

The two campuses generated numerous outreach ministries, including to the Hispanic and Filipino communities, to the homebound, to those in prison, to the poor in need of food and lodging through the Williamsburg House of Mercy, to pregnant mothers through the Hope Pregnancy Care Center, and for faith formation programs for adults, youth and students at the College. The parish offices, faith formation programs for children, adults and youth were consolidated in the DiLoreto Administrative Wing and Kaplan Parish Hall provides a home for parishioners to build community on the Ironbound campus. The annex was dedicated on March 26, 2017, by Bishop Francis X. DiLorenzo and Monsignor Timothy E. Keeney. Saint Bede is blessed today with 7,667 parishioners and 3,058 registered families.

On March 30, 2016, the Shrine of Our Lady of Walsingham at Saint Bede Parish in Williamsburg was officially recognized by the USCCB as a national shrine, the first in the Diocese of Richmond.

The original Walsingham shrine in England dates back to 1061 when a noblewoman from the central part of England was being visited by a woman the English began to call "Our Lady." This English noblewoman built a replica of the Holy Family's house on her property in Walsingham in honor of the Blessed Virgin.

In the Middle Ages, Walsingham was what Lourdes and Fatima are today — centers of pilgrimage and prayer to invoke the intercession of the Virgin. Until the Protestant Reformation, Walsingham was the most popular center of pilgrimage in the world except Rome.

While the Shrine was desecrated and the image of Our Lady reportedly burned during the Reformation, the devotion survived in England, and both Anglican and Catholic shrines have been re-established in Walsingham, England.

The "first American national shrine to Our Lady of Walsingham" was established in Williamsburg on February 1, 1942, by Father Thomas Walsh, Saint Bede pastor, with Bishop Peter Ireton of Richmond present to bless it.

Father Walsh thought it was fitting, that in a city founded by English colonists, Mary should be honored under a title that was so connected with the faith of the English people. The Shrine of Our Lady has been a part of Saint Bede Parish's fabric since that 1942 date and was, in fact, the inspiration for the Sisters of Mercy establishing and naming their Williamsburg school in September 1947 as Walsingham Academy.

In 2001, Saint John Paul II approved the Feast of Our Lady of Walsingham to be observed on September 24 each year. The Feast Day is celebrated at the Shrine and includes Mass, the Walsingham Rosary, a procession, and a special Vespers Service that includes other denominations that are devoted to Our Lady of Walsingham. The Shrine is the spiritual home to Catholic Campus Ministry serving the College of William and Mary and is also host to daily and Sunday Mass, devotions, and pilgrimages.

Saint Anthony

Norton • 1938

The beginning of the Stonega mission dates from 1896 when the Stonega Coal and Cokes Company erected "a handsome edifice" for its Catholic employees. Records state the mission was first served by Father Burke from Bristol, which was part of the Diocese of Wheeling.

Shortly after Burke's death, the Bishop of Wheeling sent the Benedictine priests of Cullman Alabama to take care of the Catholics in Southwest Virginia. In December 1902, the Bishop asked them to minister to the coalmining camps surrounding Stonega, and as far as Bristol, Tennessee. Father Vincent became the first resident pastor of Stonega.

In 1911, new missions began in Rhoda, Keokee, and Pardee, where private homes served as churches, and in Inman-Linden where a church eventually was built. The Benedictine Annals note that there were Lebanese and Italian Catholics in Norton at the time.

By the mid-1930's, Saint Anthony Church on Virginia Avenue, was built. Fr. Peter Aarts, a Dutch priest, and architect, became the pastor of the parish. He designed Sacred Heart Church in Appalachia, which was built by Bishop Swint's brothers and dedicated by the Bishop on August 28, 1938. It was the first mission parish started from Saint Anthony's in Norton.

In 1945, Glenmary priests came to Southwest Virginia and were entrusted with a parish territory of some 2,200 square miles of rugged mountain terrain. They were often assisted by Glenmary Brothers and Sisters. In time, churches were built in Dungannon, St. Paul, Coeburn, Gate City, Clintwood and Lebanon. Today there are about 750 active parishioners in these parishes.

In 1972, Saint Anthony Parish Hall was completed, providing a much-needed facility for parish functions. In 1975, the decision was made to build a new church, and it was dedicated on November 20, 1977.

With the appointment and installation of Bishop Walter F. Sullivan as the 11th Bishop of Richmond on July 19, 1974, southwest Virginia, which was part of the Wheeling Diocese, was transferred to the Diocese of Richmond. In 1979, Glenmary Missionary priests returned Saint Anthony's Parish to the care of the Diocese of Richmond.

Saint Mary

ALLELUIA! HE HAS RISEN

HE IS RISEN INDEED!

At the beginning of the twentieth century, Catholics of Montgomery County were included in the Diocese of Wheeling, West Virginia, and were served by visiting priests. When a priest was not available, people met in homes for prayer and worship. The first mention of Blacksburg appeared in the 1911 Catholic Directory as a *mission station* of Saint Mary's Mother of God Church in Wytheville also part of the Diocese of Wheeling. During World War I, when Virginia Polytechnic

Institute (VPI) became a student Army Training Corps, there was a need for more permanent worship space. Blacksburg began to grow and the need for a Catholic church was evident. Bishop Patrick Donahue of Wheeling authorized the purchase of land on Wilson Street and a small wooden church was built and dedicated on the first Sunday in June 1924 as Saint Mary's Church. It held about 135 people. In 1937, the house across the street was purchased to serve as a rectory.

Saint Mary's Parish quickly grew and on September 1, 1938, it became an official parish within the Wheeling Diocese with Father George Walter as the first resident pastor. With the influx of veterans attending VPI, and new industries in the county, the new growth of Catholics put a strain on the little church. The property across the street where the rectory was located became the site of a bigger church building which was designed to connect to the existing rectory. The new Saint Mary's was completed in 1948.

In 1974, the transfer of Montgomery County and Catholic parishes of southwestern Virginia from the Diocese of Wheeling to the Diocese of Richmond and its Bishop, Most Reverend Walter F. Sullivan, took place. In March 1976, under the pastor Father Thomas Miller and parish lay leaders, a study was done that determined the needs of the parish could not be met without more space. A new church on Harding Avenue was completed and dedicated on October 25, 1986.

By 2000, the parish had grown to about 700 families. After much searching, 35 acres of land and a house were purchased on Old Mill Road and construction of a new church building was underway. Bishop Francis X. DiLorenzo dedicated the Saint Mary's current church in 2008.

Over the years St. Mary's has welcomed many pastors of different backgrounds and ethnicities. All left their mark on the parish as they nurtured the spiritual growth of the community.

Adding to the diversity of St. Mary's parish is the influx of Catholic students enrolled at Virginia Tech. Under the leadership of an assigned campus chaplain, the Catholic Campus Ministry supports some 7,000 students each academic year, through liturgical and sacramental celebrations.

St. Mary's remains a vibrant Catholic community where a deep faith is continually fostered through Sunday liturgies, ongoing faith formation, and outreach to Blacksburg and the New River Valley community.

Saint Theresa

Farmville • 1939

Missionaries of the Precious Blood, a Religious Community of priests from Carthagena, Ohio, at the request of Bishop Andrew Brennan, Richmond's Eighth Bishop, arrived in 1939 to establish a Catholic Church in Crewe, and missions in Blackstone, Farmville, and Meherrin. The first pastor, Father Marcellus Fortman, assisted by Father Isadore McCarthy, traveled to Farmville from Crewe to celebrate Mass in a room at the Hotel Prince Edward for the first two years. At the time, there were only 20 Catholics in the area. As the membership grew, including students from the local women's college (now Longwood University), it soon became apparent that the location was no longer adequate. Longwood kindly offered the use of the French Auditorium for Sunday Masses.

In the late 1940's, Father McCarthy traveled to other parishes to preach and seek funds to build a permanent church. One major donor asked that the church be named for Saint Therese of Lisieux, an appropriate name for a mission church. On May 25, 1951, the Rt. Reverend Michael J. Cannon, on behalf of Bishop Peter Ireton, the Ninth Bishop of Richmond, officiated at the dedication of Saint Theresa Church in Farmville. It is still in use today and serves as the current commons area and office space.

Priests at the time lived in a small room above what is now the parish office. In 1964, the pastor and Newman Club Chaplain, Father Carl Reikowsky, was assigned as the resident pastor at Saint Theresa's. The remaining Precious Blood

priests returned to Ohio in the summer of 1978 and priests from the Diocese of Richmond have served the parishes ever since. Under the administration of The Missionaries of the Precious Blood, Saint Theresa's parish was no longer a mission, and both religious order and diocesan priests assigned there also assisted the other missions. As the parish grew, a new worship center was needed, and the building on Buffalo Street was completed in 1988.

In January 1997, work began on the current worship area addition and was dedicated in June 1998. The parish recently celebrated its 50th anniversary on Buffalo Street. Now the Parish is one of four parishes within the Central Virginia Cluster along with Sacred Heart in Meherrin and Immaculate Heart of Mary in Blackstone. Under the leadership of the current pastor, Father Stefan Migac, Church of the Nativity in Buckingham has merged with St. Theresa Parish. Father Migac, a priest of the Archdiocese

of Kosice in Slovakia was assigned in 2015. He also serves a large Catholic Campus Ministry for Longwood University and Hampden-Sydney College.

Since 1939, the church in Farmville has grown from a few Catholics in southside Virginia, attending Mass in a hotel room to over 300 families and vibrant campus ministries at both Longwood and Hampden-Sydney. Formed from a mission church with visiting priests it has grown into a parish with two full-time priests and two deacons serving the spiritual and sacramental needs of Catholics in the Central Virginia Cluster.

Church of Saint Therese

—— Gloucester • 1939 ——

The seeds of Christianity were brought to the Middle Peninsula by Spanish Jesuit Missionaries in the 1570's, led by Father Juan Baptista de Segura from Spain, with four brothers and four novices. They landed at present day West Point, and after five months were martyred by the Algonquins on February 4, 1571.

There was no active Catholicism until the summer of 1898, when Jesuit brother Father William Reynolds Cowardin began celebrating Mass at a resident's home near Ware Neck. In 1906, the Catholic Church of Saint Therese was built at Port Richmond (West Point) as a mission of Saint Patrick Parish in Richmond. In 1918, Our Lady of the Blessed Sacrament was established there and dedicated in 1925. Its missions extended from Tappahannock to York County and included Gloucester County, which Father Jakubowski ministered to by foot, horseback, bicycle, boat and finally automobile. Roads were few and nearly impassable at that time, so Gloucester and Mathews belonged to Saint Mary, Star of the Sea Parish at Fort Monroe. The priest from Saint Mary boarded a steamer to come up the York River for Sunday Mass.

In 1930, there were seven to ten Catholics in the area. During the early 1930's, Father Jakubowski

of West Point offered Mass at a central location for Catholics in Gloucester and Mathews, such as Edge Hill Theatre in Gloucester. In the late 1930's, an anonymous donation of $2,500 was given to finance the necessary building project of Gloucester County's only Roman Catholic Church, with the sole condition of the donor being that the church bear the name of Saint Therese of Lisieux, the Little Flower. The cornerstone was laid in 1938 and dedicated May 14, 1939. From 1939 to 1959, the Church of Saint Therese remained a mission parish of Our Lady of the Blessed Sacrament.

On October 31, 1959, Bishop John J. Russell designated Saint Therese a parish. Many Catholics came back to active participation, and the increase of the population made the need for a larger worship space necessary. A second building phase included a vestibule, social hall, and kitchen with the cornerstone being laid on July 25, 1965. Quiet growth took place between 1969 and 1980 and ecumenical services grew with neighboring churches. Saint Therese also served Middlesex and

Mathews Catholics as part of her mission until the establishment of Church of the Visitation on September 8, 1985, and Church of Francis de Sales in January 1988.

Between 1980-1987 tremendous growth occurred in Gloucester, and Sunday Masses began to overflow. A Parish Planning Committee was formed in 1983 and a master plan evolved. A larger worship space, classrooms, commons area, and offices were built, and Bishop Sullivan dedicated the new church as a diocesan parish on October 11, 1987. Over these many years the service ministries of Saint Therese have blossomed. Soup with Love and the Bread for Life Food Pantry has seen tremendous growth in the local community. Outreach through our Social Ministry and Hispanic communities continues to be strong.

We have been blessed with many generous gifts and support from our parishioners. We remain eternally grateful to the priests who have served our parish and continue to pray for God's blessings and guidance as we continue our spiritual journey of faith in action.

Saint Richard

— Emporia • 1940 —

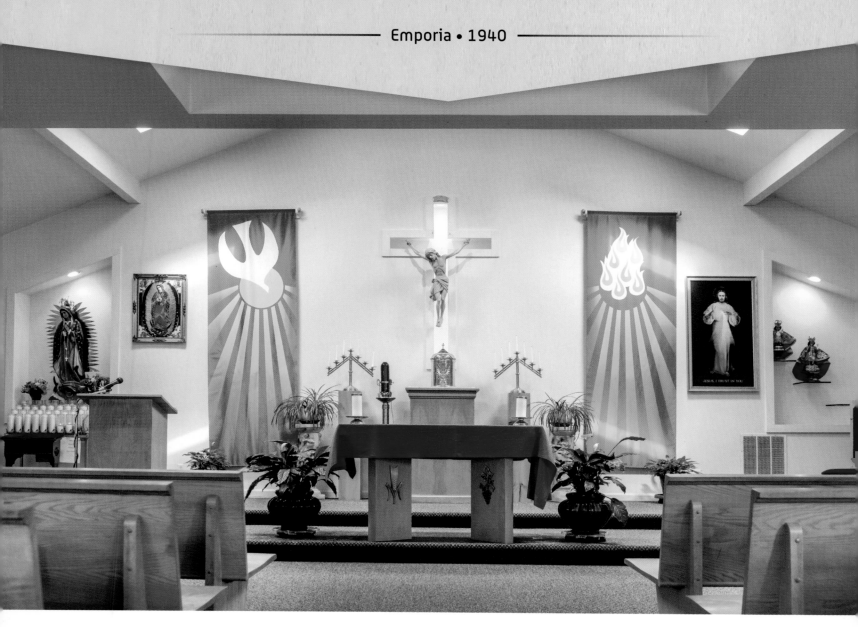

For more than half a century, the Josephite Fathers of Baltimore did missionary work along the southern border of Virginia, celebrating Mass in various private homes from time to time.

In September 1879, the cornerstone was laid for a mission church about 10 miles north of Emporia, it was called Saint Francis of Assisi and located in Jarratt. In 1913, the church building was destroyed by fire, rumored to be the work of the Ku Klux Klan. It was not rebuilt, and again Mass was celebrated in the homes of parishioners in Jarratt and Emporia.

One of these homes belonged to Gustave Kreienbaum. In 1923, Mr. Kreienbaum donated land on Park Avenue in Emporia to the Diocese of Richmond, and Mr. Markey of New York City donated money to build a church on the site. It was named Saint Richard in honor of Mr. Markey's father. The church was dedicated in 1924 by Rt. Rev. Denis O'Connell, Seventh Bishop of Richmond. Thereafter, Mass was celebrated monthly until 1939, when weekly services began.

In 1940, the Friars of the Franciscan Missionary Union of New York were welcomed into the area where they ministered to the Catholics of Emporia. Father Walter Hammon, OFM, was the first resident pastor.

In 1967, a new and larger church and rectory were constructed on Laurel Street in Emporia. Saint Richard was returned to the care of the Diocese of Richmond in 1975 when the Franciscan Fathers were reassigned by their religious order. Today, the parish continues at that location, serving approximately forty Catholic families and is a stopping point for welcoming visitors traveling into Virginia from North Carolina on the I-95 corridor.

Saint Peter the Apostle

In 1942, Saint Peter the Apostle began with fewer than ten Catholics meeting for Sunday Mass in the home of Father Bennet McNulty, a retired priest from the Diocese of Wilmington. Father McNulty had to retire early for medical reasons and so he came to live on Finney's Wharf outside of Onancock on the Eastern Shore of Virginia. Although this area is in Virginia, there was no church within 100 miles between Saint Charles Parish in Cape Charles, in the Diocese of Richmond, and Salisbury, Maryland, in the Diocese of Wilmington.

With Father McNulty's arrival, the few Catholics in the area were in his spiritual care. By December of 1947, they broke ground for a new church in Onley. The building's exterior was completed in June 1948. The dedication Mass was attended by 141 parishioners including summer visitors, and 40 guests. Over the years, Saint Peter has been a very active parish. The parishioners finished most of the interior of the church and assisted wherever possible. By 1955, the first Mexican migrant farm workers were attending Mass. Over the years, the parish developed a large and active migrant ministry, and a permanent Hispanic community. Saint Peter the Apostle Parish was transferred into the Diocese of Richmond in 1975. The congregation has grown to over 300 families in a culturally diverse community in a rural area. In addition to Mass in English and Spanish, there is an active migrant ministry including Mass at the migrant worker camps during the summer months, outreach to the poor and needy in both Accomack and Northampton counties, and a thriving Knights of Columbus and Ladies Auxiliary.

Within the parish there are vibrant Catholic education programs, book clubs, prayer group, Hispanic Ministries, Ladies Guild, choirs, lectors, ushers, altar servers, and support groups serving both English and Spanish speaking parishioners. Eucharistic Ministers not only assist at Mass, they take Communion to the sick, the shut-ins, and the elderly in a parish whose territory reaches 30 to

50 miles to the north and south. In 1991, a religious education building was installed and is also used for a large inter-denominational Hispanic Charismatic praise and worship group. In the last few years, we have been honored to be part of the eastern Virginia Simbang Gabi, a traditional Filipino Catholic Christmas celebration.

On Sunday, June 24, 2018, Bishop Barry C. Knestout, thirteenth Bishop of Richmond, dedicated the new worship space that was the vision of the parish community for several years.

Our Lady of Lourdes

In the early 1940's, a Praesidium of the Legion of Mary met at the home of Mr. and Mrs. J. A. Lyons. It was made up of parishioners from Saint Paul Catholic Church and the Cathedral of the Sacred Heart. This Praesidium was dedicated to Our Lady of Lourdes with Father Robert O'Kane as its chaplain. It was through this prayer group that the idea of having Mass at the Lakeside Community Center originated.

For some time, the Lakeside Catholic Community was a Mission of the Cathedral. Beginning in August 1943, Mass was held on Sundays and Holy Days in the Lakeside Community Center. As the community grew, a farmhouse belonging to the Stupasky family was purchased and converted into a Chapel and rectory. Once the regular communicants grew to eighty, Bishop Peter L. Ireton, Ninth Bishop of Richmond, appointed Father Thomas J. Healy as Pastor. The first Mass was celebrated at the Chapel of Our Lady of Lourdes on October 29, 1944.

Within ten years, the parishioners had outgrown the little Chapel on Clover Lane and property was purchased on Woodman Road. In June 1954, building was begun, and on May 1, 1955, the beautiful church was dedicated to Our Lady of Lourdes.

Father Healy envisioned a Church like the one at Lourdes, France, where people

would come to pray. He dreamed of a grotto at the edge of the property where weary travelers could stop and meditate and visit the Blessed Sacrament in the Church. The steeple on top of the church, sitting high on the hill, gives the impression of the building dedicated to Our Lady in Lourdes, France. The stain-glass windows depict the many "titles" of our Lady as said in the prayer, 'The Litany of the Blessed Virgin."

Shortly after the dedication of the Church, a rectory was built for the priests of the parish. The parochial school was built in two stages and completed in 1966. For several years, the Missionary Sisters of Verona (now named Comboni Missionary Sisters) staffed the school.

To comply with requests that Our Lady of Lourdes serve the disabled as does the original shrine in France, a wheelchair ramp was added to the front entrance and dedicated by Bishop Walter Sullivan on January 7, 1979. On May 4, 1980, the Parish celebrated their 25th anniversary of the dedication of Our Lady

of Lourdes Church. The dedication and blessing of the new Allen Computer Organ was the highlight of the celebration.

On Sunday, May 20, 1984, the 40th anniversary of the founding of the parish was joyfully celebrated and the parish was rededicated to the patronage of Our Lady of Lourdes. Fifteen years later, the parish gathered to celebrate its continued growth with the dedication of a new Church.

Bishop Peter L. Ireton

IN NOMINE JESU

In 1935, Father Peter L. Ireton of Baltimore (1882–1948) was appointed coadjutor and administrator of the diocese. World War II (1939–1945) and its effects on the United States shaped his episcopate. During World War II, as in previous conflicts, Catholics rallied around the flag by serving in the military and by making other contributions. Numerous diocesan priests, along with religious priests who worked in the diocese, served as military chaplains. One of them, Father J. Louis Flaherty (1910–1975), who later became an auxiliary bishop of Richmond (1966–1975), was awarded the Silver Star for his bravery on the Italian battlefield. Other priests in the diocese ministered to German and Italian soldiers who were interned in prisoner-of-war camps in Virginia.[1]

World War II and the Postwar Boom
(1935-1958)

One month before Germany surrendered to Allied forces, Peter Ireton formally became the ninth bishop of Richmond, when Andrew Brennan submitted his resignation (1945). The nuclear age dawned four months after Ireton's accession, when the United States dropped atomic bombs on the cities of Hiroshima and Nagasaki, forcing Japan to surrender. By the end of the war, the position of the United States in the world had changed. Whereas in the period after World War I the United States pursued an isolationist foreign policy, it was now a global superpower locked in an ideological and military struggle with the Soviet Union.

Father J. Louis Flaherty

These world events had practical consequences for the Richmond Diocese. In addition to a nationwide population boom after the war, Catholics from other states migrated to Virginia to work for the federal government, including the military, or in related industries—all of which continued to expand during the Cold War (1946–1989). The construction of the country's military headquarters at the Pentagon (1941–1943), located across the Potomac River from Washington, DC, symbolized this phenomenon. Tidewater also underwent significant growth as naval facilities in the region expanded.[2]

The number of Catholics in the Diocese of Richmond nearly quadrupled, from thirty-eight thousand to one hundred-and-forty-five thousand, during Ireton's tenure. He established forty-five parishes and forty-nine schools to meet the growing pastoral needs. Furthermore, several religious orders began to staff parishes because there were not enough diocesan priests for this purpose.

Seminarian Peter Ireton

Fewer diocesan priests served as military chaplains in the Korean War (1950–1953) than in World War II because they were needed at home. The appointment of a local priest, Father Joseph H. Hodges, as the first auxiliary bishop of Richmond (1952–1961) was another sign of the diocese's growth.[3]

World War II brought the Great Depression to an end, with the result that large numbers of Catholics entered the middle class and began to live in suburbs. The widespread availability of automobiles and the construction of new highways facilitated this suburban migration. In a state like Virginia, this development led to the broader acceptance of Catholics, who were a minority. But rural areas required a different approach. To evangelize there, Bishop Ireton launched a diocesan mission band (1937) to build on the work of an earlier, independent lay evangelist (1933). A designated team of priests now drove a mobile chapel, named "St. Mary of the Highways," to teach the Catholic faith and to celebrate Mass in outlying communities.[4]

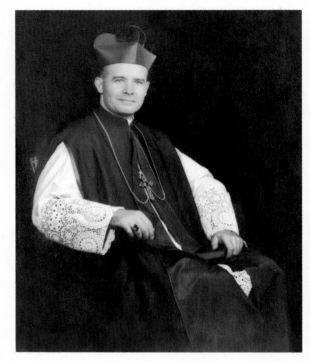

Auxiliary Bishop Joseph H. Hodges

The onset of social change was another feature of the postwar era. In this regard, Ireton distinguished himself as the first bishop in the South to integrate Catholic schools. He did so just days before the Supreme Court desegregated the public-school system (1954).[5]

Lydia Elizabeth Nichols of Columbia, recipient of the pro ecclesia et pontifice *cross (1951)*

St. Alphonsus, Newport News, Confirmation class

Diocesan mission band

*The mobile chapel
St. Mary of the
Highways*

177

Saint Gerard

— Roanoke • 1946 —

In August of 1946, Bishop Ireton saw a need to serve the spiritual needs of Roanoke's African-American Catholic Community. He appointed Redemptorist Reverend Maurice McDonald to establish a Roman Catholic mission to serve the black population in the City of Roanoke. Shortly after, on September 22, 1946, Father McDonald and a group of Catholic Missionary priests called the Society of the Most Holy Redeemer, the Redemptorists established the mission.

Father McDonald became the first pastor and celebrated the first Mass at Harrison School with seventeen people in attendance. On October 16, 1946, the Redemptorists Provincial approved the purchase of a nearby building on Moorman Road. Bishop Peter Ireton, Ninth Bishop of Richmond, named the parish after Saint Gerard, the patron saint of mothers and the poor, whose Feast Day coincides with that day. Thus, Saint Gerard became the first and only black Catholic parish in southwest Virginia.

In 1948, Bishop Ireton assigned the Redemptorists of Saint Gerard a mission in Salem and they were in charge of the mission until October of 1963 when the Salem mission became an independent parish.

Not long after Saint Gerard opened, many organizations and programs for adults and the youth where started: The Ladies of Charity, Christmas baskets for the poor, a youth football team, youth and adult baseball teams, Girl Scouts, Boy Scouts, and basketball teams.

178

In the Spring of 1950, small lots on Orange Ave, N.W., were purchased for the parish. With financial support promised from Bishop Ireton and $15,000 from the Vice Provincial, work on the new church began on May 22, 1951. Father McDonald moved the first shovel of earth. On December 16, 1951, Saint Gerard held its first Mass in the new church. A week later, on December 23, 1951, Bishop Ireton dedicated the new church.

Father McDonald was transferred in 1953. His tiny parish had grown from 11 black Catholics when he first came, to 17 families.

Father Thomas Norton came to Saint Gerald in August of 1953. On May 17, 1954, a Supreme Court decision made parochial school attendance possible and on May 31, 1954, Father Norton talked to Nazareth School, Saint Andrew School, and Roanoke Catholic school and on September 7, 1954, black children were enrolled in the Roanoke Catholic Schools for the first time.

More organizations were also created during Father Norton's time: The Holy Name Society, The Nocturnal Adoration Society, and The Legion of Mary.

Saint Gerard's congregation continued to grow. In the 1990's Saint Gerard began offering Mass in Spanish. Today the parish includes a diverse group of Catholics: African-Americans, Mexican-Americans and other Latinos, Africans, and sons and daughters of European lands celebrating together in our parish family. We speak English, Spanish, Kirundi, Kinyarwanda, and Swahili at our Masses.

Saint John the Evangelist

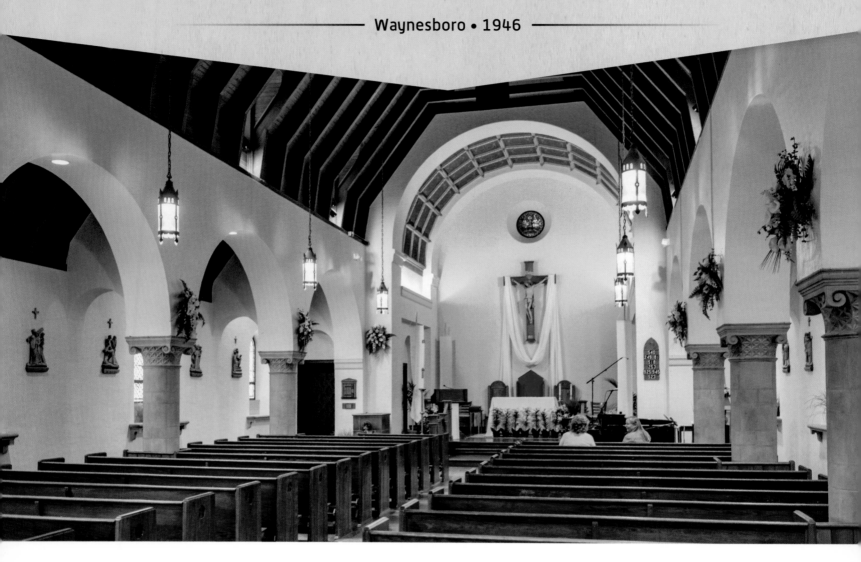

Around the turn of the century, the first Catholics came to Waynesboro during the expansion of the railroad in the valley. At first these people traveled to Saint Francis of Assisi Church in Staunton for Mass. The number of Catholics increased in the 1920's, with the establishment of new industries, especially Dupont and Crompton-Shenandoah. During this period, Saint Francis Church provided a priest for Mass in Waynesboro on a regular basis. Mass was held at the Old Star Theater in 1929.

Miss Margaret Burns of Staunton bequeathed funds in 1925 for the erection and maintenance of a worthy mission within the Diocese of Richmond. Part of this bequest was used in 1931 for the construction of a Church in Waynesboro. Bishop Andrew J. Brennan dedicated the new Church to Saint John the Evangelist on May 30, 1932. The first Mass was celebrated on June 4, 1932. Saint John remained a Mission of Saint Francis until 1946 when Reverend Eugene P. Walsh was named the first Pastor.

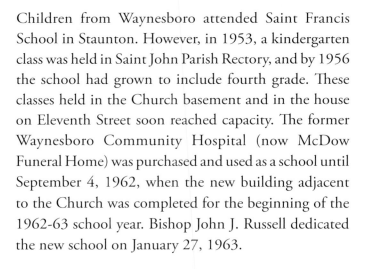

Children from Waynesboro attended Saint Francis School in Staunton. However, in 1953, a kindergarten class was held in Saint John Parish Rectory, and by 1956 the school had grown to include fourth grade. These classes held in the Church basement and in the house on Eleventh Street soon reached capacity. The former Waynesboro Community Hospital (now McDow Funeral Home) was purchased and used as a school until September 4, 1962, when the new building adjacent to the Church was completed for the beginning of the 1962-63 school year. Bishop John J. Russell dedicated the new school on January 27, 1963.

In 1967, a wing was added to the west side of the Sanctuary to relieve the overcrowded conditions. Major renovations to the exterior and interior of the Church were begun in 1988. Reverend William O'Brien was assigned as pastor to Saint John in 1990 and under his direction renovations were completed in 1992.

Saint Patrick

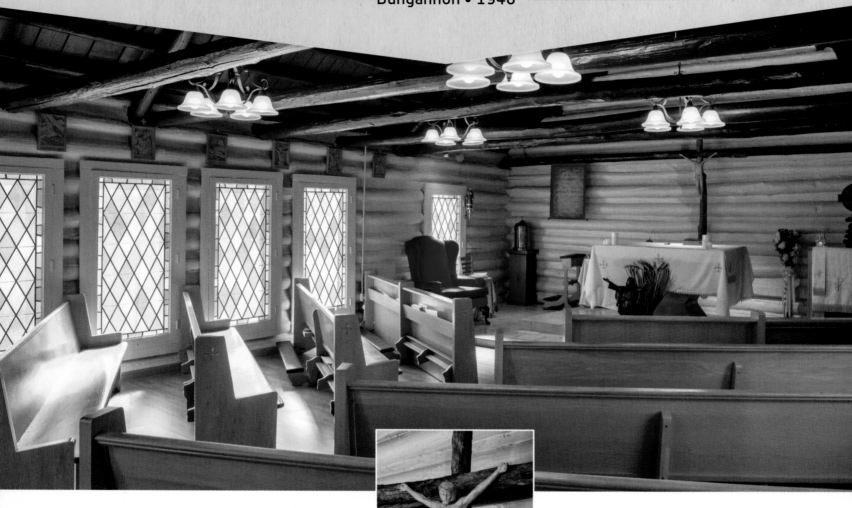

Saint Patrick Catholic Church in Dungannon had a population of 322 as of the 2010 census. An Irish settler, Patrick Hagan (1829-1917), born in Dungannon, Ireland, inherited land in Scott County from his Uncle Joseph Hagan. He purchased more land, and was the largest Scott County landholder in the late 1800's. He was influential in having the Clinchfield Railroad come through the town in 1909. By 1918 his oldest son, Charles Hagan had a town laid out and incorporated it as Dungannon, in honor of his father's Irish birthplace. This town is on the Clinch River and was formerly called Osborne's Ford.

In 1876, Patrick built an elegant seventeen-room mansion "Hagan Hall," the first brick home in Scott County. Throughout the fifty years, until Saint Patrick's log church was built, many priests came there to celebrate Mass. This landmark was destroyed by a fire in 2004.

Saint Patrick's log church exists today because Barney Hagan, a Dungannon resident and great grandson of Patrick Hagan, met Father Ed Smith a Glenmary Home Mission priest from Norton, Virginia. Barney donated the land for the construction of a new church in 1946.

Father Smith drew up plans and the triple-peaked log cabin church was built. Glenmary priests staffed Saint Patrick for 67 years, from 1946 until 2013, when the mission was returned to the pastoral care of the Diocese of Richmond.

Saint Patrick holds an important place in Glenmary history. It was the last place that their founder, Father Bishop, spoke before he died on June 11, 1953. Father Leo Schloemer remembers:

It was a hot Sunday in early June 1953. Father Bishop had spent the previous night in Hunter's Valley, Virginia. He was scheduled to speak that afternoon at the little log chapel in Dungannon to Legion of Mary members from Glenmary missions in Norton, Appalachia, Big Stone Gap, Gate City, and St. Paul. Father Bishop commended these lay people for their apostolic work of visiting the sick, the elderly, non-Catholics and fallen-away Catholics in this coal-mining area of Southwest Virginia. He emphasized that missionary

priests, brothers and sisters could not possibly do all this. They needed the hands, hearts, talents and personal contacts of these lay men and women to build up the Church in all the mission areas. He cited the important role of lay people in Communist China in keeping the Catholic faith alive in that hostile atmosphere where priests were imprisoned. He envisioned that lay people would be equally important in spreading the gospel and the Catholic faith throughout our home missions. Later that week he had a heart attack and died at Saint Mary's Hospital in Norton.

Considering the Second Vatican Council's later emphasis on evangelization and the role of the laity, it is interesting that Father Bishop's last public address, in a backwoods area of the Appalachian Mountains, was on this very topic.

Father Rollie Hautz arrived in 1953 and served the people living in Appalachia for the next 70 years. He pastored two Virginia missions — Saint Bernard in Gate City and Saint Patrick in Dungannon. Saint Patrick remains today a place for people to gather and celebrate Eucharist as Roman Catholics in an area where they are still a minority.

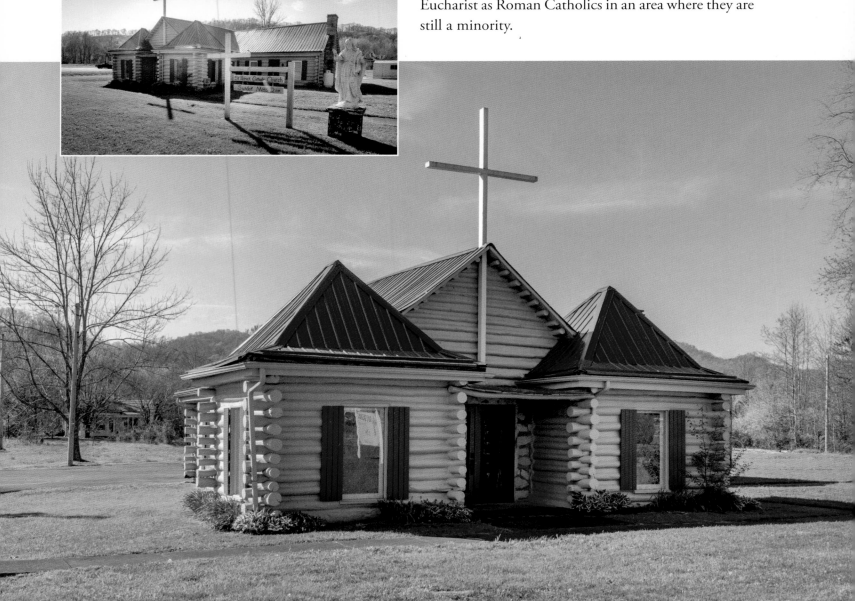

Immaculate Heart of Mary

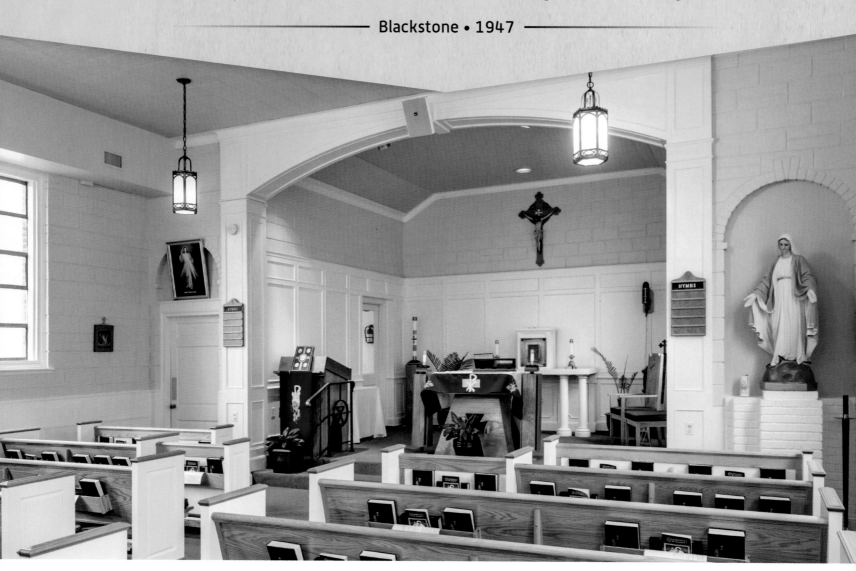

Prior to 1941, there were few Catholic families in the Blackstone area, and those families traveled to Saint John the Baptist in Crewe to worship with parishioners from the surrounding five counties. Occasionally, Father Isidore McCarthy would travel to local homes or a community center within the five counties to celebrate Mass. Camp Pickett was established in 1942 and the Catholic population began to steadily increase. The Priests of the Precious Blood Order were assigned to the parish and as auxiliary chaplains to Camp Pickett.

In 1947, a large home on South Main Street in Blackstone was purchased to serve the Catholics living in the area. The home was used to hold Mass until Immaculate Heart of Mary was constructed and dedicated by Bishop Peter Ireton on May 5, 1954. The building included a connecting breezeway to the house which became the church hall.

Father William Donohue became priest in 1968. He and a few religious sisters performed community outreach by obtaining buses and picking up children who wished to attend Catechism (and playtime) during the summer. The Precious Blood Fathers left the parish in 1977.

In 1979, the pastor began reading parts of the Mass in Spanish to include many of the Hispanic migrant workers who would attend. The parish worked to coordinate transportation for the migrant families. The parish grew through fellowship by beginning new traditions such as covered dish dinners, community Halloween parties, and gatherings after Midnight Mass.

The pastor of Immaculate Heart of Mary was assigned to travel to Saint John and to Sacred Heart. The challenges of scheduling three churches along with other ministries often led the three churches to join for special occasions such as the youth-centered Mass on Christmas Eve or the candlelit Easter Vigil.

In 2010, Immaculate Heart of Mary became a part of the Central Virginia Catholic Cluster and is served by the two priests who are located at Saint Theresa in Farmville. The parish was awarded diocesan grants in order to repair and update the 110-year-old Bethany House and the 63-year-old church. The Church was restored to its original form, the Tabernacle and the original altar were returned to the sanctuary.

Today, parishioners continue to fellowship through church sponsored festivals/bake sales, Easter egg hunts, and picnics. The parish family sponsors Thanksgiving meals for multiple families, provides gifts for a Christmas family, and supports the Pregnancy Support Center. As the parish population continues to grow, the functions of Bethany House have grown to include an overflow area with audio and video of Mass as it is celebrated.

Our Lady of Perpetual Help

Our Lady of Perpetual Help Catholic Church has a rich history, with its origins dating back to 1893. In that year, Bishop Augustine Van de Vyver secured a plot of land in Salem near the railroad station to be used for a place of worship for the Roman Catholic Church. As more Catholics moved into Roanoke rather than Salem, however, the Bishop felt the need for a church in Salem no longer existed and he sold the land.

The struggle to secure a parish in Salem continued for many years until a Catholic Women's Club was formed in 1947. Taking a census, the women secured 100 signatures which they sent to Bishop Peter Ireton along with a request to establish a church in Salem. Bishop Ireton approved their request and entrusted the new parish to the Redemptorists, who were already serving at Saint Gerard in Roanoke.

The Redemptorists brought a chapel up from Durham, North Carolina, and placed it on a parcel of land located on West Main Street. The first Mass was held on April 18, 1948.

In 1969, Father Tackney, known as the "building priest," arranged for the purchase of 5.73 acres of land on Turner Road, where Our Lady of Perpetual Help now stands. A groundbreaking for the new building was held in August of 1972. The new church was dedicated on May 27, 1973 by Bishop John J. Russell.

The Diocese of Richmond took over staffing the parish from the Redemptorists in 1980. Father Mark Richard Lane, who later became the Vicar General of the Diocese, was the first Diocesan priest at Our Lady of Perpetual Help.

Today, Our Lady of Perpetual Help parishioners report their parish is flourishing and are eager to sing its praises.

Saint Catherine of Siena

— Clarksville • 1947 —

Clarksville is in Mecklenburg County, 112 miles southwest of Richmond near the North Carolina border. In 1946, when Colonial Mills decided to build nearby Clarksville, many Catholic labors followed the company. The need for a Catholic Church was realized by Bishop Ireton of Richmond and the Franciscan Provincial. Bishop Ireton gave the job of building a church to Father Walter Hammon. Soon after, Father Hammon hired a local contractor, Otis Wilkinson, to build the church and on November 15, 1946, building began. The Church is located at 805 Virginia Avenue.

Since this was shortly after World War II, building supplies were scarce. Yet, Mr. Wilkinson was able to find the supplies. Much of the roof came from an old church in Keysville (Barnesville), along with an altar, pews, windows, and doors. However, the builders had many problems with flooding and by June 23, 1947, records show that $14,471.81 had been spent on the Church.

Bishop Ireton was concerned since he had hoped to spend $10,000. The Catholic Church Extension Society gave generously and asked for the right to name the Church. Saint Catherine of Siena Parish was established officially on Sunday, September 28, 1947.

On April 20, 1950, Father Provincial gave permission to build the friary at the back of the Church. The friary was officially dedicated on November 14, 1950. By April of 1977, the Franciscans decided to turn the Church over to the Diocese of Richmond.

Since then the Church had an administration office as well as the parish rectory added. The parish is currently home to 292 members from 134 families within a 60-mile radius. Expansion and renovations to the Sanctuary in 2015 added 1,300 square feet, 65 seats to the Church, and handicap access to the Church and social hall. The new renovations help especially during the summer months when vacationers to Bugg's Island and Lake Kerr visit. The Church was blessed by Bishop Francis DiLorenzo on December 13, 2015.

Our parish is an active, close, and vital one. Many groups are active in infusing God's word through the community.

The Saint Catherine Knights of Columbus and Knights of the Patrick Henry Assembly participate in local events. A dedicated staff of volunteers provide religious education for our youth and work with Backpack Buddies which provide food to elementary school children for the days they are not in school. Many of our services, organizations, and religious groups provide structured opportunities for active discipleship in our community. Other groups include Small Christian Communities, Prison Ministry, Food Pantry, Craft groups, and Extraordinary Ministers of Communion. Pastoral Council provides resources as well as counsel to the pastor. Office of Justice and Peace coordinates food baskets to the poor at Thanksgiving and Christmas and organizes an Angel tree at Christmas. Saint Catherine also offers Spanish Mass on the first Sunday of the month.

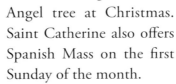

Saint John Neumann

Most parishes establish a church first and later their parochial school, but the history of Saint John Neumann Catholic Church in Powhatan County is the reverse. Their roots began with two schools established by the Drexel daughters, Louise Drexel, who married Colonel Edward Morrell and Louise's sister, Saint Katharine Drexel, founder of the Sisters of the Blessed Sacrament. In 1894, the Morrells purchased Belmead, a 1,600-acre estate formerly belonging to Confederate General Philip St. George Cocke. Upon this site, they built Saint Emma's Industrial and Agricultural Institute for young Indian and Black men. In 1899, a school for Indian and Black ladies, Saint Francis de Sales, was opened by Saint Katharine. These schools were served by various orders of brothers and priests and Powhatan's first Catholic communities began there. In 1928, a beautiful memorial chapel,

Saint Edward's, was built by Mrs. Morrell in memory of her husband.

This chapel served students, faculty, and Powhatan Catholics until its destruction in 1970. At that time, with desegregation, Saint Emma's could not find financial backing to continue, and its beautiful and sound classrooms, labs, shops and mills were destroyed. The parish then moved to Saint Emma's chapel. Records of baptisms, First Communions, etc., were kept at Saint Francis de Sales, which became the parish church for Saint Edward's and now being staffed by priests of the Diocese of Richmond. In 1976, the name of the parish was changed to Saint John Neumann in honor of the Fourth Bishop of Philadelphia. From 1976 to the present, the parish has worshipped in the following sites: Saint Francis de Sales (1976-1982), Powhatan Rescue

Squad (1982-83), the original Powhatan United Methodist Church (1983-86), and the present facility at Flat Rock since its dedication on November 2, 1986.

The Flat Rock site began modestly with a multi-purpose center hall serving as both the worship area on Sundays and Holy Days and a social hall for parish functions. A full-service kitchen adjoins that room, and the parish chose to utilize the rest of the space as a small chapel, classrooms, an office for the pastor, and a large narthex. Since that time, the parish has had two more building campaigns: the first focused on more classrooms and the second on a worship center, pastor's office, business office, formal multi-purpose room appropriate as a parlor for brides or for families during funerals. The parish's generosity and commitment to building campaigns has allowed them to provide a fully operative building and out buildings that serve religious education, various parish ministries and committees, Boy Scouts,

and the county's Food Pantry of which we are heavily involved as a parish.

As the parish continues to grow it has added a Columbarium, a children's recreation area, and expansion of its parking facilities as well as a new rectory.

More importantly, as Saint John Neumann parish grows, it chooses to focus on serving the goals of the parish and of Christ: to show Christian love.

Saint Jude

— Franklin • 1948 —

In the early 1940's, Catholics in this area gathered for Mass in private homes and in the old USO building located on the corner of Fourth Avenue and Franklin Street. In 1945, the lot was purchased and in 1947 a contract was signed to build a Shrine to Saint Jude and an attached Parish Hall for $30,000, to serve the spiritual needs of about 80 Catholics within a thirty-mile territory. Our mission church was pioneered by Father Julius Schmidhauser, pastor of Saint Mary of the Presentation in Suffolk. Records show that as our first pastor, he was instrumental in acquiring the lots and raising money to build the church. Bishop Peter Ireton, Ninth

Bishop of Richmond, officiated at the blessing of the church on April 25, 1948.

Saint Jude was named a parish on May 1, 1955. The church building remained unchanged until its renovation in the Spring of 1987. Additional classrooms for religious education were built and dedicated by Bishop Walter Sullivan, the Eleventh Bishop of Richmond. It was followed by the construction of the Commons as an addition to the front of the Church and was dedicated by Auxiliary Bishop David Foley. The parking lot was also enlarged and paved.

Our present Church was constructed in 1994. The pews with kneelers from the original Sanctuary were replaced with our current oak chairs. Bishop Walter Sullivan presided at its dedication on December 4, 1994. Our first Worship space became our Fellowship Hall.

In 1996, the Saint Jude Parish added a garden honoring Mary, the Blessed Mother, on the northeast side of the church property. We celebrated our 50th anniversary in 1998 and later in the decade stained-glass windows were designed and installed.

A prayer group meets to recite the Rosary and the Chaplet of Divine Mercy. Christian Formation classes for children are held before the Sunday Mass. The ChristLife series for adults is done after the Sunday Mass. Formation classes are done for RCIA, First Communion and Confirmation.

Our Social Ministry includes collecting donations, food, and household items for the Franklin Cooperative Ministry. We participate with our local Social Services agencies in their Christmas Angel Tree, Thanksgiving, and Christmas food baskets. The diocesan Fuel and Hunger Fund helps to augment our resources to help the needy who come to our door. We support a twinning project with Haiti, with Saint Mary of the Presentation Church in Suffolk.

Saint Jude Eucharistic Ministers also give Holy Communion to homebound parishioners. Sunday Mass at Saint Jude is held at 11:00 a.m. from the first Sunday after Labor Day and ends on Memorial Day. Our summer schedule for Sunday Mass time is at 9:30 a.m.

We are a welcoming community and continue to give service through the different ministries of Saint Jude Church. April 25, 2018, marked the 70th anniversary of the dedication of Saint Jude Church.

Shrine of the Infant of Prague

Larry Monahan, a Catholic whose ancestors came from County Cork, Ireland, found himself suffering from severe job-related stress. He had worked for the Kroger chain since he was 14, doing every job from bagging potatoes to supervising 38 stores. He was advised by his doctor to take an extended leave of absence and hitchhike around the country. With his family's blessing, he decided to follow his doctor's orders and leave his home in Detroit, Michigan.

A ride from a trucker ended with Mr. Monahan drinking a cup of coffee at the Virginia Diner in Wakefield. After telling the restaurant's owner, Darcy Davis, how much he liked the area, Davis offered to sell him the business, which he had started in an old train car in 1929.

Monahan set out to make the Virginia Diner one of the most famous restaurants in the United States. Business was very slow at first. Unable to meet the first weeks' payroll, he made a promise to Saint Jude that, if he was successful, he would build a Catholic Church.

At that time, there were very few Catholics in the Wakefield area. However, when the "Mission Trailer" came to town, it was evident that quite a few Catholics would attend Mass, if it was available. When the crowd was too large for the trailer, the Monahans opened their home until the growing number of members outgrew the home.

Mr. Monahan approached the Bishop asking to build the church in Wakefield. The Bishop asked how much it would cost to build the church. Mr. Monahan replied: "if we knew, we would be afraid to build it." The Bishop gave his approval.

Mr. Monahan said that while digging the footing, they noticed Bill Broderick unloading cinderblocks. The idea struck them that if they could sell these blocks at $10 apiece, they could build a nice little church. Mr. Mario Campioli, then head architect at Williamsburg, gave the plans and offered his advice and counseling as the building progressed. They called John Daly at *The Catholic Virginian* to put an ad in the paper with a picture of the proposed Shrine and asked for buyers of the cinderblocks offering to put a name in every block as the church was built. John Daly and *The Catholic Virginian* were responsible for over $30,000 in revenue to build a beautiful Shrine.

The Secretary and Treasurer, Gloria Smith and her husband Chuck, at the Virginia Diner worked together, answering hundreds of letters and selling the cinderblock and appointments. Donations came from Catholics and non-Catholics; Senator Peck Gray gave the rafters for the roof.

A beautiful hand-built pipe organ was installed and since this was the first organ built by their newly formed Southeastern Organ Service of Suffolk, the owners were willing to forego their profit, making it possible for the Shrine to purchase a world-class instrument.

The idea for the Church's name, Shrine of the Infant of Prague, was born on Christmas Eve, 1950. On that day, Virginia Monahan gave her husband a beautiful statue of the Infant of Prague, which has continued to grace the Shrine Chapel. The groundbreaking for the new church on October 19, 1952, was well attended. One year later, the completed Shrine was dedicated on Wednesday, October 28, 1953, by Bishop Peter L. Ireton.

Visitors from all over the world stop at the church to pray as they travel in the area, as the church is open daily. Parishioners from churches in Virginia Beach and Petersburg make a pilgrimage to the Shrine each year. The Shrine sponsors a young child with a yearly donation to be used for schooling and assistance. At Christmas, presents and food baskets for the needy are prepared and given to the Sussex County Social Services for distribution. The parish is blessed with a growing membership.

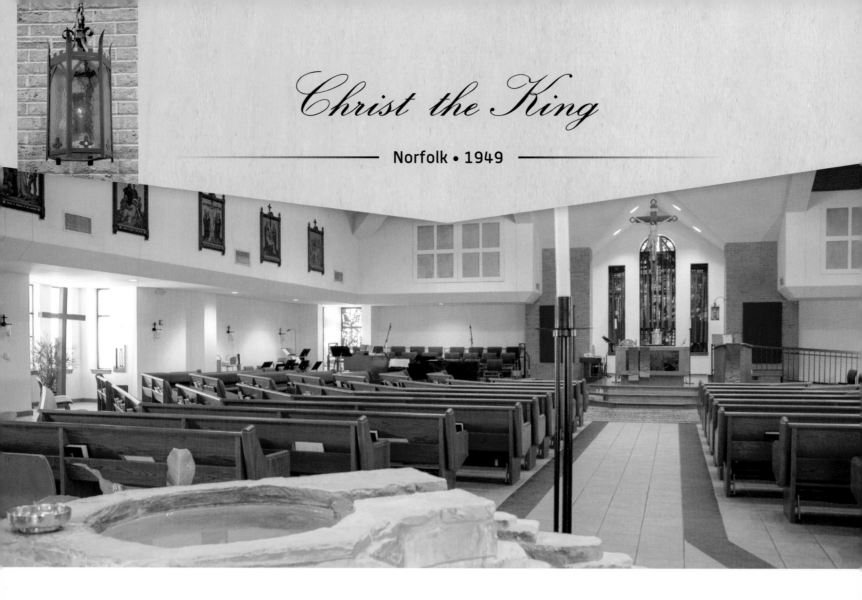

Christ the King

In September 1937, Reverend Edward A. Brosnan, pastor of Saint Mary of the Immaculate Conception, Norfolk, broke ground for construction of a mission chapel. On Passion Sunday, 1938, the mission chapel was completed and dedicated to Christ the King. In June 1949, Christ the King Mission Chapel became an independent parish with Reverend Conrad C. Hoffner as first resident Pastor.

Father Hoffner acquired land and made plans for a rectory, church, and school while the parish participated in a Rosary crusade. In 1953, construction began on new school and auditorium. Christ the King School,

staffed by the Franciscan sisters of Baltimore, was opened in September 1954. The old chapel became the Parish Hall. The first class of Christ the King eighth graders graduated in June 1959 and placed a statue of Christ the King on the grounds in honor of Sister Austin, the first Principal.

Having outgrown the small mission chapel, liturgies were celebrated for 40 years in the school auditorium. The church was completely renovated

in the early 1970's and also acquired a new organ. In September 1989, Bishop Walter F. Sullivan, approved the parish's request to construct a new church on the space envisioned by Father Hoffner 40 years before. In April 1994, construction began, and on the Feast of Christ the King, November 20, 1994, the new church was formally dedicated by Bishop Sullivan.

The new church incorporated furnishings from the original chapel, the "temporary" church, and the convent: the tabernacle, the tabernacle stand (which was the original Baptistery), the Sanctuary lamp, and the angels. The marble on the altar, the ambo, and the tabernacle stand were cut from larger pieces of the previous altar. The stained, carved, wooden doors depicting the Holy Family were plaques mounted on the walls on each side of the altar in the "temporary church." The altar stone was from the previous altar. The Credo table was the sisters' altar in the convent. The former church building was renovated and became the church hall/auditorium/gymnasium.

The Corpus from the original church was restored and hung on a new cross over the altar. The Stations of the Cross that hang in the church were also acquired, plus many icons. In June of 2010, two mosaic icons were purchased from a Byzantine Church in Chicago and

placed on either side of the altar – one of Christ the King enthroned and one of The Virgin holding the Christ Child.

In the last decade, a confessional was added in the alcove, where the tabernacle used to be. The sacristy was enlarged, a statue of Saint Joseph was placed in the northern alcove, and a statue of Our Lady of Fatima was put in the southern alcove. The convent house is used for the youth activities and faith formation.

Under the leadership of our pastors, Christ the King parish has always been a faith-filled community with a vision for the future. Our history is a testament of God's many and frequent blessings.

Saint Andrew the Apostle

— Chincoteague Island • 1949 —

In 1949, Father Bennett McNulty of Saint Peter in Onley, celebrated Mass on Sunday mornings in various locations for Catholics on Chincoteague Island until 1958 when Father Rudolph Miller, Pastor of Holy Name of Jesus Church, celebrated Mass for Saint Andrew's Mission Congregation.

Father Bennett McNulty blessed the newly purchased Saint Andrew Mission Church in July 1965.

In 1975, Virginia's Eastern Shore Catholic Churches transferred to the Diocese of Richmond from the Diocese of Wilmington. Saint Andrew's Mission was therefore reassigned to Saint Peter's Church. The Parish, small in number but stout-hearted, survived transient Mass locations, times, and visiting priests. Various ministries continued to thrive benefiting the community.

In September 1977, the Parish of Saint Andrew the Apostle Catholic Church was established, and Father John Murray was named first Pastor. Many church improvements followed including custom-designed stained-glass windows. A newly acquired parish house and rectory were dedicated in February 1982. A new roof was installed on the church in 1985.

Father John Prinelli arrived in 1986 and was the first to organize visits to nearby migrant camps. Overseeing renovations in the Church included professional restoration and installation of the Blessed Virgin and Saint Joseph statues and a new steeple on the Church roof by 1990.

Parishioners continued working with migrant camps and organizing donations for workers and their families requiring a Justice and Peace Committee formation with outreach programs for the poor and oppressed.

Father Paschal Kneip, OSB, arrived in June 2003 from Saint Vincent Archabbey. During his tenure, a hall was built accommodating 300 additional people for Mass. He oversaw construction of a columbarium in the cemetery. In December 2010, he returned to the Archabbey. From January 2011 to October 2014, Father Richard Chirichiello, OSB, from Saint Vincent Archabbey served as Pastor.

Our Church reverted to a Mission Parish in October 2014. Father Michael Imperial, a priest from the Philippines serving the Diocese of Richmond, developed an interfaith fellowship throughout Chincoteague Island and the entire Eastern Shore, receiving President Obama's Gold Service Award for Eastern Shore Migrant Ministry Encounter 2016.

Saint Bridget

— Richmond • 1949 —

The foundation of Saint Bridget Parish was made possible by the generosity of Annie Irvin, who died December 21, 1948. Her will provided more than $200,000 for building a church on property owned by the Diocese of Richmond at Three Chopt and York Roads. She asked that the church be named in honor of Saint Bridget, in memory of her mother, Bridget Murphy Irvin.

The first Mass for the parishioners of Saint Bridget was offered in the Westhampton Theatre, September 11, 1949. Meanwhile, plans for the new church were done by architects, Gleeson and Mulrooney of Philadelphia, Pennsylvania, and ground was broken on the Feast of the Assumption of Our Lady, August 15, 1949. Construction was begun by Doyle and Russell, Richmond contractors.

The new church was dedicated by Bishop Peter Ireton on May 21, 1950. The marble in the church, including the altar, statues and the baptismal font, was imported from Italy. Rambusch Studios of New York City did the interior decoration. The Stations of the Cross were done by Hildreth Meiere of New York City. They show an art deco influence and are painted in vibrant color on wood panels.

The school building was completed in 1952 and dedicated in the fall of

the same year. However, before the school was built, in August 1951, five Religious of the Sacred Heart of Mary (RSHM) came from Tarrytown, New York, to staff Saint Bridget School. Mother M. Gonzague, began classes in September, with three grades in temporary classrooms in the church basement and kindergarten in the convent building. In Fall 1952, classes moved to the new building for the kindergarten and seven elementary grades. The eighth grade was added the following year.

As the parish celebrated its 25th anniversary in 1974, the church interior was repainted, gold-leaf decorations and a second altar were added. The decoration was done by Rambusch Studios who did the original work.

A Skinner Organ from the deconsecrated Monumental Episcopal Church was brought over, and it took two weeks for parishioners to dismantle the organ and move it to the church. The dedicated volunteers spent numerous Friday evenings and Saturday mornings reassembling the organ piece by piece before being lifted onto the balcony.

The parish underwent a renovation of the church sanctuary in 1987 and built a Commons for fellowship by filling in the convent garden and building on top of it. The convent became the parish offices and meeting rooms with doors opened into the convent exterior walls to connect the offices and meeting rooms to the Commons. Nurseries and accessible restrooms were added.

A new Buzard Opus 42 pipe organ was built for the church and installed in September 2013. It continues to provide world class music and reveals the church's great west window. Following that, the church's original

tabernacle was located and restored to its location on a new altar. A new entrance and a bell tower were added to the church and dedicated on January 12, 2019, by Bishop Barry C. Knestout, Thirteenth Bishop of Richmond.

Saint Joseph

Saint Joseph Catholic Church began as a mission of Danville in 1938. Father Brennan would travel weekly to Martinsville to say Mass in the homes of some of the parishioners. Eventually, a hall over a bakery on Bridge Street was rented to hold Catholic liturgies and celebrations.

In the 1940's with the opening of the DuPont Company, the number of Catholics in Martinsville and Henry Counties grew. Saint Joseph finally became a parish in 1948 and was housed in the Rives Theater. Rev. Robert O'Kane was assigned as our first pastor in 1949. This new parish was home to about 125 Catholics when property was purchased

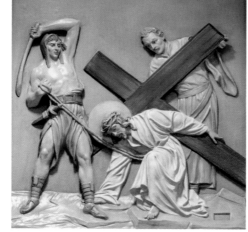

on Myrtle Road to serve as our church building. This home later became the parish rectory.

A more permanent home was purchased in 1952 on the corner of Booker Road and Church Street. This former Baptist Church became Saint Joseph Catholic Church and remained so for the next 50 years. At that site, the parish continued to flourish and grew to more than 300 families. Also growing were the number of Hispanic Catholics in the area. In December of 1996, the parish began a monthly Mass in Spanish. In 2001, the Spanish Mass became a weekly celebration that continues today.

At the turn of the century, plans were made to build a new Catholic Church to replace the current building which needed costly repairs. In 1999, a five-acre tract of land off of Spruce Street in Martinsville was purchased and construction began. On November 25, 2001, our current church building was dedicated by Bishop Walter Sullivan. And in 2011, we were clustered with Saint Francis of Assisi in Rocky Mount.

As we continued to grow in numbers and in spirituality, we added on to the current church building and expanded the parking lot in 2015.

Our parish is a diverse, spiritual, devoted family of faith. We continue to be active in many social, spiritual and outreach programs in our parish and in the Martinsville/Henry County area.

Holy Infant

The Church of the Holy Infant traces its origin far back in the early 19th Century as part of the satellite mission of Saint Francis in Staunton and Blessed Sacrament in Harrisonburg.

Harry and Kathryn Wade moved to the town of Shenandoah coming from a predominantly Catholic area in Baltimore. The family found themselves to be the only Catholics there. The Ku Klux Klan, in an effort to scare the Wades out of town, staged a large demonstration that included burning an eight-foot cross in front of their house. Mrs. Wade was not intimidated.

The Bishop of Richmond contacted the monastery in Winchester to minister to the few Catholic families in the Shenandoah Valley. The families organized for the celebration of Mass at their homes. This practice continued until World War II.

The Bishop of Richmond organized another pastoral approach as he dispatched two mission vans to the area in the Summer of 1948. The back of each van opened to reveal the altar on which priests celebrated Mass as people gathered around in the open air. The van also had sleeping accommodations for the priest.

Father Conrad Hoffner, then pastor of Blessed Sacrament, requested the mission van team visit the Elkton area. The response was very encouraging, and this prompted Bishop Peter Ireton to contact Father Joseph Driscoll the Vice Provincial of the Redemptorist Order in the South to establish a new mission in Elkton.

In March of 1951, Father Driscoll made a quick survey in the towns of Luray, Stanley, Shenandoah, Elkton and Grottos. It indicated 36 Catholics living in the area. The Provincial gave permission and recommendation to staff the new mission.

A thorough census of the area had disclosed that there were 186 baptized Catholics. Reverend Raymond Govern and his assistant, Reverend Lawrence Murphy, arrived at the mission in May 1951 and made their headquarters in Elkton, living in the old Gables Hotel. Through the kindness of the proprietors, Mr. and Mrs. Armentrout, arrangements were made for weekday and Sunday Masses in the hotel's basement. Bishop Peter Ireton gave special permission to reserve the Blessed Sacrament in one of the hotel rooms upstairs that was turned into a chapel. Religious education and Catechesis were conducted for the children and adults on Friday and Saturday.

After a vigorous search and despite the opposition and resistance to have a Catholic Church in the area, a four-and-three-quarter lot of land was approved for the construction of the Church. The Diocese of Richmond purchased this property from Elkton Improvement Company. The architectural plans were comprised of the church, rectory and social hall. In May 1952, the Diocese of Richmond purchased the property where the church would be built. The groundbreaking took place on February 22, 1953. The church, rectory and hall were constructed as a single unit according to the plans

drawn up by the architect, Mr. Frank Martinelli.

A generous benefactor, Mr. John Gaetano of Milford, Connecticut, made the largest individual cash donation of $5,000 and suggested the name "Holy Infant" in honor of the Infant of Prague. The large stained-glass front window was designed specifically for the church.

On November 4th, 1953, the new church was dedicated and presided over by Bishop Peter Ireton.

The Redemptorist Fathers ceded the administration of the parish in 1968, and it has since been staffed by priests of the Diocese of Richmond.

Major renovations to the Sanctuary were done in 1989 and again in 2006. This is when stained-glass windows of the four Evangelists were installed behind the tabernacle and on the side windows of the church. Among the changes made during renovation was the replacement of most of the stained glass with clear windows. Beginning in 2005, unique hand-crafted stained glass windows were created and installed in the nave and church hall by parishioners Jim and Shirley Shirron. This was completed in 2014.

Holy Rosary

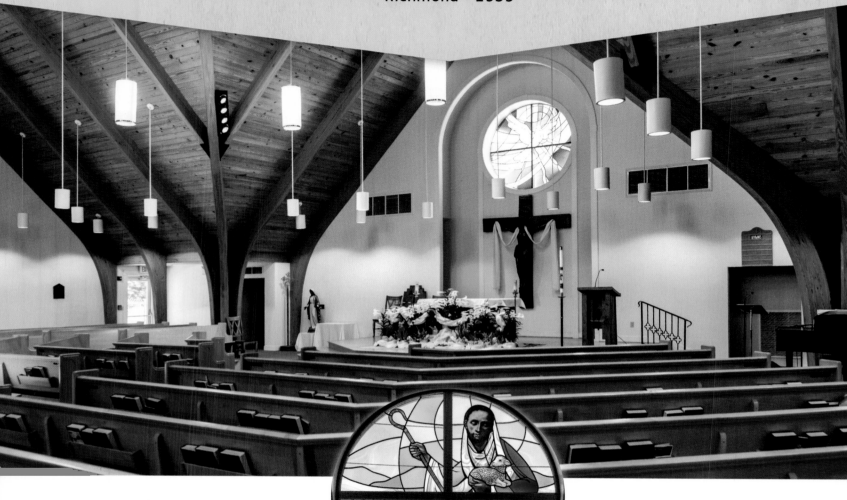

In the heart of Church Hill, the roots of the Holy Rosary Catholic Church go back to the 1930's, when the Redemptorist Fathers started the Church Hill Catholic Mission on North 27th Street.

During that time, the Redemptorist Fathers gathered at the home of George Pollard at 27th and P Street. The Mission was an outgrowth of Saint Augustine parish, which was located in the Fulton section of Richmond. The Redemptorists found great interest among the African-American families to further develop the mission into a full parish. Continued progress motivated Bishop Peter Ireton, Ninth Bishop of Richmond, to formally establish Holy Rosary Parish in 1953.

Over the next few years, property earlier purchased at North 33rd Street between R and S Streets, was developed. The first church on the current property was built at 33rd and R Streets. It served as church office, Worship Center and child care center, run by the Missionary Sisters of Verona (now known as the Comboni Missionary Sisters.) The parish grew and, in the early 1960's, the previous Church was built; in the 1970's the child care center was built and the Bishop Russell

Center was renovated and became the Parish Hall. Most recently, the parish completed at $2,500,000 expansion including a new Sanctuary and Chapel, new offices and renovated Parish Center and Commons.

The people of Holy Rosary have gathered to give praise and thanks to God for over fifty years. During that time, through the births and deaths, baptisms and marriages, the opportunity has been given to deepen our relationship with God and one another. The transformations occurring in society and in the Roman Catholic Church universally, are reflected in both this worship space and our worship gatherings.

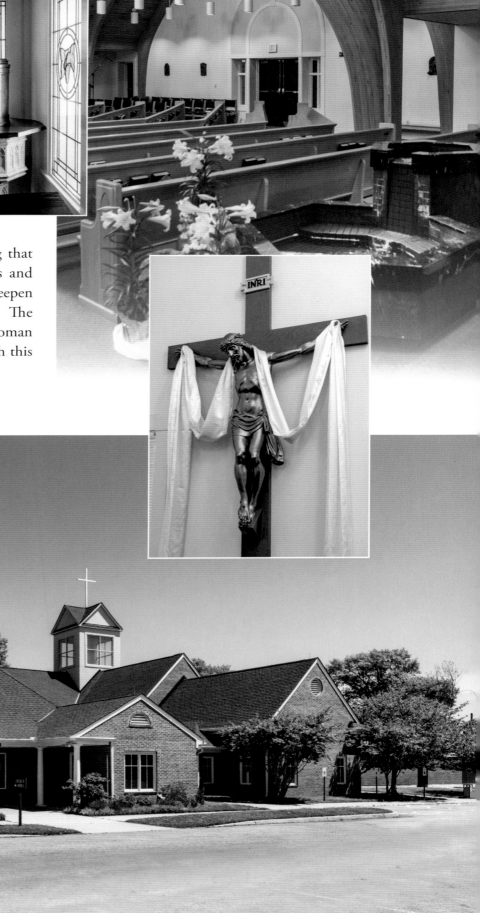

Our Lady of Mount Carmel

Our Lady of Mount Carmel parish was established in 1953 by the Carmelite Fathers under the leadership of its beloved first pastor, Fr. Norbert Piper. The parish school opened the following year, and from that time has been beautifully guided by the Dominican Sisters of St. Cecilia. During the same period the Poor Clares established a monastery just down the street from the parish, and for nearly fifty years were a vital part of the life of Mount Carmel; although now removed to Barhamsville, Virginia, the Poor Clare nuns remain close to our parish. Thus, Mount Carmel has been shaped by three different religious communities throughout its existence, a distinction that may be unique in the Diocese of Richmond.

«We find Christ here. We bring Christ to the world.» For many years these words have guided the mission of Mount Carmel parish. Jesus teaches us that we are formed to be like him through three inter-related experiences: worship, word, and witness. We worship God in Mass and the life of prayer, and meet him in the sacraments, and from this «source and summit» flows everything else. We come to know the Word of God through studying the Scriptures and the teachings of the Church. And we witness to Christ by going forth beyond the walls of the parish, identifying with the poor and learning from them, and proclaiming in our lives and words the love and mercy of Jesus which we have ourselves received. Mount Carmel parish is known throughout Newport News and beyond as the key place that

provides help with material needs--food, rent and power payments, layettes for newborns, prescriptions for the elderly--but also, and at the same time, for compassion, a caring word, and, always, prayer. Likewise, parishioners and priests constantly visit the sick at Riverside Hospital, as well as shut-ins and residents of half a dozen retirement and nursing facilities, bringing them the Eucharist, companionship, prayer, and a smile.

At the time the parish was established, there was concern that it might be too far from town to succeed. As Newport News has grown, the parish has grown up with it. For the first decade, the parish worshipped in an unfinished wing of the school, until the school gym was finished and served for worship for nearly twenty-five years. The current church was dedicated in 1986. More recently the parish hall, built in 2004, has provided vital space for every imaginable program, and as the place to host PORT one week each year, the winter shelter for the homeless.

Renovations to the church in 2014 provided an expanded Blessed Sacrament Chapel, which has inspired a constant flow of visitors for prayer before Jesus' Eucharistic Presence. Increasingly parishioners and visitors point to Adoration as a constant encouragement and strength as they seek to become like Jesus. The parish continues to thrive now as always, with a growing diversity of parishioners and increasing numbers of young families whose children love to climb the crape myrtles on the front lawn after Mass. We look forward to meeting Christ here and bringing him to the world for many decades to come.

Church of Saint Thérèse

— Chesapeake • 1954 —

In May 1942, Monsignor Joseph F. Govaert, pastor of Saint Paul's Catholic Church of Portsmouth, purchased a plot of land on Oregon Avenue in Portsmouth. Twelve years later, Little Flower Elementary School opened on the site and the parish of Saint Thérèse of Lisieux was established by the Bishop Peter Ireton with Father Thomas Finnegan appointed pastor on June 16, 1954.

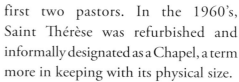

The new parish, which was quartered in a small chapel in the Little Flower School for nearly 16 years, first opened its doors on Sunday, September 5, 1954. Father Finnegan was succeeded by Father Joseph Leitch in 1959 and religious and social activities thrived during the tenure of these first two pastors. In the 1960's, Saint Thérèse was refurbished and informally designated as a Chapel, a term more in keeping with its physical size.

When the three local Catholic grade schools combined in 1970 to become Portsmouth Catholic Elementary School, Saint Thérèse was asked to relinquish its space. On June 8, 1970, the last liturgy was celebrated in the chapel of the Little Flower School. From June 16, 1970, until June 24, 1972, the parish family of Saint Thérèse gathered for Mass in the auditorium of Chittum Elementary School. The groundbreaking for Saint Thérèse's present church took place on August 1, 1971, on Portsmouth Boulevard in the Western Branch area of Chesapeake, and the new church was dedicated on June 24, 1972. Shortly after, an office wing and a residence wing were added to the main structure.

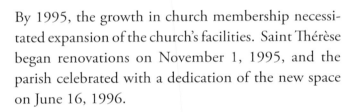

By 1995, the growth in church membership necessitated expansion of the church's facilities. Saint Thérèse began renovations on November 1, 1995, and the parish celebrated with a dedication of the new space on June 16, 1996.

Throughout 2015, the church celebrated 60 years of doing "small things with great love" and how, like our patron saint's humble beginnings, the Church of Saint Thérèse had grown from a parish of 285 households gathering in an elementary school chapel to a

parish of over 1,000 households with its own recently expanded structure. We are a parish committed to living out Christ's Gospel challenge. Although we cannot know the future, our present continues to be exciting and Spirit-filled.

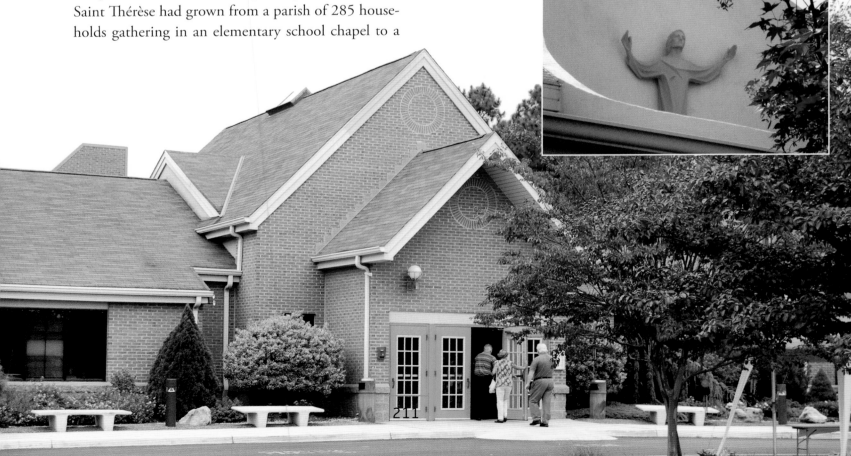

Saint Joan of Arc

Catholicism had been practiced in York County since the 16th century. However, it wasn't until 1910 that a permanent Catholic population settled in the County. This came with the arrival of 42 Polish Catholics to build a cement factory at Waterview. The first priest to serve the community was Father Ladislaus Cynalewski who came by boat from Baltimore to celebrate Mass in a large house on the York River. In 1918, Bishop Denis O'Connell established a more permanent foundation for the parish by appointing Father Ceslaus Jakubowski as the first pastor of West Point and the surrounding Tidewater communities. He was known as "Father Jack" the "horse-and-buggy-priest." Father Jack traveled by boat twice a month on Saturdays to Yorktown where the men of the parish met him and travelled by horse and buggy to the "big house." Early on Sunday mornings he celebrated Mass and spent the rest of the day visiting and teaching. He would leave on Monday mornings at 2 a.m. to catch the morning boat to West Point.

In 1941, the Navy assigned a Catholic chaplain to the Naval Mine Warfare School near Yorktown and a Navy bus transported Catholics to Mass on Sunday to the chapel. This practice continued throughout World War II and until 1953.

An attempt to form a civilian parish came with a mission from Saint Bede in Williamsburg headed by Father Thomas J. Walsh. Under his leadership the land on which the present church stands was purchased. On September 5, 1954, Bishop Peter Ireton dedicated Saint Joan of Arc as a mission of Saint Bede Parish. It was through the generous outgrowth and ministry of the Carmelite Fathers who first began to serve the Catholic Community in Newport News, that Father Norbert Piper, O.Carm. and his Carmelite community took over the administration of the parish soon after it was founded.

Located in historic Yorktown where the Battle of Yorktown occurred in 1781, thus ending the American Revolutionary War with Great Britain, the parish mission statement declares Saint Joan of Arc is "a community dedicated to the teachings of Jesus Christ as passed down through the Apostles and the Traditions of the Catholic Faith. We are devoted to the mission of the Church to "go and make disciples of all nations" (Matthew 28:19).

A new worship space was built in 1998 and dedicated on March 12th of that year by Bishop Walter Sullivan, 44 years after its founding. In his homily, the Bishop stated "I am sure because of the connection with France in the Revolutionary War, the parish was fittingly named after the Maid of Orleans, Joan of Arc, who won France her freedom from England in 1429."

Saint Therese

St. Paul • 1954

Although Saint Therese did not become a parish until 1951, Glenmary Home Missioners priests from Saint Anthony in Norton began coming to St. Paul in 1946 to celebrate Mass with a small group of believers at the local "Lion's Den" clubhouse.

Mr. and Mrs. Melvin C. Matthews, parish community members in nearby Dante, donated the land the brick church would be built upon. Their son, Fred, directed building operations and used much of his time, energy, materials, tools, and machinery in the actual building of the church. He was assisted by friends. Many furnishings and substantial donations for the church were received from local individuals and businesses, and also from Glenmary contacts throughout the United States.

The Most Reverend Thomas J. McDonnell, Coadjutor of the Wheeling Diocese, was celebrant at the church dedication on August 12, 1951. In 1955, Father Roland Hautz became Saint Therese's first permanent resident priest. He converted the basement of the church into a "recreation hall" for meetings and so teenagers could have dances and a general place to meet on Saturday nights.

Father David Glockner became pastor in 1977 and was instrumental in arranging for the presence of the Sisters of St. Joseph in the area. Sisters Mary Keane, Loretta Scully, and Martha Sirois, known as the "Dante Damsels," ran the Neighbor's Aid Store for more than 17 years. Lillie Peters, a local resident, took over in 2001. Sacred Heart Catholic Church in Glyndon, Maryland, continuously provided funds to assist the church with expenses, in addition to many donors from the North who mailed donations to the Store. Before the Sisters took over the store operations, it was said long-time parishioner "Pauline Molinary was Neighbor's Aid."

The "Dante Damsels" also assisted with religious education, Bible schools and community efforts. Others who followed them in this area were Sisters John Bosco and Mary Bowman. Laywomen Marty Huber and JoAnn Detta came to the area in 1975 providing programs for the children, teens, and adults.

Brother Vince Wilmes helped start a local Little League baseball with as many as 120 children participating at one time. Although few of his Little Leaguers were Catholic, he'd march them into church before a game and teach them a prayer. Brother Bernie Stern is remembered for his tremendous love of music, often playing his accordion at Mass and church gatherings.

In 1989, Father Tom Charters, became the Church's last Glenmary pastor.

Saint Therese had been a part of the Wheeling Diocese, but after the Region IV Bishops Conference in Maryland, in 1974, the parish was transferred to the Richmond Diocese along with all counties in Southwest Virginia. In 1994, Glenmary Home Missioners returned the satellite parish of Saint Therese to the Diocese of Richmond's Bishop Walter Sullivan.

In November 2012, Father Charles Ssebalamu from Uganda was the parish's first African priest by way of a program set up by then Bishop Francis DiLorenzo. When Father Charles was transferred, he was replaced in September 2016 by Father Zaverio Banasula, also from Uganda.

Saint Mary

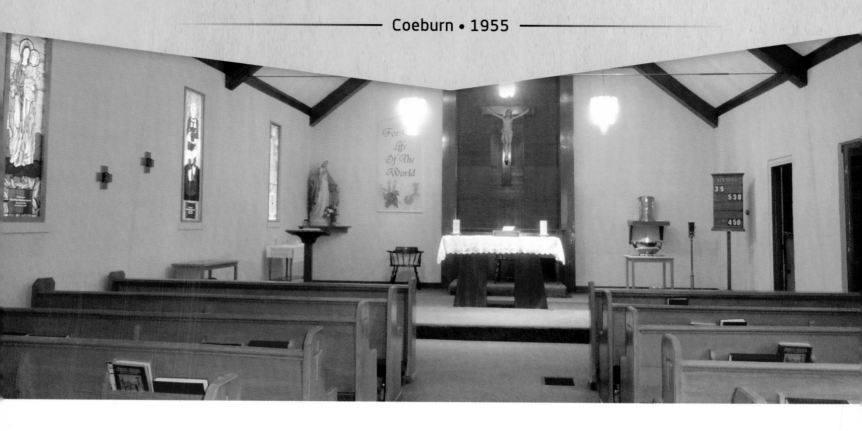

Saint Mary in Coeburn had a unique beginning. From the mid 1940's through 1955, a small group of parishioners held Mass first at the Women's Club House, then in a beauty shop belonging to parishioner Mattie Payne, then in individual parishioner's homes such as Alton and Rose Lawson, Sr., and Bill and Gen Hunsaker. Finally, in a common community effort, the present church building was erected and dedicated in 1955. Parishioners donated equipment for excavation as well as their time and energy to make the dream of a Catholic Church in Coeburn a reality.

Since neighbors near a site selected for the church were leery of selling land to the Catholic Church, Alton Lawson, Sr., bought the land for the church to use. He also provided a bulldozer and, along with several other parishioners, helped blast rock out of the side of a hill to prepare the site for construction.

Reverend Roland Hautz, a Glenmary priest, was instrumental in the direction of the building operations as he had drawn the plans for the new church. Before completion of the building, Father Hautz was transferred to another parish. His successors, Fathers Gardner and Berson, both Glenmary priests, directed the final phases of construction.

Many people contributed to the building and furnishings of Saint Mary. Substantial donations for the building were made by the Saint Vincent de Paul Society of the Diocese of Brooklyn, New York. The altar and altar cloths were donated by Mrs. Nicholaus McManany of Kansas City, Missouri, in memory of her husband. The tabernacle was donated by Mr. Edward Jiru of Waukegan, Illinois. The statue in the niche was donated by Mr. and Mrs. Raymond Hautz of Milford, Ohio, (parents of Father Hautz). The statue of the Blessed Virgin Mary was donated by Mrs. John Riehele of Milford, Ohio. Other generous donations were made by the Glenmary Missioners, Dr. and Mrs. Hugh Clement, Mrs. H.C. Brann, Rev. Sheehan, and Mr. and Mrs. Bill Hunsaker. In addition, Benedict Barta, John Barta, Peter Catron, and Alton P. Lawson, Sr., all of Coeburn were instrumental in the construction and preparation of the building site for Saint Mary Church.

The Saint Mary Church building was dedicated August 7, 1955 by Rev. Thomas J. McDonnell, Coadjutor Bishop of the Diocese of Wheeling followed by Confirmation of several parishioners.

The Glenmary Home Missioners continued to serve at Saint Mary for 24 years until its acquisition by the Diocese of Richmond in September of 1979. Under the direction of diocesan priests, Saint Mary celebrated its 25th Anniversary on October 26, 1980, with Bishop Walter F. Sullivan as celebrant.

On October 8, 2005, Saint Mary's celebrated its 50th Anniversary with a special Mass celebrated by Bishop Francis X. DiLorenzo which was attended by close to 100 people.

Saint Mary's Catholic Church continues to serve the needs of the people of Coeburn with weekly Masses on Tuesday evenings and Saturday evenings.

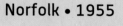

Saint Pius X

Norfolk • 1955

Saint Pius X was established on July 8, 1955, by Bishop Peter J. Ireton. He then requested the Missionary Servants of the Most Holy Trinity to staff the parish. Father Michael Giblin, S.T., arrived on July 18, 1955. Over the ensuing years, additions to the school, church, and rectory were undertaken. The convent underwent addition of several rooms for the arrival of the Sisters of the Immaculate Heart of Mary (IHM) over the summer of 1958. Their arrival saw the departure of the Trinitarian Sisters who had temporarily staffed the school since its opening in September 1956. The groundbreaking

for the new church took place on April 28, 1968, and the first Mass was held in the new Sanctuary on December 19, 1970. Saint Pius X continued to grow and in 1983 the Missionary Servants of the Most Holy Trinity ended their stewardship and Father Francis Toner S.T., pastor for 20 years, departed. Saint Pius X had transformed from a small missionary church to one of the largest Catholic communities in the area.

Saint Pius X parishioners have been an integral part of the growth of the parish, beginning with the Men's and Women's Clubs which foster the start of the Nocturnal Adoration Society, the Altar Society and the Rosary Society. Boy Scouts and Girl Scout troops were added for the youth.

The parish supports the local community with donations of food distributed through our food pantry. Special Thanksgiving and Christmas food boxes are prepared, as well as gifts parishioners

have contributed. Christmas stockings and gifts are also part of the migrant ministry that was started by Saint Pius X. Several local area churches work in conjunction with parishes on the Eastern Shore to help the migrant population with food, clothing, and toys.

The parish has ongoing religious education for students who do not attend Saint Pius X School with the addition of the Edge Program for our Middle School students and LifeTeen for our students preparing for Confirmation. Adults also participate in ongoing study, including RCIA classes, Bible study, and small group studies.

Saint Pius X School has grown with the parish over the years, adding additional wings and a new gym. It has recently completed a major renovation.

Church of the Holy Spirit

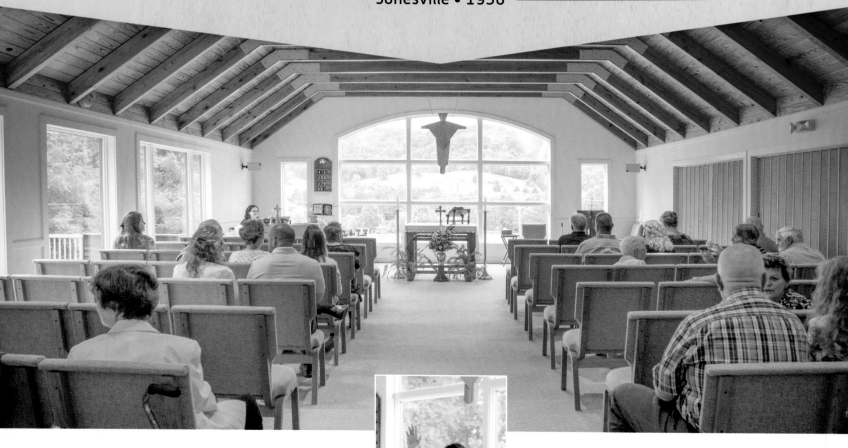

Holy Spirit Catholic Community in far southwestern Virginia is wedged between Tennessee and Kentucky. The western-most parish in the Diocese of Richmond, Catholics number less than one-half of one percent of the approximately 25,000 souls in Lee County.

The number of Catholics in Southwest Virginia reflects the economy and has varied over the years, with reports of between two and four thousand in the early 1900s, to about 400 following the Great Depression.

Prior to the 1950's, Catholics in Lee County traveled to Middlesboro or Harlan in Kentucky or to Sacred Heart in Appalachia, Virginia, for Mass. In 1945, the Glenmary Home Missioners assumed the pastoral duties of five counties in the southwest Virginia region, including Lee County.

At that time, there were 150 Catholics in the area. The Glenmary priests ultimately started many of their own churches, including Saint Pius X in Pennington Gap.

On May 12, 1956, the parish celebrated its first Mass in a converted rental property on West Morgan Avenue. Established as a mission of Sacred Heart in Appalachia, Saint Pius X was in the Diocese of Wheeling. Along with priests, Glenmary Sisters and Brothers were also ministering in the parishes.

Even after the opening of Saint Pius X Chapel, parishioners continued to travel to Appalachia for religious instruction and special events. This continued even after Sacred Heart moved to Big Stone Gap in 1966, with both communities sharing pastoral and religious education resources.

Lee County was blessed with its first and only resident priest and brother. They lived among the poor. A Sister of Mercy resided at the Chapel, which was utilized as a food stamp distribution center. She evangelized among the poor and the imprisoned. In 1972, the Congregation of Notre Dame began a decades-long ministry, which continues to this day.

By October of 1974, the Diocese of Richmond encompassed all southwest Virginia. Worship at Saint Pius X included celebration of Sunday morning liturgy, with Mass, pot-luck suppers, and prayer on Wednesday evenings. In 1978, the parish moved out of the rental property to a house down the street from the original structure. The first Mass was celebrated at that location on January 29th of that year.

Glenmary turned Sacred Heart and its mission back to the Diocese of Richmond in 1984. The number of active Catholics has remained constant through the years. An influx of Catholics during the late eighties and nineties, however, made it financially feasible to build a church. The new construction, located in the geographic center of the county, was designed to fit in well in the pastoral setting. A name change followed, and Saint Pius X became Holy Spirit Catholic Community. The parish's new home was dedicated on May 26, 1997.

Holy Spirit became one of a three-parish cluster in 2005, along with Sacred Heart in Big Stone Gap and Saint Anthony in Norton. Saint Joseph in Clintwood was added in 2006.

Saint Bernard

Gate City • 1956

Saint Bernard was built in 1956 and dedicated in 1958 by Archbishop Swint of Wheeling, West Virginia. It was the first Catholic Church in Gate City, Virginia, and the fourth Catholic Church built in Scott County.

In 1833, Joseph Hagan, an Irish Catholic, purchased 35,000 acres of land in the rugged wilderness of southwest Virginia. His nephew, Patrick Hagan, was responsible for introducing Catholicism into the region. He built a beautiful mansion in Hunters Valley, and it was the only Catholic home in the area. He generously opened his home and offered it as a haven for many bishops, priests, and nuns. Patrick Hagan was also instrumental in building the Catholic churches in this region.

Patrick Hagan's first wife died and shortly thereafter he married a widow. Together they had a combined eight children, four sons and four daughters. Patrick's stepdaughter, Mary, wed Marion Stapleton of Dungannon, Virginia. Mr. Stapleton converted to Catholicism and they moved to the Wood Settlement in Big Moccasin Valley at the foothills of the Clinch Mountain. This is where they raised their family and became instrumental in the conversion of many people in this area to the Catholic faith.

In 1918, Father Clement from the Benedictine Abbey of Saint Bernard in Cullman, Alabama, came to this area to care for the Catholic faithful. It is speculated that this is where we got the name for our parish.

Around 1920, a rough road was finally forged thru Big Moccasin Valley from Gate City to Russell County, making it possible for wagons to travel to the county seat. It was around this time that Father Clement retired. The Benedictine Priests continued to serve southwest Virginia.

In 1946, Father William Howard Bishop, founder of Glenmary Home Missioners, decided it was time to begin an Evangelical movement in Scott County. In 1954, Father Eugene Ryan and Father Pat Breheny were sent to Gate City to offer Mass. Father Ryan covered the Gate City area and Father Pat Breheny was appointed to Saint Patrick in Dungannon.

In 1956, land was purchased in Gate City, and the construction of

Saint Bernard began. Many of the men of the parish worked alongside Father Ryan in the construction of the church. The members had much pride in their place of worship and maintained the church and grounds themselves. Priests and nuns gathered the young people and tended to their religious education.

The present congregation is an older population and, even though small in numbers, we are large in our hopes and faith in our church community.

Around 2014, we became a mission parish and depend on others to assist with our support. We are so thankful for the support of Saint Anne in Bristol, the Diocese, the Glenmary priests, and all the dedicated people who have been instrumental in keeping our doors open.

Saint Gregory the Great

— Virginia Beach • 1957 —

The history of Saint Gregory the Great is unique. From our church's founding in 1957 to the present day, it is the story of a shared alliance between the civilian and military population of Virginia Beach and the Order of Saint Benedict. We have always been an inclusive parish family that blends the spirit of Vatican II with traditional Catholic practices while embracing ethnic and cultural differences.

Our story starts in 1957, when the then rural Princess Anne County had only one parish, Star of the Sea. Located at the oceanfront, it served the entire county. But during the 1950's, areas far from the oceanfront experienced a population boom. A second parish was needed and the people living in this growing area, led by the residents of the new subdivision called

Aragona Village, petitioned for one. Since the Benedictines served the nearby Barry Robinson Home and School for Boys, it was decided to invite them to administrate the new parish. In 1957, the parish of Saint Gregory the Great was canonically established and thus was born the long and fruitful alliance of the new parish and its staffers, the Order of Saint Benedict.

In 1958, a 14-acre parcel of land and its accompanying house were purchased on Virginia Beach Boulevard. In 1959, a cornerstone was laid, and our parish journey began. In 1964, a school was added and staffed by the Sisters, Servants of the Immaculate Heart of Mary. Building continued with a new rectory, convent, gymnasium, and food pantry/thrift store. By 1981, a larger church was needed, and in 1988 the new church was dedicated. A Middle School building and a child day care center followed. However, one must remember that buildings do not a "parish make" and that it is the people who worship, learn and serve in those buildings that are the true parish. Our people, both from the civilian and military sectors, have always been, and continue to be, committed to their faith and work selflessly in being "God's hands on earth." Today, over 4,700 registered households are part of our parish, and the cultural tapestry of our parish is rich with members from all corners of the globe.

We have more than 40 ministries and organizations including Liturgical, Social Justice, and Pastoral Care. The Filipino American Ministry, Persons with Disabilities Liaison, Haiti Twinning Committee, Parish Funeral Ministry, and a full time Hispanic Ministry Coordinator are just a few. The local community benefits from the parish's Blood Drives, Meals on Wheels, and assistance at local shelters. We also have a myriad of opportunities for spiritual growth, including RCIA, PREP Program, adult faith activities, youth groups, small faith communities, Benediction, retreats, lectures, prayer and outreach groups. We have seven Masses per weekend and, although based on traditional practices, we enjoy diversity in all religious services and activities. Through God's grace and the work of our parishioners, both civilian and military, we are an active, vibrant, multicultural parish built on the Benedictine values of prayer, hospitality, community, and service. All are welcome here.

Bishop John J. Russell

John J. Russell (1897–1993) became Richmond's tenth bishop following the death of Peter Ireton in 1958. Russell was from Baltimore and was a priest of that archdiocese (and later of the Archdiocese of Washington that was created in 1939). He was the bishop of Charleston at the time of his appointment to Richmond.

Vatican II and Social Upheaval (1958-1973)

Like his predecessor, Russell oversaw significant changes in the diocese during his tenure. It was the story, in miniature, of the Church's initial adaptation to modernity. Just three months after being elected pope, and four months after Russell came to Richmond, St. John XXIII surprised the world by announcing an ecumenical council (1959). The thrust of this council, called Vatican II (1962–1965), was to renew the Church for the sake of evangelizing the modern world.[1]

Prior to Vatican II, Bishop Russell supported official efforts already underway to equip the Church for its contemporary mission. This support included a wider use of the dialogue Mass to facilitate lay participation in the liturgy (1960), a practice Ireton had restricted three years earlier (1957). In another significant achievement, Richmond became the second diocese in the country to form an ecumenical commission (1962). Russell then attended the Vatican Council. Upon returning to the diocese, he promoted its teachings and implemented its reforms: liturgical renewal, greater ecumenical cooperation and interfaith dialogue, emphasis on the laity's vocation to holiness, and even the restoration of the permanent diaconate (1972–1973).[2]

The bishop and auxiliary bishops of Richmond with Pope St. Paul VI

Groundbreaking, St. Mary's Hospital, Richmond

The Diocese of Richmond developed in other ways around the time of Vatican II. More parishes and schools were built in the northern Virginia suburbs to accommodate a growing white population that was becoming more affluent. In Goochland County, St. John Vianney minor seminary opened (1960); it was the first such institution in the diocese since Bishop Richard Whelan's brief initiative a century before (St. Vincent's, 1841–1846).[3] A cook at St. John Vianney Seminary, Mother Maria Bernadetta of the Immaculate (1918–2001), a Poor Sister of St. Joseph from Italy, was remembered for her everyday kindness and practical wisdom. The cause for her canonization was introduced in 2019.[4]

Mother Maria Bernadetta of the Immaculate

The second Catholic hospital in the Richmond Diocese opened several years after the minor seminary: St. Mary's in Richmond (1966), run by the Bon Secours Sisters. The Daughters of Charity had founded the first Catholic hospital a hundred years before in Norfolk, during the yellow fever epidemic (1855–1856). Notably, too, a series of auxiliary bishops helped Russell govern the expanding diocese: Ernest L. Unterkoefler (1962–1964), J. Louis Flaherty (1966–1975), and Walter F. Sullivan (1970–1974).[5]

Despite the optimism surrounding Vatican II and the election of the first Catholic president, John F. Kennedy (1960), the Church faced increasing turbulence as the decade unfolded. The quest for racial equality was one source of upheaval, as the civil rights movement (1954–1968) gathered momentum across the South, including Virginia. In July 1963, Dorothy Day (1897–1980), co-founder of the Catholic Worker movement and a candidate for canonization (2002), came to Danville to demonstrate in favor of integration. Danville was a historically significant location, having been the last capital of the Confederacy (April 3–10, 1865). More recently, municipal authorities there had closed the public library rather than allow African Americans to use it (1960), and black protestors had suffered violence during the course of a peaceful protest on "Bloody Monday" (June 10, 1963).[6]

Dorothy Day

Bloody Monday, June 10, 1963, Danville

Vatican Council II

From Richmond, Bishop Russell vigorously supported the civil rights movement, advocating for both racial equality and fair housing. He also reversed the policy of his predecessors, who had established separate churches for black Catholics. Russell, seeking integration, closed some black parishes and turned others into territorial ones (1961–1970). Most black Catholics, however, were opposed to losing their distinctive communities as a result of these decisions.[7]

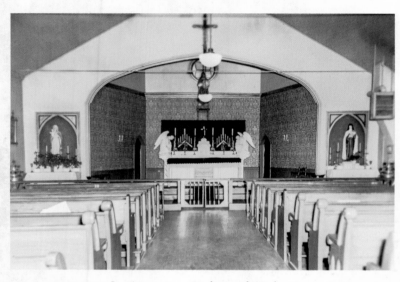

St. Augustine, Richmond (Fulton)

St. Joseph, Richmond

St. Augustine, Richmond (Fulton)

Pope St. Paul VI

The decade's unrest peaked in 1968. That cataclysmic year witnessed the assassination of civil rights champion Martin Luther King Jr. and presidential candidate Robert F. Kennedy; race riots in major cities; public disorder and police brutality at the Democratic National Convention in Chicago; growing opposition to the Vietnam War (triggered by the Tet Offensive); and controversy surrounding the Church's teaching on contraception.

Notably, whereas Catholics had sought to show their patriotism through military service in earlier wars, the Vietnam War (1955–1973) proved bitterly divisive. Some Catholics in the Diocese of Richmond, including priests and religious, protested the conflict as part of the antiwar movement (1964–1972).

At the same time, another movement was overturning sexual mores. The prevalence of artificial birth control and the influence of the youth "counter-culture" propelled the sexual revolution. But despite expectations of change, Pope St. Paul VI upheld the Church's prohibition against contraception (1968),[8] a decision many Catholics opposed. Finally, at the end of Bishop Russell's tenure, the Supreme Court legalized abortion (1973). American society and the Catholic Church had undergone dramatic changes in just two decades.

Good Shepherd

Lebanon was a mission stop for priests serving Saint Therese Catholic Church in St. Paul. Father Roland Hautz, a Glenmary Missionary priest and pastor at neighboring Saint Therese Parish, first came to Lebanon and said Mass on Christmas Day 1957 in a trailer chapel. It was the first of its kind in the Diocese of Wheeling, in which Lebanon was situated.

The trailer chapel was named in honor of Saint Vivian in memory of the wife of Larry Welsch of Cincinnati, Ohio, who donated the fully equipped mission trailer chapel. Mayor John McAvoy, a local Catholic, allowed Father Hautz to park the trailer on an empty lot next to the

elementary school, however a more permanent structure was needed. The Diocese purchased a lot in 1960 on Lebanon's West Main Street. By 1962, funds were raised through the Diocese of Wheeling. Parishioners and Glenmary priests and brothers helped prepare the foundation by manually hauling dirt and rock to build up the swamp area and digging a ditch for the water and sewer system of the new church.

Raymond Hautz, the father of Father "Rollie" helped build the present-day church. They built the steeple in the basement of the church in St. Paul and hauled it to Lebanon in the back of a dump truck. Father Rollie talked a local

crane operator into hoisting the steeple into place on the church roof. Living space adjoining the church served as a rectory. Father Hautz will always be remembered for his energetic and deeply devoted service to the church and people of Good Shepherd.

In July 1985, Father Rademacher brought in lay women, JoAnn Detta and Marty Huber to serve the local Catholic community as Ministers of Religious Education. They worked in several Southwest Virginia parishes sharing their skills and resources.

Good Shepherd will forever be indebted to a substantial legacy from parishioner Dr. Albert delCostillo received during the mid-80's. A house on Brumley Circle in the Lebanon Manor Subdivision was purchased for use as a rectory. The invested funds are used to this day to subsidize the upkeep of the church.

Father Tom Charters was the final Glenmary pastor. He will be remembered for his weekly question-and-answer column in two local newspapers to evangelize and teach the Catholic faith in a rural area which is 99.5 percent non-Catholic.

In November 2012, the parish welcomed Father Charles Ssebalamu from Uganda, the first international priest serving in the parish. Today Father Zaverio Banasula is Administrator of the parish consisting of 28 Catholic families.

Saint Edward the Confessor

— Richmond • 1959 —

Saint Edward the Confessor Parish was established by Bishop John J. Russell on June 8, 1959. Over the next seven months 350 founding families had registered. The faithful assembled in the auditorium of Bon Air Public School for Sunday Mass. Ground was broken in February 1961 for a combined church and school building to be erected. The local Catholic population and mission grew rapidly during the 1970's and a new worship space was dedicated in October 1976. With continuing growth in the Catholic population, Saint Edward parishioners were called upon to support and attend new foundations and new parishes were generated including Church of the Epiphany, Saint John Neumann, and Saint Gabriel.

The Census of 1990 revealed over 2,500 households called Saint Edward their faith home. In September 1999, the worship complex was expanded and renovated to accommodate the growth. The building of a gym emphasized our close bond with Saint Edward Epiphany School (SEES), which has become a regional school. A final interior restoration of the church in 2005 graced us with the facility we have today.

The Saint Edward faith community boasts a rich variety and diversity of people. We are welcoming, talented, active and generous. It is our aim to help everyone find their niche and feel at home. The staff is collegial, competent and friendly and provides the leadership that makes Saint Edward a vibrant and successful parish.

Our parish community comes together in great, spirited assembly during our five weekend Masses.

Every weekend, approximately 150 volunteers participate in our liturgical ministries. A dynamic Music Ministry composed of volunteer singers, instrumentalists, adult, youth and children choirs, and cantors service each of these celebrations. The healing sacraments of Confession and Anointing of the Sick are administered in the Healing Chapel each weekend.

Human Concerns/Justice and Peace Ministry gives parishioners opportunities to serve in prisons, an inner-city school, food pantries and providing meals to shelters. Parishioners and staff assist refugee families, have opportunities for outreach to Appalachia, host the homeless for two weeks at Christmas, participate with Habitat for Humanity and work on a nearby farm which supports food justice. We are active in interfaith activities with neighborhood congregations, advocacy efforts with the Virginia Catholic Conference, and educational programs on Catholic Social Teaching. The gifts of generosity and outreach are hallmarks of the parish.

Saint Edward Haiti Ministry is one of the oldest in the diocese, having been twinned with the Haitian parish of Holy Family in Cerca Carvajal for 30 years. The ministry helps support the parish, a 900-student school, and a medical clinic with a doctor, lab tech, dentist, and a midwife. Several parishioners make a yearly pilgrimage to Haiti and their pastor graces us with his annual visitation during Haiti Solidarity Week.

Journeying together as the Catholic community of Saint Edward the Confessor Parish, we embrace the mission of Jesus Christ by sharing our gifts through discipleship, liturgical celebration, spiritual formation and outreach.

Saint Mary
of the Holy Family Parish
── Richlands · 1962 ──

Establishing a Catholic Church in Richlands took faithful parishioners a long time to accomplish. In the end, their efforts paid off and the church was built and is still in use today. The first Catholics to arrive in Richlands were Mr. and Mrs. Fred Amato and their children, who came from West Virginia in 1909. Mr. Amato was employed as a construction worker in the Seaboard mines. Father Emilie Olivier, a native of France, traveled by horseback and train from Bluefield to serve the family in Richlands.

Over the next three decades there was a small but growing Catholic community. By the late 1940s there were about 10 families. Bishop John Swint of the Diocese of Wheeling (in which Richlands was situated) was asked to establish a church in Richlands. For the next 13 years – from 1941 to 1954 – Mass was celebrated in the Forrest Family's home whenever a priest was available. Mrs. Forrest continued to make the request for a church, however it was not until 1953 that the dream of having a church building in Richlands began to materialize.

In 1950, the Pallotine Fathers from Ireland were assigned to serve the Catholics in Pocahontas, Tazewell, Richlands, and Grundy which were considered missions. Dr. A. del Castillo donated land for the building site and on November 16, 1953, ground was officially broken for the new church building. James Skewes was the architect and Nick Amelia, of Bluewell, West Virginia, was the builder for the Northfork Supply and Lumber Company. The building was completed in April 1954 and dedicated in honor of the Immaculate Conception of the Blessed Virgin and was officially named Saint Mary's.

The community grew and in 1959, Dr. Castillo gave two additional lots for a rectory and driveway. The rectory was completed in 1961, but it wasn't until February 5, 1962, that St. Mary Church was established as a new parish with missions in Tazewell and Grundy. In 1971, Dr. Castillo gave the remaining lots which make up the present-day parish grounds.

In August 1974, the parishes of southwest Virginia were transferred to the Diocese of Richmond from the Diocese of Wheeling. From the beginning, the Catholic community has been dedicated to handing on the faith. In October 2006, Bishop DiLorenzo dedicated the new worship space, and in 2010, Saint Mary was officially merged with the parishes of Saint Elizabeth in Pocahontas; Saint Joseph in Grundy; and Saint Theresa in Tazewell to form Holy Family Parish. Each of the four churches maintained their own worship sites, but in diocesan and administrative functions became one Parish together forming a *holy family.*

Saint Mary

— Richmond • 1962 —

From its first liturgy in a high school gymnasium in 1962, Saint Mary Catholic Church has grown from 350 founding families to a 2,300-family parish with an award-winning K-8 school. As the Second Vatican Council ushered in an era of transformation throughout the Catholic Church, parish founders accepted the mission to serve the developing West End of Richmond.

Saint Mary's pastor and parishioners helped initiate Vatican II practices in the Richmond Diocese. This included a contemporary architectural style for the parish's first building, a multipurpose structure that served as church, parish hall, gymnasium and classrooms. Funds were raised to build Saint Mary's Catholic School, which opened in 1966.

The parish has grown with western Henrico County, expanding from the original multipurpose building to its first permanent worship space in 1984. The parish had grown to more than 1,000 families by the mid 1980's and by the end of the decade had established two nearby communities to serve the disadvantaged and elderly. Marywood, a 112-unit independent living apartment complex for low and moderate-income elderly and disabled persons, opened in 1983. Saint Mary's Woods opened in 1988 and provides independent and assisted living facilities for senior citizens.

The parish expanded its facilities again in 2007 with its current worship space, school additions, columbarium and consolation garden.

Parishioners established a tradition of welcoming refugees and immigrants. They helped refugees from southeast Asia establish new homes in Richmond during the 1970's and 1980's. Today immigrants from around the world participate in English as a Second Language classes taught at the parish, which also offers job workshops, cultural field trips and helps immigrants prepare to become naturalized U.S. citizens.

In addition to helping those who come to the parish from distant lands, parishioners regularly travel to those in need. Saint Mary parish joined other churches in the Diocese and established a twinning relationship with parishes in the Diocese of Hinche, Haiti. This fruitful ministry continues with parishioners making regular trips to Haiti to share medical, education and humanitarian support.

In 1994, Saint Mary became one of the first churches in suburban Richmond to participate in CARITAS (Congregations Around Richmond Involved to Assure Shelter), serving those who are temporarily homeless. The parish hosts 30-40 guests each year for a week or two at a time. Between 400 and 500 parishioners of all ages volunteer to provide comfort, meals and fellowship.

Joyfully responding to Pope Francis' call to evangelize, the parish offers a wide array of ways to share and learn more about the Catholic faith. The Monsignor Kelly Faith Formation Forum, established in 2015 in memory of former pastor Monsignor Charles A. Kelly, brings nationally recognized speakers to Richmond to foster opportunities for people to grow in their love for Jesus Christ and to respond to Christ's love through a life of service.

Saint Nicholas

─── Virginia Beach • 1963 ───

aint Nicholas Catholic Church, located in Virginia Beach, was founded in 1963 and named after Bishop Nicholas of Demre, Turkey. The first congregation of 40 parishioners began celebrating Masses at a neighboring elementary school. Soon after, a hunting lodge was moved to church property and refurbished as a sanctuary. Fr. Nicholas Habets celebrated the first Mass in the hunting lodge on Palm Sunday of 1963.

By 1965, Mass attendance had increased to 2000. Consequently, additional weekend Masses were celebrated at a nearby movie theater for two years. Later, a building campaign raised money to build a provisional church and rectory. Bishop John Russell dedicated the newly constructed church on May 28, 1967.

A remodel of the Sanctuary began in the 1980's, relocating the altar to the center of the Sanctuary and adding a new entrance. The expansion added a Social Hall, Commons, Kitchen and new Rectory. Mother Seton House, a non-profit shelter for troubled teens, moved into the former rectory. The church was rededicated in 1988.

As the community grew together as the Body of Christ, a growing Music Ministry enhanced liturgies and produced dinner theater fundraisers. These community events fueled a Thanksgiving Basket drive and Winter Shelter for the homeless. M.E. Cox Adult Day Care moved into the church in 1975 and St. Nicholas entered into one of the diocese's first twinning relationships with Saint Anne's in Maissade, Haiti, in 1985. In 2002, a Columbarium was built, inspiring the creation of new grief support ministries.

During the Great Jubilee Year, Saint Nicholas hosted ecumenical services, liturgies, and events including the Week of Prayer for Christian Unity and Jubilee Justice, focusing on topics such as the abolition of the death penalty and our response to poverty and racism.

For its 50th Anniversary in 2013, the parish celebrated with a pilgrimage to the Church of Saint Nicholas in Myra, Turkey, becoming the first Americans to celebrate Mass at his burial place. The parish also unveiled a stained-glass window above the altar - a replica of Bernini's "Holy Spirit" - and celebrated an Outdoor Mass with Bishop Francis DiLorenzo.

St. Nicholas remains an ever-growing community, both physically and spiritually. Recently, the Living Our Mission Campaign addressed urgent repairs and renovations that connected the second story hallway and added an elevator lift, bell tower, and a new

stained glass window depicting "The Baptism of the Lord" to the church exterior. The newly renovated building was blessed by Bishop Barry Knestout on January 20, 2019. Pope Francis's call to the New Evangelization also led parishioners of all ages to renewed participation in Catholic devotions, liturgies, Parish Life ministry, Religious Education, Adult Faith Formation, and Youth Ministry.

The parish mission, "Stewardship as a way of life," led decades of parishioners, touched by the Holy Spirit, into loving service of the church and others. By God's grace, we at St. Nicholas celebrate this Bicentennial Diocesan Anniversary as a parish rooted in joyful service, ready to shine inextinguishable light upon the world. For all this, to God be the Glory.

Saint Thomas Aquinas

— Charlottesville • 1963 —

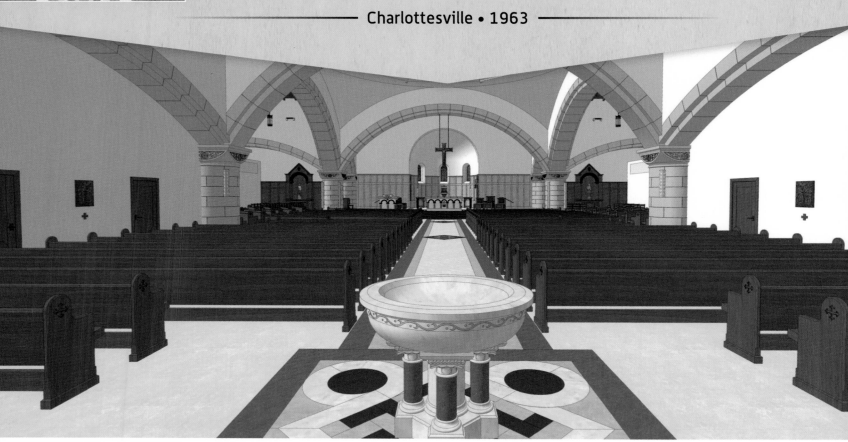

The two most distinctive qualities of Saint Thomas Aquinas University Parish – its definitional association with the students, faculty, and staff of the University of Virginia and the evangelical and pastoral ministries of the Dominican Friars – are discernable in its origins as a Newman Club and Center. In 1942, this center established a Catholic presence at UVA. In 1948, the center acquired an official location on Jefferson Park Avenue, a major thoroughfare for the southern part of the University's Central Grounds. The location was well-suited to both John Henry Cardinal Newman's desire for "an intelligent well-instructed laity" and to the high academic values of the University. As the Catholic population of the University and surrounding area grew, the Dominican friars welcomed the increased opportunities to address pastoral, catechetical, and evangelical issues. Charlottesville, which had been predominantly Southern Baptist, witnessed a strong Catholic influx. The dedication of Catholic students joined with the strength of Dominican preaching to attract many throughout Central Virginia – even in their selection of the secular University.

In 1959, when they first began their service at the Newman Center, these Friars from the Dominican Eastern Province of Saint Joseph, headquartered in New York City, established a close partnership with Bishop John J. Russell, Tenth Bishop of Richmond. Together with him, they developed plans for the establishment of the University Parish. In 1962, the Dominicans purchased land on Alderman Road with the aim of eventually constructing a church on that site. The following year Bishop Russell established Saint Thomas Aquinas Parish and ratified the special character of this uniquely non-territorial parish. The Dominicans would provide a pastor and parochial vicars for the parish, as well

242

as chaplains for the University Hospital. Their mission was to the University. The Bishop dedicated the new church on Alderman Road in October 1967.

By 1990, it was necessary to construct a new church to serve the expanding population of the Parish. Bishop Walter Sullivan, Eleventh Bishop of Richmond, dedicated the new church in November 1995. A parish center was completed in the Spring of 2004. In 2013, the Dominicans and Bishop Francis DiLorenzo celebrated fifty years of Dominican ministry at UVA. This historic moment was one of renewed commitment and ecclesiastical vision, as the Bishop blessed and formally opened the Dominican Priory constructed beside the church.

Within a few years of the priory's dedication, parish growth and growing pastoral needs required special consideration. Once again, Saint Thomas Aquinas University Parish initiated a plan for a new and lasting church building.

The 800-year-old apostolic charisms of Dominican spirituality along with the support and cooperation of the Diocese of Richmond for over fifty years, strengthened their shared mission in spreading the Gospel of Jesus Christ in Central Virginia. The parish continues to be a place where graces flow and faith increases. Parishioners and clergy alike anticipate and embrace their new church building as an offering of praise to God, where their past is honored while they build their future on the one true foundation, Jesus Christ. *Duc in altum!*

Saint Edward

In 1939 the Catholic community in Pulaski consisted of three families who had just moved to Virginia from Pennsylvania. They traveled to Blacksburg and Wytheville to attend Mass. Occasionally a priest said Mass in one of their homes in Pulaski. At the time, all of Southwestern Virignia beyond Roanoke was in the Diocese of Wheeling.

The advent of World War II and the construction of Radform Army Ammunition Plant in Montgomergy and Pulaski Counties resulted in the influx of people from places heavily populated with Catholics, thus causing the need for a place to worship. Following WWII Saint Edward became a mission of Saint Mary Parish in Wytheville whose pastor was Father John J. O'Reilly.

In the early 1950's Pulaski was again affiliated with Saint Mary's in Blacksburg, making Pulaski and Radford missions of that parish. Father Leo R. Fohl, a U.S. Army Chaplain during the war, was assigned as pastor of Saint Mary's in Blacksburg. His duties extended to Radford and Pulaski as well as to serving the students at VPI and Radford College. He was responsible for the construction of three churches in Blacksburg, Radford, and Pulaski.

Father Fohl and his assistant, Father Edward Sadie conducted religious education for the school children during the summer. Mothers in Pulaski formed car pools to drive the children to Radford for their daily instructions.

The Catholic Women's Guild formed various groups in the parish that continue to function without interruption, taking responsibility for all parish social gatherings, help for those in need, providing services for the physical necessities of the church and community, and raising the necessary financial resources for a future church building. In 1964 the little mission realized its dream and Saint Edward was built on the corner of Washington Avenue and Seventh Street.

In 1974 all the parishes located beyond Roanoke were transferred from the Diocese of Wheeling to the Richmond Diocese. Many changes have come about over the years and growing to 80 families in 1998. After years of planning and pledging, major gifts from the Diocese of Richmond and the Catholic Extension Society, the dream of constructing a new sanctuary was realized.

Saint Victoria

Over sixty years ago Catholic families in the Altavista-Hurt area attended Mass at Holy Cross Catholic Church in Lynchburg, and in 1955, a traveling mission band of priests called, "Saint Mary of the Highways" was sent by the Diocese to serve Catholics in the Altavista-Hurt area. Soon the Bishop realized that a resident priest was needed to minister to this growing community.

The first Masses in Altavista-Hurt were held in the community room of the Campbell County Bank, and priests came from Holy Cross in Lynchburg to celebrate Mass, alternating early and late Masses. At first there were fifteen to twenty people at the bank during 1955. Some of the original families that attended were the Hurt, Key, Rolfes, Hall, Hubbard, Lewis, Arthur, and Dickerson families.

The community slowly grew to more than fifty people in early 1961 and began meeting at the Moose Lodge. During this time, construction on Leesville and Smith Mountain Dams brought new Catholic families to the area. The land for the new church was given by Mr. and Mrs. John L.

Hurt along with a sizable donation. The official groundbreaking ceremony was held on April 1, 1962. Bishop John J. Russell, 10th Bishop of Richmond turned the first spade assisted by Msgr. F. Harold Nott, pastor of Holy Cross Catholic Church.

The name of the church was requested by a family that had donated money through the Catholic Extension Society. They chose Saint Victoria in memory of their young daughter Victoria who had passed away. To help the church get started, Catholic Extension also donated vestments, statues, robes for the altar boys, and linens for the altar. The women of the parish made the altar cloths, tabernacle veils and other needed items.

Saint Victoria, considered a mission of Holy Cross in Lynchburg, was dedicated on Saturday, September 29, 1962, by Bishop Russell. In August of 1964, Saint Victoria was established as a parish with a resident pastor, Father DePaul Landrigan of the Missionary Servants of the Most Holy Trinity.

With deep gratitude, we thank our parishioners and benefactors who have given so generously of their time, talents, and treasure to the church over the years.

Holy Family

Prior to 1941 the early roots of Holy Family Parish lie in the occasional visits of missionary priests from Sweet Springs and Bluefield, West Virginia, and Wytheville and Blacksburg, Virginia, who came by horseback, railroad and automobile to celebrate Mass and provide pastoral care for the scattered Catholic families of the New River Valley. Three original families identified in church records were the Coles, Santollas, and Phlegars.

In 1941, through the efforts of Bishop Swint of the Diocese of Wheeling, West Virginia, a parish was formally organized with priests of the Congregation of Oblates of Mary Immaculate serving the pastoral needs of several counties in West Virginia as well as Giles, Bland, and Craig counties in Virginia. Mass was celebrated in the old "soup kitchen" near downtown Pearisburg.

Parishioners worked together having spaghetti suppers, white elephant sales, and other projects to raise money to build a church with a parish hall and rectory. The buildings were dedicated July 6, 1966, by Bishop Joseph Hodges of the Diocese of Wheeling.

In June 1970, Father Charles Beausoleil, OMI (Oblates of Mary Immaculate) was named pastor and quickly became a leader and active advocate for social justice in the church and county. From that time parishioners continue serving the needs of the poor and indigent people of Giles County by providing direct assistance and sponsoring a food ministry and toy collection at Christmas. Father Beausoleil also developed a ministry to the Appalachian Trail hikers, encouraging them to use the parish hall overnight as a place of rest. With the great increase of hikers in the mid 1970's, the hall became overcrowded and a grain barn was moved to the parish grounds and the Holy Family Hostel was established. Two to three hundred hikers a year make our hostel their trail home for one or several days – an unusual dimension of ministry in our parish. Since the early 1970's the parish hosted high school and college students during their spring breaks who work under direction of the towns of Pearisburg and Narrows to serve those citizens and non-profits in need of help.

In 1974, Holy Family Parish transferred to the Diocese of Richmond from the Diocese of Wheeling, and in 1988 the Oblates of Mary Immaculate moved to other areas and priests of the Diocese of Richmond were assigned to serve the parish.

Because of the rural nature of Giles County and Holy Family's warm and welcoming nature, the parish is recognized as a true example of Christian presence, and voice of the spirit of Jesus in the larger community.

Saint Jerome

In June 1966, our first pastor, Father Frank Hendrick, celebrated Mass with 135 parishioners in the auditorium of R.O. Nelson Elementary School on Moyer Road. At that time, the Denbigh Courthouse served as the meeting place for the Men's and Women's Clubs and various parish events. In 1967, Bishop John Russell approved plans for the church on eight acres of land on Denbigh Boulevard. Bishop Russell dedicated the church and the parish center on September 2, 1968, for our parish of 200 families. By 1972, the parish had grown to 600 families and was very active in the Denbigh Community.

The church where we currently worship was built and was dedicated on May 3, 1987, by Bishop Walter Sullivan. We transformed the

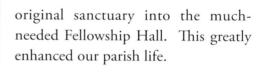

original sanctuary into the much-needed Fellowship Hall. This greatly enhanced our parish life.

Our parish continued to grow throughout the 1990's commensurate with the Newport News population growth in the Denbigh area. This growth and the redirection of religious education towards family education led to rapidly increasing numbers of parishioners in our Christian Formation classes. We built the Faith and Life Center, which was dedicated November 5, 2000, by Bishop Walter Sullivan, to meet our growing parish. This increase in facility spaces also allowed Saint Jerome, as part of our mission of "loving service to all people," to join the PORT emergency winter shelter program in 2009. Since then we have provided shelter for the homeless of the peninsula area for one week during the winter months annually as part of an interfaith community program. Other examples of our commitment to community partners in the Denbigh neighborhood and throughout Newport News as we strive to live the corporal and spiritual works of mercy include the school backpack program, assistance to refugee families and our financial assistance for the needy.

The last major facility added to the Saint Jerome parish is the columbarium. Once the columbarium was dedicated, Saint Jerome parish established the initial New Evangelization Garden in 2015. The garden includes a rosary walk.

Our parish has grown during these years, with over 1100 families. We have seen a five-fold increase in our population. Saint Jerome has robust ministries and Christian Formation programs that reach out to every element of our parish as we work to spread the love of Christ. Our mission statement is: "We, the faith community of Saint Jerome Roman Catholic Church, are called to holiness. We dedicate ourselves to the on-going mission of Jesus Christ by celebrating the Sacraments and by proclaiming the living gospel, in loving service to all people."

Saint Joseph
of the Holy Family Parish
— Grundy • 1966 —

As early as 1951, a handful of local residents who sought to continue in their Catholic faith, began meeting in area homes. Luke and Sue Owens and Tom and Mary Holland opened their homes for Mass when a priest could be located. Attendance was based on word of mouth, three to four families gathered together. As the number grew, a large banquet room owned by the Bohinskis became the first regular location for Mass outside of area homes.

In May 1959, Buchanan Catholics moved to a school building at Dry Fork rented by parishioners of the church for $15 and Saint Joseph was formally named a station of Pocahontas in the Diocese of Wheeling in 1961. Its "mission" status followed almost six years later in 1967, just after the first formal church building was constructed and dedicated – the same building used today.

Fathers James Maher and Michael Gormley, of the Pallottine Order, from Pocahontas, celebrated Masses. Later, Father Daniel Hayes, Father Alphonsus Hayes, Father Paul Laub, and Father Vincent Cunningham said Mass on a rotating basis with Father James Walsh, who became the first priest officially assigned to Saint Joseph in 1967 as it gained "mission" status.

In the late 1950s and early 1960s, Buchanan Catholics began looking for a permanent place to hold Mass and in 1961, Sue Owens wrote to Bishop John Swint in the Diocese of Wheeling in April of that year with a simple request – "that something be done about the church facility in Grundy."

Her letter was answered, and on February 6, 1962, Grundy, Richlands and Tazewell split from Pocahontas and for the first time, a priest was specifically assigned to the two-county area. Father James Walsh then moved to the rectory at Richlands and became pastor for the Richlands, Tazewell, and Grundy churches.

In 1965, two lots in the Tookland area were purchased from George and Marlene Mitchell. Some $6,500 came from the Diocese for the purchase of the land, and fundraisers were held to raise the money to build the church.

Father Walsh wrote to the Catholic Church Extension Society and his letter was given to Mrs. Estelle Hartnett of Brooklyn, New York, interested in helping to build new churches. She chose the one planned by the Grundy Catholic community as one of her projects. The Extension Society had a $6,000 limit, but Mrs. Hartnett wanted to give $10,000 in memory of her late husband, Joseph Hartnett. She later donated an additional $10,000, and her daughter, Mary, donated a pipe organ to the church.

John Kodak of Harman Mining and Frank Salak designed the church building. Ken Fletcher was the contractor who built it. The first Mass was said in the new church building on Christmas Day in 1965. The formal dedication of the church did not occur until October 1966 when the bishop could attend. At that time, Bishop Hodges praised the Saint Joseph congregation for its dedication and assisted in the ceremonial laying of the cornerstone.

The first religious sisters arrived in the area in the summer of 1976 with three members of the Congregation of Notre Dame. They established a residence in the Hurley community.

In 2010, Saint Joseph was officially merged with the parishes of Saint Elizabeth in Pocahontas; Saint Mary in Richlands; and Saint Theresa in Tazewell to form Holy Family Parish. Each of the four churches maintained their own worship sites, but in Diocesan and administrative functions became one parish.

Saint Joseph
Shrine of Saint Katharine Drexel
— Columbia • 1967 —

Saint Joseph Shrine of Saint Katharine Drexel started with the William Wakeham family who influenced the town of Columbia and were key to building Saint Joseph Chapel in 1884. Well-known in Fluvanna County as a clothing manufacturer and landowner, the Wakeham family was blessed with six children. Their son, Alfred, became a Josephite Brother and missionary, and his brother, Richard, studied for the priesthood and dedicated his life to training young men for the priesthood.

Father Richard was granted a corner lot in Columbia to build a home and a chapel for Roman Catholic worship. The property became known as "Free Hill," and in 1885, Father Richard deeded the property to the Rt. Rev. John J. Keane, Fifth Bishop of Richmond.

In 1900, Mother Mary Katharine Drexel, foundress of the Sisters of the Blessed Sacrament was traveling to Lynchburg in search of a site for a school for African American children. The train stopped in Columbia and she noticed a gilded cross gleaming through the trees. Mother Katharine inquired if there was a Catholic Church in Columbia and was told there was one, but it was no longer in use. On a following trip, the Sisters decided to investigate and found a well-kept structure that would seat about two hundred. The church had been maintained for many years by Uncle Zack Kimbro, in hopes that someday Mass would be said again in the chapel.

Mother Katharine contacted Bishop Augustine Van de Vyver who readily gave permission for the Sisters to conduct a Sunday School there and suggested that the Sisters contact the Josephite Fathers to see if a priest would be available to say Mass there once a month. Twenty-five children and seventy-five adults gathered in the church for Mass.

Saint Joseph began attracting African American members, many of whom converted to Catholicism. Four years later, a school was opened for those families under the guidance of an Ohio missionary, Miss Lydia Nicholas O'Hare. She taught school, cleaned the church, and cooked for the priests. Miss O'Hare remained for fifty years teaching, serving as a catechist, organist and sacristan in the one-room mission school. At seventy-five, her health forced her to retire from mission work and in 1951 at the age of 95, she received the Papal Medal Award "Pro Ecclesia et Pontifice," one of the highest marks of honor to be bestowed by the Holy Father.

In 1981, Saint Joseph built its parish gathering place and made it available to the town for local elections and a community meeting place. Bishop Walter Sullivan of the Richmond Diocese celebrated a special Mass on October 15, 2000, honoring the canonization of Saint Katharine Drexel and added to the name of Saint Joseph the title "Shrine of Saint Katharine Drexel."

The heart of the Saint Joseph Church/Shrine of Saint Katharine Drexel continues through the warmth of people over the past 120 years. In keeping with the past, we continue to rejoice and remain hopeful for the future. We commit ourselves to the vision set in 1884 by the Wakeham family to love and serve our community in faith.

Saint Jude

Catholicism arrived late in the valleys of southwest Virginia. By 1923, a chapel existed in Blacksburg. In the 1930's, the first Catholic family arrived in Radford and Father George Walter from Blacksburg sometimes said Mass in their home. Father Walter, considering the possibility of building a church in Radford, chose the name Saint Jude, the patron of hopeless cases, because it seemed a rather hopeless undertaking.

In 1939, Radford and Pulaski became missions of Saint Mary in Blacksburg as part of the Diocese of Wheeling. Mass was celebrated twice a month in Radford at various locations. For many years, Saint Jude existed only on paper until the Bishop of Wheeling initiated a fund drive for a Radford church. Dr. Garrett Dalton, a convert to Catholicism, and his wife Madeline were a major force in making the dream become a reality. By this time, there were about 100 Catholics in the area. On August 3, 1952, the original church on Tyler Avenue was dedicated.

Saint Jude became a separate parish, no longer a mission of Saint Mary in 1967, and a period of rapid growth followed. In 1974, southwest Virginia became part of the Diocese of Richmond, and with the arrival of Father Tom Magri in 1983, an era of continuity and stability began. The parish grew to 511 members, and a great number of activities and numerous projects to serve the disadvantaged were initiated.

Committees and parishioners were mobilized to make a reality of this new dream, and in January of 1994, the shell and the lower level of the church were completed. On January 16, the coldest day of the year (-12 degrees F), Bishop Walter Sullivan celebrated the dedication liturgy.

Five years later, the upper level, the actual liturgical space, was dedicated on September 19, 1999, with Bishop Sullivan. At this point, there were 260 families and it was wonderful to be able to use the downstairs as a social hall. Saint Jude continued to grow: a columbarium was added inside the church and a new rectory was built nearby.

Saint Jude Church on Tyler Avenue, opposite Radford University, was bursting at its seams. There was the need for a new church and plans accelerated when a 17-acre site on Rt. 177 outside Radford was acquired.

The Catholic Campus Ministry at Radford University has always been a focus of Saint Jude parish, and we now have a strong prison ministry as well. Today the parish has 355 families. Our parish continues to grow and be blessed with generous parishioners, giving of their time, talent, and resources as we continue to further the work of Christ in bringing his message of hospitality, peace, justice, and reverence for God.

Immaculate Conception

In August 1968, Bishop John J. Russell reorganized Saint Mary Parish at Fort Monroe and the parish of Saint Rose of Lima in Hampton to form a single parish to be built on 15 acres of land on Cunningham Drive in Hampton. On March 13, 1969, the first organizational meeting was held, the name Immaculate Conception was chosen and the community began celebrating liturgy in the Riverdale Theater. Bishop Walter Sullivan celebrated the groundbreaking on the new facility on December 27, 1970 and Bishop John Russell dedicated the new Immaculate Conception parish on December 12, 1971. However after consideration, Bishop Russell determined that three Catholic parishes in Hampton were needed and on March 27, 1972, Immaculate Conception became an independent parish.

For many years, mass and other parish functions were held in this multipurpose facility. Eventually, after more than eight years of planning, preparation and construction, the new worship space was dedicated on May 22, 1988. With the growth in the parish community and surrounding Catholic population, it was determined that even more space was needed. On June 7, 1992, the Pastoral Center was dedicated which provided classrooms, meeting rooms, nursery and administration areas. Later, the parish columbarium was constructed in the daily mass chapel and our beautiful stained-glass windows

were installed in the chapel a few years later. With the addition of the proceeds from the capital campaign fund, our parish kitchen was renovated and remodeled to satisfy the growing needs for more efficient food preparation space.

From its earliest days, this newest parish in Hampton was formed and dedicated to outreach to the poor, the elderly and those living in need. Coupled with this outreach focus, adult formation in the faith was seen and known of utmost importance in the journey to true discipleship. For fifty years, these two foci have helped the parish with a clarity of vision and goals.

Immaculate Conception was a founder in the formation of Hampton Ecumenical Lodging and Provisions (H.E.L.P.) the leading faith-based service organization in Hampton, and Seton Manor and Somerset Apartments, two low income senior living facilities adjacent to the parish property. Outreach ministries through the years include: resettlement of refugees from Cambodia, Vietnam, and Bhutan, a weekly Food Pantry, a monthly bag lunch for residents of a low-income senior residence, our Young at Heart luncheon and prayer which hosts local nursing home residents, a monthly nursing home prayer service, weekly food collections and distributions, financial assistance outreach as well as a weekly "Sunday Supper" that provides about 150 persons week a hot meal, life skills workshops, and a small bag of groceries to take home. The parish's pioneering work with diversity and inclusion has earned it top awards by the City of Hampton's Citizen's Unity Commission.

Immaculate Conception is known in the Diocese for providing opportunities for quality adult formation. From its earliest days in the 1980's and 1990's the parish

brought Catholic speakers to the parish that challenged and stretched the parishioners and those outside of the parish. Since 2015, the best national and internationally known theologians and experts have come to Immaculate Conception's Bishop Keane Institute. Catholic and non-Catholic presenters have continued to share wisdom and help the parish to reflect and grow.

In 2019, the parish affirmed its commitment to caring for God's creation by installing solar panels on the building roof. The parish continues to live out its mission as a community of imperfect men and women who strive to be faithful to the promises of our baptism by living the Gospel of Christ and gathering to give praise and thanksgiving to God in our celebrations of the Eucharist.

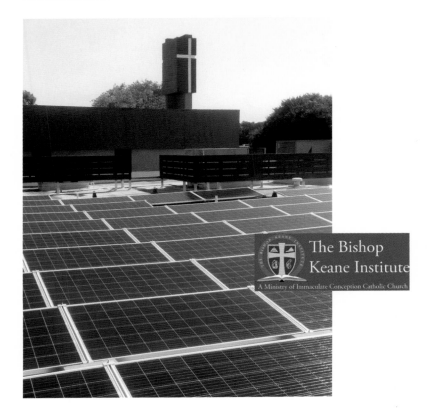

The Bishop Keane Institute
A Ministry of Immaculate Conception Catholic Church

Saint Joseph

Beginning around 1870, Buckroe Beach Catholics fulfilled their Sunday obligations by traveling five miles to Saint Mary Star of the Sea at Fort Monroe. By 1950, the influx of resident military and civilian Catholics, and the ever-increasing number of summer vacationers to Buckroe Beach justified a place of worship closer to Buckroe parishioners.

The church and parish of Saint Joseph evolved from a nucleus of about 150 faithful parishioners. Summer Sunday Masses for this nucleus of parishioners began in June 1950 at the Community Center of the Buckroe Civic Association. Loans from Bishop Peter L. Ireton of the Diocese of Richmond and Saint Mary Star of the Sea Church were the seed money used by the Buckroe Catholic Chapel Project to raise funds for a church in the Buckroe area.

Three lots on Buckroe Avenue and Fifth Streets were purchased. The groundbreaking ceremony took place on February 6, 1955, and the first Mass was offered five months later on July 3, 1955. The dedication of Saint Joseph Chapel, now Cordier Hall where the parish offices are located, followed on October 16, 1955.

Saint Joseph remained a mission of Saint Mary Star of the Sea Church until 1968, when it became an independent parish under the direction of the Redemptorist Fathers. From 1971 to 1977, however, Saint Joseph and Saint Mary Star of the Sea were merged into one parish. On July 1, 1977, Saint Joseph regained its status as an independent parish and planning began for a new church on land acquired in 1974.

The Saint Joseph Building Committee was appointed in January 1978. Bishop Walter F. Sullivan signed a contract in October 1979 with the architectural firm of Rancorn, Wildman, and Krause to build the new church. The groundbreaking for this new church building took place on the Feast of Saint Joseph in March 1982. The dedication of the new Saint Joseph

Catholic Church in Buckroe (Hampton) finally took place on June 26, 1983.

In 2011, the Diocese of Richmond clustered three parishes: Saint Joseph, Hampton; Saint Vincent de Paul, Newport News; and Saint Mary Star of the Sea, Fort Monroe, into the Peninsula Cluster of Catholic Parishes. Monsignor Walter Barrett was assigned as the Pastor of the Peninsula Cluster of Catholic Parishes.

In 2016, Saint Joseph Catholic Church was selected for the Best of Hampton Award in the Place of Worship category by the Hampton Award Program. The Hampton Award Program identifies organizations that have achieved exceptional success in their local community. Saint Joseph was recognized for their service to their parishioners and to the community.

Church of the Resurrection

The Most Rev. John J. Russell, Tenth Bishop of Richmond, established the Church of the Resurrection Parish in 1971. He contracted with C. L. Pincus, Jr. & Co. to build a new parish center on 8 acres of land purchased in Hatton Point Estates. Lamm and Associates Architects created the drawings for the 5,300-square-foot building. The new parish began with 376 families.

Phase I was completed in August of 1972. In just two years, the parish grew to 531 families.

Bishop Walter Sullivan presided at the dedication of the new parish worship center in October of 1974. This second phase of building was scaled back to contain the debt that the parish would incur. In 1988, the Church of the Resurrection began the third phase of building. The parish had paid off the debt and the architect Hunter Bristow finished plans for the new building and renovation of the current fellowship hall. On May 6, 1990, Bishop Walter Sullivan dedicated the new building.

In the Spring of 2005, Bishop Francis DiLorenzo created the Cluster Parishes of Portsmouth and Chesapeake: Church of the Resurrection, Saint Paul, and Church of the Holy Angels in Portsmouth and Saint Mary in Chesapeake. Father Anthony Morris is the current Pastor of all four Parishes.

Church of the Ascension

— Virginia Beach • 1972 —

Church of the Ascension, located in the heart of Virginia Beach, was established in 1972, in the aftermath of Pope John XXIII Vatican II Council. That renewal inspired the parish to develop and enjoy a rich history of ecumenism. It impacted the unique vision and design of Ascension as a faith community and the church's architectural design. Called by Jesus to become One even as He and the Father are One, the church space was built to be a place for God's people to become one, to know each other, to care for each other, to discuss and explore how to carry out the mission of the Gospel together. The design of Ascension promotes both worship and interaction through large open gathering spaces. The Commons facilitates multiple functions to create a sense of community before entering the worship space to celebrate liturgy.

The parish vision was for the people to take ownership of their church, recognizing that it is our church. From this vision, a commitment to self through faith development and education, and a commitment to others through ministry is foundational. The parish mission is to *Proclaim the Word of God, Celebrate the Eucharist, and Serve our Local Community.* As a result, Ascension challenges the parishioners to live their faith by reaching out to those in need and offers them over 70 ministries ministries in which to serve.

A vibrant religious formation program is called Emmaus II. There are programs that support youth and adults, as well as those returning to the church after an absence, and those inquiring about the faith and practices of the Catholic faith tradition.

The Social Justice Ministry operates a food pantry, financial outreach, winter shelter and advocacy programs to serve those who are in need. These ministries are grounded in Catholic Social Justice teachings in hopes

that God's justice and peace will reign in our hearts, in our families, in our parish, and in our world.

Ascension has been blessed with many charismatic and caring pastors, deacons, lay ministers, and staff to nurture and shepherd our congregation. Our current pastor, Father Daniel Malingumu from Tanzania, is challenging our parish towards more global solidarity by learning more about our brothers and sisters in faith worldwide.

To complement our vibrant liturgies, we have a wonderful music ministry with both talented musicians and choir members.

There is a meditation garden and columbarium just outside the Eucharistic Chapel. Here also is a large sculpture of the risen Christ.

The Church of the Ascension seeks to stay true to the ecumenical vision through which it was formed, and the strong foundation laid by those who have gone before us. It is this rare and unique combination that allows our faith community to be so vibrant and endure as such a beacon of hope.

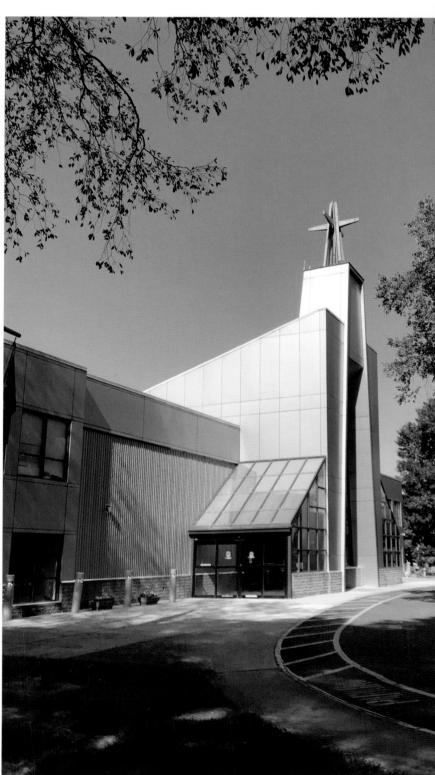

Church of the Risen Lord

The Church of The Risen Lord is a mission parish in Stuart, the seat of Patrick County. Risen Lord is clustered with Saint Joseph in Woodlawn and All Saints in Floyd. All three parishes are nestled in mountainous southwest Virginia, near the Blue Ridge Parkway. Fairy Stone State Park is in Patrick County, so during the summer and fall it is common for tourists and campers to attend Mass at Risen Lord Church.

The present parish was formed in 1972 when a group of approximately ten families began meeting

for church services in individual homes under the care of the pastor of Saint Joseph in Martinsville. After about a year, the services were relocated to the Recreation Building in Stuart. Then, in May 1975, services were relocated to the Stuart Presbyterian Church. Religious education classes were held at Blue Ridge Nursing Home following Mass. The pastor in Martinsville made the drive to Stuart. In 1981, the current cluster of the parishes was formed. Over the next ten years, the plans and fundraising efforts to build the Church of the Risen Lord took place. The land for the church had been donated by parishioner Dr. Manuel E. Tayko, a surgeon at the local hospital in Stuart.

On December 22, 1985, the new church building was dedicated by Bishop Walter F. Sullivan. At that time, the parish had grown to approximately 31 households, half of which were younger couples with growing families. There were 37 school age, or younger, children attending Mass and religious education.

The pastor was a "Circuit Rider" in the hills and mountains of southwestern Virginia, driving from Saint Joseph in Woodlawn, to All Saints in Floyd, to celebrate Mass, and back to Woodlawn after Mass over windy, hilly, two-lane roads. The round trip takes nearly two hours. Sunday morning, a similar commute to Risen Lord in Stuart for 8:30 a.m. Mass takes place, with a return to Saint Joseph in time for 11:00 a.m. Mass.

As the 1990's unfolded, the economic situation in Patrick and surrounding counties deteriorated rapidly, as textile plants closed, and jobs disappeared. Those Catholics who had moved south with the industry, had no choice but to move to where the jobs were. As jobs and young families left the area, Risen Lord's membership declined as well. While many of the families with children moved on, retirees and others seeking a less hectic lifestyle remained and more retirees continued to move into the area. We continued our Adult Education programs; modified our youth education programs, instituted our Sunday dinners, and maintained our outreach programs.

In 2005, we replaced the roof on the church. In 2008, we replaced all the windows and put vinyl siding on the building. Our outreach efforts continued, with an emphasis on providing food and healthcare for those in need in cooperation with other churches and social services, with involvement from all in the parish. Church membership is now 39 households with 15 children.

Risen Lord Parish is truly blessed. While we have had our share of ups and downs, we remain in the Holy Spirit.

Saint Timothy

In 1940, the Catholic community began to organize in Tappahannock. From its inception, Saint Timothy was under the care of the Missionary Servants of the Most Holy Trinity, the Trinitarians, as part of their mission territory of the Northern Neck and Tappahannock. They served Saint Timothy parish until 1992. Saint Timothy's original church was completed in 1949 and served as a part-time residence for the priests serving here as a mission church first to Saint Elizabeth, Colonial Beach, and then Saint Francis de Sales in Kilmarnock.

In 1971, Saint Timothy became an independent parish and saw the planning and completion of Saint Jude hall and a rectory for the pastor. At that time, Saint Paul in Hague became a mission

church of Saint Timothy. Under the Trinitarian pastors, Saint Timothy parish continued to grow in numbers and the foundation for a solid religious education program began. The Missionary Sisters of the Blessed Trinity traveled from Washington, D.C., and then later joined the parish staff to help with the religious education.

In 1988, after 9 years as pastor, Father Colin Cooke, S.T., died leaving a legacy of dedication and loving service. Saint Timothy Knights of Columbus Council is named Father Colin Cooke Council.

By 1992, the Trinitarians completed their work in developing the parish of Saint Timothy. The Diocese of Richmond sent priests to staff the parish and began the building of a larger church to accommodate the ever-growing parish. The parish saw the completion of the new church in 2000.

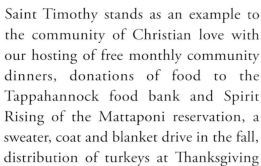

Planning for the Father Richard Dollard Memorial Garden and Columbarium began in 2005. The garden was completed and dedicated March 3, 2012, by Bishop Walter Sullivan, a longtime friend of Father Dollard.

Over the years, the original church was converted into office and meeting space. The wooden statue of Saint Timothy, that was above the entrance, was restored and now stands above the baptismal font in the new church. Saint Jude Hall was renovated twice and is now totally new again with work that was completed February 2017. It was rededicated June 11, 2017, by Bishop Francis DiLorenzo.

In 2013, the parishioners repainted the interior of the new church and a wooden outline of a cross was installed behind the altar helping to draw attention to the Rose window.

Saint Timothy is a small, vibrant, diverse parish. There is a growing Hispanic community within the parish, an active Boy Scout troop, Knights of Columbus Council, and religious education program for students through high school.

Saint Timothy stands as an example to the community of Christian love with our hosting of free monthly community dinners, donations of food to the Tappahannock food bank and Spirit Rising of the Mattaponi reservation, a sweater, coat and blanket drive in the fall, distribution of turkeys at Thanksgiving and hams at Easter, an angel tree at Christmas and participation in community outreach projects through Essex Churches Together.

All Saints

The only Catholic Church in Floyd County has roots that go back more than 40 years when itinerant priests would visit the area once each month. One of All Saint's first members recalls celebration of Mass in the homes of parishioners at a time the assembly was known as Floyd Catholic Community. Bishop Walter Sullivan assigned a neighboring pastor at Saint Mary in Blacksburg the responsibility for the fledgling community.

In 1982, Bishop Sullivan officially declared Floyd Catholic Community a mission of Saint Joseph in Woodlawn. He assigned a resident pastor to both parishes in addition to Church of the Risen Lord in Stuart. This cluster of parishes continues today. At that time, Bishop Sullivan purchased the present building site – five acres of land at the corner of Needmore Lane and Christiansburg Pike. Until the completion of a building, the Catholic congregation met in the Zion Lutheran Church for worship and fellowship for over 25 years.

In 1992, the parish elected to change its name to All Saints Catholic Church. A massive fundraising campaign took seven years. Grants were received from the Diocesan Annual Appeal and from the Catholic Extension Society to help the parish meet their goal. Bishop Francis DiLorenzo presided at the dedication of the church and altar on June 7, 2008. Because of the many benefactors, All Saints raised the funds to complete the church debt free. The marble altar was donated by College of the Holy Cross in Worcester, Massachusetts.

Recently the cluster of parishes completed a new rectory for the pastor. The previous rectory was in serious disrepair so members

of the three parishes of Saint Joseph in Woodlawn, Risen Lord in Stuart, and All Saints in Floyd came together to coordinate the project. The new rectory was finished in the Fall of 2018.

Saint Augustine

Bishop John J. Russell expressed the desire that a new parish be established, comprising the Chesterfield County section of Sacred Heart Parish and a part of Saint Ann Parish in Colonial Heights, and that it be known as Saint Augustine. The name was to honor a little Black Catholic parish in Richmond's Fulton Bottom, run by Redemptorists Fathers with a school run by Dominican Sisters, which had been closed in the late 1960's.

Bishop Russell donated ten acres of land at the intersection of Hopkins and Beulah Roads, and the Diocese made available a grant by Mary Shaughnessy, who willed $245,000 for the first Catholic parish to be established in the Richmond area after her death. Architect Louis Legnaioli designed the new church, church hall, and rectory.

Meanwhile, a house at the corner of Hopkins and Falstone Roads was purchased to serve as offices, meeting space, and living accommodations for the priest. The chapel in the house was where daily Mass was celebrated and the parish arranged with the Chesterfield County School Board to rent Bensley Elementary School for weekend Masses for three years beginning in April 1973. During our first year, Masses were also celebrated at the Bliley Funeral Home Chippenham Chapel, the Defense General Supply Center, and in our homes. Our parish marks June 10, 1973 as the official date of founding.

The groundbreaking for the church was held on May 5, 1974. The rectory was completed in March 1975 and the church and hall were finished in June of that year. Bishop Sullivan, assisted by retired Bishop Russell, conducted the dedication of the new church on June 7, 1975. There were 430 registered families in the parish, with 240 children enrolled in religious education.

Faith Memorial Baptist Church and our good neighbors at Beulah Methodist Church for making meeting rooms available. Bensley Fire House was also used for meetings as our parish grew. And so, while Masses were celebrated and building plans discussed, others began building the essential network of committees which hold the family together and which provides the smaller communities where spiritual growth and ministry happen. Today's

Worship Committee, Christian Formation Committee, Justice and Peace Committee, and such diverse groups as Saint Augustine Women's Guild, the parish bingo teams, hospital ministry and many others owe their start to the good and careful committee work of our founding pastor and families.

In the early 1980's, the on-site rectory was turned into office space and a new residence for the priests was purchased in the Fuqua Farms neighborhood. By August of 1991, the parish had 935 registered families and was debt free.

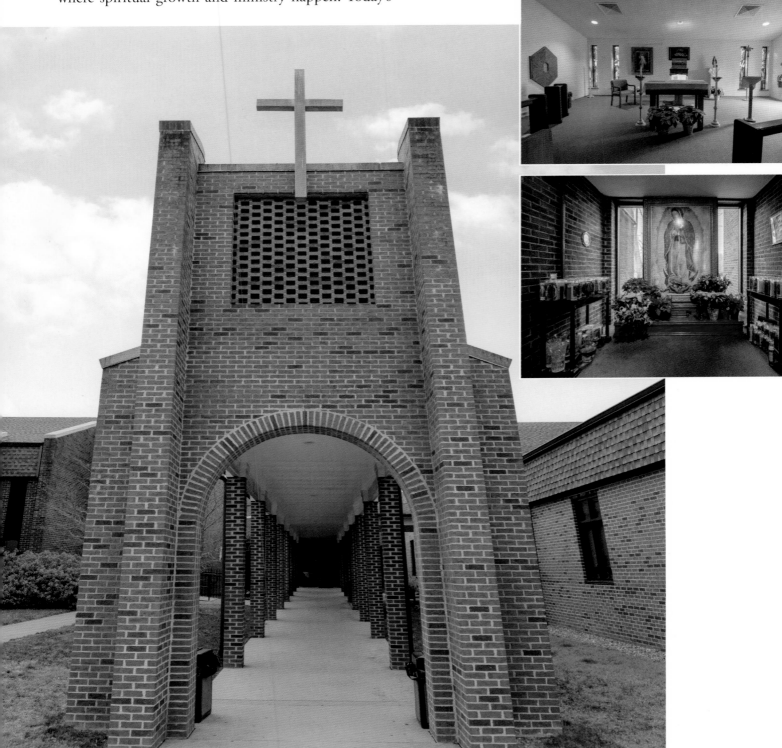

Bishop Walter F. Sullivan

W alter F. Sullivan (1928–2012) of Washington, DC, a priest and auxilia-ry bishop of Richmond, became administra-tor of the diocese following the retirement of John Russell. Sullivan was named the eleventh bishop of the diocese in 1974. His episcopate overlapped with a tumultuous period in the American Church. There were debates about the meaning of Vatican II, and reactions to the changes being made in the council's name were mixed. At the same time, aftershocks were felt from the seismic decade that had ended (ca. 1963–ca.1974). The ongoing implementation of Vatican II in this environment shaped the Church in the United States for a generation. During his twenty-nine years at the helm of the Richmond Diocese, Bishop Sullivan steered a course with bearings set on a relatively progressive view of the council's legacy. He retired as the longest-serving bishop in Richmond's history (2003).

Implementing Vatican II, Social Justice, and Secularism (1974-2003)

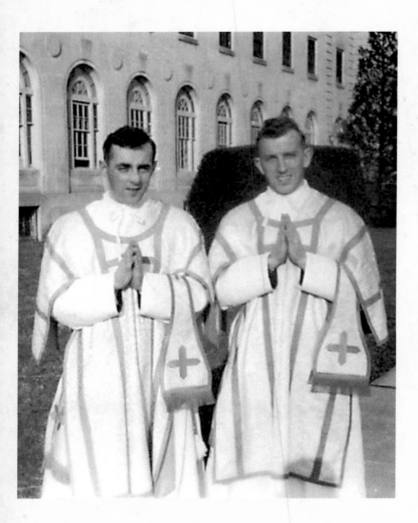

*Newly ordained
Father Walter Sullivan on right*

The diocese experienced a significant change when its boundaries were modified just one month after Sullivan's installation (1974). First, the Richmond Diocese transferred northern Virginia to the newly-created Arlington Diocese. Second, the boundaries of the Dioceses of Richmond and Wheeling (soon renamed Wheeling-Charleston) were finally made to coincide with state lines. As a result, Richmond acquired southwest Virginia and ceded the northeast panhandle of West Virginia to Wheeling. Third, the Diocese of Wilmington returned the Eastern Shore of Virginia to Richmond. The reconfigured Diocese of Richmond comprised thirty-three thousand square miles in the southern three-fifths of Virginia. At its extremes, the diocese stretched from the Atlantic Ocean on the east to the Appalachian Mountains on the west—the same width as at its creation 150 years earlier (1820).[1]

This rearrangement involved more than geography. The Richmond Diocese now returned to its earlier history by becoming more missionary (with the reacquisition of southwest Virginia) and poorer (with the loss of relatively affluent northern Virginia). Furthermore, the territorial changes marked an ideological division, as more traditional priests generally went to the Diocese of Arlington, while more progressive priests opted for the Diocese of Richmond.[2]

Diocese of
Richmond

Diocese of
Wheeling-Charleston

Diocese of
Arlington

At the time of its establishment in July 1820 the Diocese of Richmond encompassed the entire area shown above. In July 1850 the Diocese of Wheeling was erected. It was redesignated the Diocese of Wheeling-Charleston in 1974. At that same time, the Diocese of Arlington was established.

Among the characteristics of Bishop Sullivan's tenure, both in parishes and in the diocese at large, were social justice activism, including such causes as the abolition of capital punishment, prison reform, nuclear disarmament, the

alleviation of poverty, outreach to Haiti (specifically the Diocese of Hinche), and care of the elderly; ecumenical and interfaith worship, dialogue, and collaboration; and the greater involvement of lay persons, especially women, in the ministry and governance of the Church.[3]

Some activities in the diocese aroused suspicion and led to a Vatican investigation (1983). The probe focused on liturgical irregularities; the practice of general absolution (that is, without individual confession) in the Sacrament of Penance; a joint Catholic-Episcopal church (Holy Apostles, Virginia Beach); and questionable teaching about priestly celibacy and women's ordination to the priesthood. The matter was finally resolved with the appointment of Monsignor David E. Foley, a priest of Washington, DC, as auxiliary bishop of Richmond

Bishop Sullivan in Haiti

Bishop Sullivan with the Little Sisters of the Poor

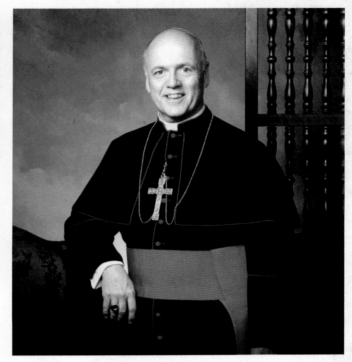

Auxiliary Bishop David E. Foley

(1986–1994). Foley exercised authority over particular aspects of the diocese in this capacity.[4]

Other developments affecting the Richmond Diocese included the rising tide of secularism, which led to fewer Catholics practicing their faith. The doubling of Hispanic immigrants in the diocese between 1990 and 2000 helped to offset the trend of declining religious practice.[5] Dozens of parishes responded to the influx of Latin American immigrants by offering Mass and pastoral care in Spanish. In what was another national trend, the diocese began to experience a decline in vocations to the priesthood and religious life (ca. 1980). Noteworthy too was the ordination of permanent deacons to assist parishes (1973, 2003).[6]

The national crisis of clerical sexual abuse, centered in Boston, battered the Church at the end of Bishop Sullivan's tenure (2002). Americans were shocked to learn about the extent of the abuse, and that some bishops had concealed the abuse and allowed offending priests to remain in ministry. In keeping with the norms adopted by the US Conference of Catholic Bishops—the *Charter for the Protection of Children and Young People* (2002)—abuser Richmond priests were removed from ministry and safeguards were instituted to protect children.

Vietnamese Refugees

Bishop Sullivan at a Mass celebrating Hispanic heritage

Saint John the Evangelist

— Marion • 1974 —

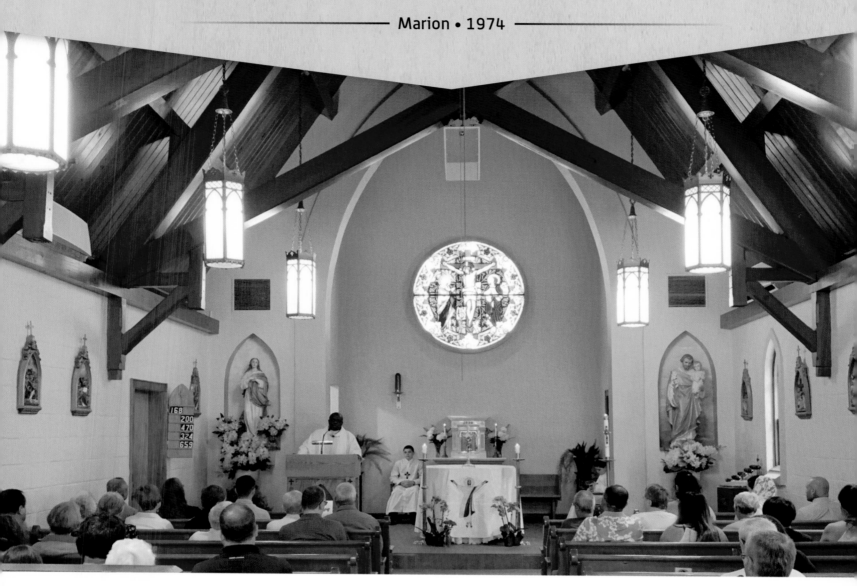

The first Mass celebrated in Marion was likely by Father Devine. After 1887, when the Southwest State Hospital was established, Mass was celebrated annually for the small number of Catholic patients along with two or three nearby Catholic families. In the 1940's, with the introduction of furniture and textile industries, more Catholic families moved into the area. Initially, they traveled to Wytheville each Sunday to attend Mass at Saint Mary Catholic Church. Father John O'Reilly, the pastor at Saint Mary, began to make trips to Marion for Mass.

In May 1951, Cardinal Spellman, Archbishop of New York, came to Wheeling, West Virginia, and learned that the mission territory of the Diocese of Wheeling (of which Saint Mary and the Marion area were a part) had 24 counties with neither churches nor priests. He decided to donate $25,000 to erect a new church in the county that was deemed to be the most deserving. The church would be named Saint John the Evangelist, the patron saint of Bishop Swint of Wheeling. In August of 1951, Joe Scalise received a letter from Bishop Swint announcing Marion as the location of the new church.

Land was purchased at the corner of Park Boulevard and Route 11 in September 1951. The building of the new church was completed by March of the following year. The pews, marble altar, statues, stations of the cross, and the large cross over the altar all came from the convent of the Sisters of the Visitation in Wytheville. On Easter Monday, April 14, 1952, Cardinal Spellman dedicated the new church.

Saint John became a mission church of Saint Mary Catholic Church in Wytheville, and Sunday Masses were alternated between the two churches. Soon new plans to construct a parish hall addition to Saint John Church were announced. The parish hall was to be used for extra seating for Mass, religious education, an office for the priest, restrooms, a kitchen, and space for social activities. In May of 1962, construction began on the new addition to Saint John.

In 1974 the parishes of southwestern Virginia were officially transferred from the Diocese of Wheeling, to the Diocese of Richmond. Saint John became a parish, and on that same day the mission church in Abingdon came under the administration of Saint John Parish. Father Daniel Bain became the first resident pastor.

In preparation for the 25th anniversary celebration of the dedication of Saint John Church, the men of the parish did remodeling; placing the tabernacle in the wall where Saint Joseph stood, plastering the walls, carpeting the Sanctuary, and replacing two marble altars with a square wooden one.

In the 1990's, more renovations were done on the church: pews were refinished, new carpeting was laid in the church, a forced-air gas heating system was added, a new outdoor sign, new light fixtures were installed, air-conditioning was added, the front doors of the church were replaced.

In June 2002, the family of Saint John's marked the 50th anniversary of the dedication of the church with a week-long celebration.

Saint Jude

— Mineral • 1974 —

Saint Jude Church in Mineral, Louisa County, existed as a mission church in the late 1960s, when an Army barracks from Fort Lee was renovated for use as a mission. It was served, along with Immaculate Conception in Buckner, by Saint Mark Catholic Church in Gordonsville, by the Missionhurst Fathers from Belgium. In the Summer of 1974, the Diocese of Arlington was erected. Saint Jude remained in the Diocese of Richmond and was erected as a parish in November 1974. The new parish was entrusted to care for the mission of Immaculate Conception. Saint Jude parish embraces all who live in Louisa County.

When Saint Jude became an independent parish in 1974, a mobile home was placed on the site for a rectory. From these humble beginnings, the parish continued to thrive and grow. The startup of the North Anna Nuclear Power Station in the county in the late 1970s brought more families to the parish. A new multi-purpose building was built in 1981 for use as church and parish hall.

The old barracks was then refurbished to provide classrooms and meeting space.

During the 1980s, the parish grew to about 90 families, and bought a small house in town for a rectory. In the early 1990s, the women of the parish formed a Women's Guild and the men of Saint Jude and Immaculate Conception formed a Knights of Columbus Council (Sacred Heart Council).

The parish continued to grow, helped in part by the development of property at nearby Lake Anna.

Parishioners began the design and construction of a much-needed church that seats 300. The new church, still in use today, was dedicated on March 21, 1999, by Bishop Walter F. Sullivan. The multi-purpose building was renovated to serve as office space and parish hall, and Verbeke Hall continued to be used for religious education and meetings.

In 2002, the parishioners continued to develop the parish property using two acres for a parish cemetery and building a rectory behind the cemetery to replace the house in Louisa. Men of the parish constructed a decorative entrance to the cemetery and a memorial to the unborn. Later, they constructed a ramp and deck for the new rectory.

In 2014, the parish established a building committee, selected an architect, and began design on a new project. However, a fire destroyed the existing parish hall, offices, and bathrooms. Suddenly, the new building project had just doubled in scope. The project became one that would provide a larger parish hall and modern kitchen, storage rooms, offices, classrooms, choir room, and an expansion to the worship center. The new facilities were completed and dedicated by Bishop Francis X. DiLorenzo in December 2016.

The whole project was a major commitment for this small parish, but the parishioners recognized the need to provide for the future of the parish and continue to provide generous support.

Saint Jude has now grown to over 270 registered families. We are big enough to have many active ministries and small enough to need everyone's help to accomplish our missions to the parish and the community.

Church of the Holy Spirit

— Virginia Beach • 1975 —

On Pentecost Sunday, June 8, 1975, Bishop Walter F. Sullivan established the Church of the Holy Spirit, appointing Rev. William H. Carr as founding pastor. The first liturgies were held at Holland Elementary School with 315 families. A Saturday liturgy was soon added at Plaza Methodist Church. As the congregation increased, Plaza Junior High School became the new worship site. With no permanent building to call home, religious education classes for 600 children and first sacraments took place in parishioners' homes. As the community grew stronger, parishioners formed groups that would come together for prayer, outreach service, and fellowship, including: The Sunshine Club, the Men's Club and the Women's Guild. Ministries started to flourish.

On August 6, 1978, ground was broken at 1396 Lynnhaven Parkway, and one year later, on August 22, 1979, Holy Spirit Parish was dedicated. New ministries quickly emerged including many Peace and Justice/Social Ministries (Food Pantry, Soup Kitchen, Meals on Wheels, Right to Life), Children's Liturgy of the Word, and the addition of a Preschool for ages 2-5.

In the early 1990s, Holy Spirit began participating in the Winter Shelter Program which provides food and shelter to the homeless throughout the coldest months of the year. Spirit House, a transitional home for women dealing with mental disabilities, striving to move from homelessness to self-sufficiency, was established in 1993.

Also at this time, Holy Spirit's Youth Ministry program was significantly expanded to encompass spiritual, service, educational, social, and leadership opportunities for the young people of the parish.

In 1996, Holy Spirit established a twinning relationship with Our Lady of Mt. Carmel in Saut d'Eau, Haiti, a ministry in which, in addition to providing financial

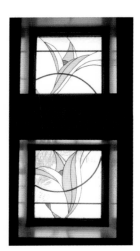

support, also promotes standing in solidarity through prayer and in the sharing of rich diversity.

On April 18, 1999, Bishop Walter Sullivan joined the pastor, Rev. Thomas Caroluzza in celebrating a special liturgy at Holy Spirit to dedicate a new Worship Space, Blessed Sacrament Chapel, Commons area, and new education wing. Two years later, a beautiful memorial prayer garden and columbarium were added outside the Blessed Sacrament Chapel.

A vibrant and active parish, known for its hospitality and warm and welcoming atmosphere, Holy Spirit Catholic Church is now comprised of over 2,300 families, rich in diversity and ethnic backgrounds. Hundreds of dedicated volunteers participate in one or more of the nearly 50 faith and service based ministries at the parish, striving to live a sacramental way of life through their active commitment to ministry, Christian fellowship, and outreach to those in need.

Prince of Peace

── Chesapeake • 1975 ──

During the summer of 1967, a group of Catholic women from the parishes of Holy Angels in Portsmouth and Saint Matthew in Virginia Beach began to meet in their homes in the Great Bridge area of Chesapeake for fellowship in their Catholic identity. Their group came to be known at Saint Matthew and their activities encouraged a parish mission.

On September 15, 1969, Saint Matthew's pastor asked Bishop John J. Russell to place the entire Great Bridge area under one jurisdiction at the persistent urging of the original group of women. On June 3, 1970, Bishop Russell designated the whole lower portion of Saint Matthew and Holy Angels parishes as a Mission which he called "Prince of Peace." In July 1970, the Chesapeake School Board granted the Mission's petition to use the Great Bridge Elementary School auditorium, and the first Mass for the Prince of Peace Mission was celebrated at 9:00 a.m. on September 6, 1970.

The Prince of Peace Mission also celebrated Mass at Saint Thomas Episcopal Church in Mann Street, Apostles Lutheran in Johnstown Road, Twiford's Funeral Home Chapel, and at the defunct Village Flick Theater. On April 11, 1971, Easter Mass was celebrated at the historic Great Bridge Congregational Christian Church which became the Prince of Peace Mission's temporary home. During the next two years, the community grew with a variety of activities that included the inception of the Men's Club and the Women's Club.

In May 1975, Bishop Walter Sullivan granted permission to begin a building program and officially named Prince of Peace a parish. Ground was broken for the Prince of Peace worship space in February 1976; Father Timothy Drake became the first pastor of Prince of Peace Parish on May 30, 1976. On December 18, 1977, Bishop Sullivan celebrated the Liturgy of Dedication for Prince of Peace Catholic Church.

The parish grew rapidly reflective of the expanding population of the City of Chesapeake. By 1988, Town Hall meetings were held to discuss the need for building expansion. On December 5, 1993, Bishop Sullivan dedicated a new worship space. Ground was broken again in July 2001 for an expansion project that included an enlarged worship space and commons area, a small worship chapel, new offices, a renovated kitchen, and a new wing for catechetical meetings.

The Parish grew in its commitment to community outreach. As early as 1996, participation began in a program that offers two weeks of meals and shelter to the homeless. The Haiti Project began in 1997, providing funds and hands-on help for the Louverture Cleary School in Croix-des-Bouquets, Haiti, and the Maison Fortune Orphanage in Hinche, Haiti. On October 24, 2010, the Food Pantry was dedicated, serving countless needy families in the community.

Prince of Peace Parish continues its life in the Lord by celebrating the Holy Eucharist and other sacraments and likewise, educating, serving the needs of others, and continually building and supporting the community.

Saint George

— Scottsville • 1975 —

Saint George is a mission parish of the Catholic Diocese of Richmond located in southern Albemarle County on Scottsville Road and established in 1974. Mass was held in a parishioner's home, then in a room over the firehouse in Scottsville, with religious education classes meeting for one hour before Mass. The small, rural community benefits from the dedication and enthusiasm of the parishioners. The parishioners determined that the building they needed would serve for community worship, but also for social, educational and cultural functions. Set in a circle of trees, it has a panoramic view of the Blue Ridge Mountains.

The Cooper-Lecky Partnership designed the new worship center and the contractor Rittenhouse Brothers, Inc., of Scottsville, built it. The total cost of the building project was just over $200,000. A generous donation of $30,000 from the Catholic Church Extension Society helped the parish to accomplish their fundraising goal. Saint Bridget Catholic Church in Richmond also helped to support the mission parish. On November 23, 1980, the Most Rev. Walter F. Sullivan, Eleventh Bishop of Richmond, dedicated the new building at Saint George. In the early 1980's, Saint George opened a cemetery. A rectory for the pastor was dedicated on April 1, 1984.

On November 1, 2011, Bishop Francis DiLorenzo requested the Dominican priests serving at Saint Thomas Aquinas in Charlottesville to provide for the sacramental and spiritual needs of the parishioners at Saint George Parish.

Church of the Redeemer

— Mechanicsville • 1976 —

For 40 years, the Church of the Redeemer has been a visible Catholic presence in Mechanicsville, reaching out to parishioners and to the wider community with open doors, welcoming smiles, and helping hands. The church itself is "in the round," with a round altar at its center, flanked on all sides by a brick "Walkway of the Saints," each brick engraved with the name of a deceased parishioner or other loved one. It is beautifully simple and simply beautiful.

Parishioners take seriously the Mission Statement's mandate to ". . . nurture the spiritual growth of all our members through vibrant celebrations of the sacraments, daily prayer, lifelong study of our faith, hospitality and compassionate service to each other and to the world beyond our doors." Priest, deacons, prayer leaders, musicians, and other ministers work together to ensure that liturgies are lively and meaningful. Wednesdays are days of prayer, with Morning Prayer at 7 a.m., a rosary service at Noon, and various other prayer services in the evening (Taizé, Benediction, Stations of the Cross, etc.) And in addition to religious education for children, teens and catechumens there are more than 15 adult classes that provide ongoing faith formation, plus retreats and outside speakers. Each year the church welcomes approximately 40 Confirmands and First Eucharistic recipients as they take the next step on their faith journeys.

Redeemer parishioners also know how to play together. They have celebrated at potluck dinners, after-liturgy coffees, welcoming meals, pancake suppers, Lenten fish fries, and soup suppers, barbecues, seafood and spaghetti dinners and multi-cultural get-togethers. They have come together for casino nights, Christmas Eve and Easter Vigil receptions, Easter egg hunts, for needlework and tole painting classes, and every team sport imaginable. Stamping Angels meet weekly to create greeting cards for the sick and bereaved. There have been Mardi Gras dances, Spring Flings, and sock hops. Parishioner artistry has been showcased at musical concerts, talent shows, Friendship Art Galleries, and annual children's Christmas programs. Many men are involved in the parish's Knights of Columbus Council, ladies in Catholic Daughters, and there are Scout troops for both boys and girls.

From its earliest days, Redeemer has reached out to others. It was one of the churches that helped to found MCEF (Mechanicsville Churches Emergency Fund), supports CARITAS and blood drives, and has resettled refugee families. Thanksgiving and Christmas collections provide meals and gifts to hundreds of those less fortunate. The annual Haiti yard sale is eagerly anticipated, and there is a waiting list of vendors who wish to be a part of the Craft Bazaar. No Room at the Inn, at which hundreds of nativities are displayed, raises thousands of dollars for local charities and for building houses for the women of Lascahobas, Haiti, with whom the parish is twinned.

Church of the Redeemer is now, always has been, and will continue to be a church of welcome for those seeking a spiritual home or for anyone who needs a helping hand.

Church of the Incarnation

Incarnation Catholic Church was previously part of Holy Comforter Parish which built a school and purchased the 93.7-acre Branchlands Estate in 1954. The school closed in 1969, but Holy Comforter continued to use it on Sundays for religious education, celebrating Mass both in the Stone Chapel, which had been a horse barn, and in the auditorium. Within four years, a new worshiping community had developed at Branchlands joining the Holy Comforter community in downtown Charlottesville.

In June 1975, Most Reverend Walter Sullivan directed Holy Comforter's Parish Council to plan a new parish community.

The existing school property was sold with 8 acres retained for the new parish. A parcel of land was sold to Branchlands Senior Independent Living, providing partial funding for the construction of the new parish. The third parcel of land was utilized by the Diocese of Richmond for the construction of Our Lady of Peace Retirement Community.

On April 12, 1976, the parish was named Incarnation. Three other names honor our past: the church was dedicated to Saint Anthony, from a bequest from the estate of Anthony Rives. The school wing was named Saint Margaret Mary, recognizing a Charlottesville

Black Catholic parish which closed in 1966, and the auditorium was named Father Bernard Moore Hall. On December 21, 1980, the first Mass was celebrated in the new church.

In the 1990s, the parish participated in the Diocesan Haiti Twinning Program, partnering with the Little Brothers and Little Sisters of the Incarnation in Pandiassou, Haiti. The Haiti ministry completed construction of a butchery, primary schools, a medical clinic and continues to provide support. The parish began a ministry to Charlottesville's growing Hispanic population. On July 16, 1996, Bishop Remi De Roo, the Bishop Emeritus of Victoria, British Columbia, celebrated the first Spanish Mass.

Incarnation expanded its narthex and added a daily Mass chapel. The charity and justice ministries grew with an active food ministry and by joining in an Interfaith program (PACEM) taking turns providing shelter for the homeless during the winter months. Incarnation became an area leader in IMPACT, an interfaith movement addressing root causes of poverty and empowering local leaders. The clerical staff expanded, the Hispanic community has grown, and the parish continues to follow its mission statement to be "motivated by God's love to transform our homes, our communities, and the world around us into places of peace and justice." For a week in August 2010, under the leadership of its fourth pastor, Father Gregory Kandt, Incarnation held the first ever old-time Catholic tent revival. Incarnation endeavors to foster a culture of witness to the Gospel in keeping with the new evangelization.

Church of the Holy Apostles

Anglican/Roman Catholic Congregation of Tidewater

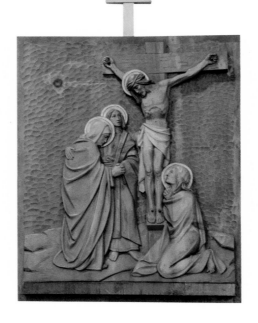

The people of Holy Apostles, Episcopalians and Roman Catholics, shared a vision with their Bishops and Priests to form a visible sign of Christian unity. To this end, meetings and correspondence throughout 1975 and 1976 addressed the canonical implications of the formation and operation of an ecumenical community.

In the Fall of 1977, the Anglican and Roman Catholic Church shared the Barry Robinson School Chapel. The statement regarding this new venture was signed by the Rt. Rev. C. Charles Vaché, the Seventh Bishop of the Episcopal Diocese of Southern Virginia, the Rt. Rev. David S. Rose, the Sixth Bishop of the Episcopal Diocese of Southern Virginia, and the Most Rev. Walter F. Sullivan, the Eleventh Bishop of the Catholic Diocese of Richmond.

Reverend Raymond A. Barton was named Catholic co-Pastor of the Anglican/Roman Catholic congregation on October 3, 1977. Reverend Donald W. Gross was named the Episcopal co-Pastor. With multiple communications between the Bishop of Richmond and the Congregation for Clergy, it was made clear this experiment would be designated a "community" and not a "parish."

In 2006, a letter from His Eminence, Cardinal Kasper, President of the Pontifical Council for Christian Unity, affirmed the Diocese of Richmond for providing a community to minister to ecumenical families. Bishop Francis DiLorenzo gave the assurance that this experimental community would be reviewed and evaluated in regular visits with the leaders and lay people, ensuring

that the congregation reflected the standards and norms of Catholic Ecumenical practices.

In 2014, Bishop DiLorenzo announced that the search for a Catholic priest for Church of the Holy Apostles was not meeting with success. However, Reverend Rene Castillo, a priest of the Diocese of Richmond, incardinated in 2012, accepted the assignment as Chaplain at Church of the Holy Apostles in August of 2015. He serves there with the Episcopal Chaplain, Reverend Mario Melendez.

Church of the Holy Family

— Virginia Beach • 1977 —

In the early 1960s, Virginia Beach was a small resort town in the southeastern part of the Commonwealth. When the town merged with Princess Anne County in 1963 to create the City of Virginia Beach, Bishop John J. Russell purchased several tracts of land throughout the city including a parcel at the intersection of North Great Neck and First Colonial roads that had previously been the Conrad family farm.

Arrangements were made in June 1975 to use Francis Asbury United Methodist Church for a Saturday evening Mass, and soon a Sunday Mass was started at Trantwood Elementary School on Inlynnview Road. By June 1977, nearly 200 families were attending weekend Masses in Great Neck.

That same month, Bishop Walter F. Sullivan approved establishment of a new parish, Church of the Holy Family, and appointed Reverend Thomas Reardon as its first pastor. The parish outgrew the temporary facilities, with more than 400 families. In May 1979, weekend liturgies moved to Cape Henry Collegiate School on First Colonial Road. The parish hired the Norfolk architectural firm Oliver, Smith, and Cooke to design the church and its adjoining buildings. On June 22, 1980, ground was broken on the parcel at Great Neck and First Colonial Roads, and on August 27, 1981, Bishop Sullivan dedicated the new church.

By its 20th anniversary, Holy Family had become one of the ten largest parishes in the Diocese of

Richmond with over 1,000 registered families. Virginia Beach General Hospital was becoming a major-medical center and several assisted-living facilities opened within parish boundaries. A full-time healthcare minister position was created to assist with visits to the sick. In 1997, the parish began an ambitious expansion project that included a parish life center, meeting rooms, classrooms, and additional office space that was completed in 2000.

The Haiti ministry was launched, and Holy Family welcomed the Church of Saint Jude in Baptiste, Haiti, as its twin parish. Several projects, including a fresh water system and a school were built in Haiti.

In 2002, the parish opened Holy Family Day School and began offering year-round Catholic education for preschool age children.

The parish contracted with the Barnes Group to design and build an open-air columbarium adjacent to the church with dedication occurring in 2010.

Parishioners also constructed a small storage building on parish grounds for the teen clothing ministry (4 Teens by Teens) that is operated entirely by parish youth who provide clothing for at-risk teens. In 2012, the parish began hosting the Chosen Ministry, a group for special needs people of all ages to congregate and enjoy fellowship. The parish also began implementing its long-term improvement plan aided by the financial assistance of the Living Our Mission fund drive. The parish had nearly 1,500 registered families in July 2017. From its humble beginnings in 1975, the Church of the Holy Family has grown and adapted to meet the needs of a burgeoning Catholic community.

Saint Mark

Virginia Beach • 1978

Known initially as the Indian River Catholic Community, there were initially 54 families gathering for Mass in backyards or in garages and family rooms during inclement weather. By Fall of 1998, a house in the Indian Lakes neighborhood was to serve as a rectory and the parish name Saint Mark selected. By October 1978, Masses were celebrated at Brandon J. High School on Sunday mornings and at Community United Methodist Saturday evenings.

In February 1981, the purchase of 6.58 acres of land was completed and the groundbreaking for Phase I ($1,047,883) occurred on November 6, 1983. Phase One (17,088 sq. ft.) of a two-phase plan included a great hall as a temporary worship space and for fellowship, a chapel for daily Mass, a commons area, parish offices, a kitchen area and a nursery. Phase One was dedicated on October 6, 1984. By 1988, there were 979 registered families. On September 22, 1991, thirteen years after establishment, ground was broken again for the Sanctuary (14,146 sq. ft.). Dedication was May 24, 1992, all without asking for a single pledge. The spirit of the community was captured in a song, "By Cross and Water Signed," composed by Del Ridge for Saint Mark.

Discussions began concerning support to the Haitian people as an outreach ministry. Working with other local parishes Saint Mark helped contributed to the purchase of the initial campus for what was to become the orphanage of Maison Fortune. This association lead to a twinning agreement

with the orphanage. A Food Pantry served the local community. The Food Pantry expanded to include working in conjunction with other pantries in the area, local grocery and food establishments to provide bags of groceries to the area hungry. A pastoral need for deceased loved ones to be closely remembered was addressed. In the summer of 2007, a Columbarium was constructed adjacent to the church building and dedicated by Bishop Sullivan. Saint Mark joined an area ecumenical group of

churches, Chesapeake Area Shelter Team (CAST) to provide overnight shelter and meals to area homeless for a week during the winter months.

Saint Mark embraces the future with joy and excitement to serve God in His Church, the Diocese, and the community. In the years to come, aided by the Spirit, we will continue to provide Liturgy and Catholic Formation, welcoming all … imaging Jesus Christ.

Saint Thomas More Parish still thinks of itself as "new" although it celebrated 40 years in 2018. More modern by design, it has grown in grace through the stewardship of its property, as well as its people, by many wonderful men and women of God. The history of Saint Thomas More Parish should be looked at first from its physical space, the building, and then its congregation, the body of Christ.

Early in 1970's, there was need for another Catholic church in Lynchburg. Holy Cross in downtown Lynchburg was celebrating extra liturgies at the regional school to ease crowding. The

Diocese began exploring the idea of building a church in the Timberlake/ Brookville area, with Mass being celebrated at Whitten Timberlake Chapel in early 1971.

Bishop Walter Sullivan announced in July 1978 that he would open a new parish as soon as a priest was available and, on September 5, 1978, a house on Deerwood Drive was purchased and became the first parish center, rectory, and office. Fundraising began in the spring of 1979 after Bishop Sullivan acquired 20 acres of pasture and forest land on Roundelay Drive, and construction began in June 1980. The church and rectory were completed and dedicated in May 1981. The parish grew from 25 families in the late 1970's to 535 families by 1985.

Realizing a need for offices and classrooms, the parish began planning and fundraising once again. Construction started in November 1990 and, at the same time, the parish started building Nott Homes, a group housing center for those with special needs. The new classrooms, offices, and Nott Homes were dedicated in September 1991.

In June 1994 the parish experienced Mass attendance spilling over from the Nave into the church foyer. Bishop Sullivan suggested that the parish should consider building a new worship space. Building began in 2002, and the new nave and chapel were dedicated, and the old nave and chapel were repurposed to become the fellowship hall and kitchen in September 2004. The rectory next to the church was torn down, and a new rectory was purchased in 2008 on Smoketree Lane, one street over from the church.

In 2013, stained-glass windows were added to the columbarium. The first of 14 stained-glass windows for the nave, Jesus in the Eucharistic Feast, was installed on Corpus Christi 2017. More renovations and improvements began in July 2017, to the nave, kitchen, and bathrooms with the addition of a More Aid office, Learning Center and elevator.

The parish of St. Thomas More has grown to over 1000 families. Ministries include Meals on Wheels, More Aid Food Pantry, Vacation Bible School, Feeding with Faith, Habitat for Humanity, Diocesan Work Camp, to name a few. The parish has been twinned with Our Lady of the Nativity Parish in Savanette, Haiti, since 1992, helping to build schools, a chapel, a water treatment plant, and in paying the teachers' salaries.

The people of Saint Thomas More are a Eucharistic people having celebrated the Mass over 12,000 times, ever becoming what they have received.

Church of the Epiphany

Richmond · 1979

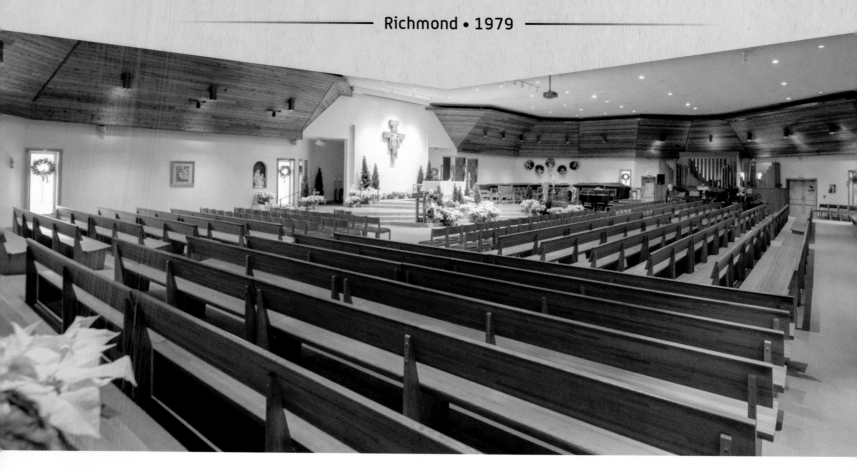

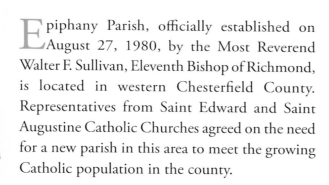

Epiphany Parish, officially established on August 27, 1980, by the Most Reverend Walter F. Sullivan, Eleventh Bishop of Richmond, is located in western Chesterfield County. Representatives from Saint Edward and Saint Augustine Catholic Churches agreed on the need for a new parish in this area to meet the growing Catholic population in the county.

Meetings were held that Fall with parishioners from Saint Edward and Saint Augustine who lived within the boundaries of the new parish and 275 families registered. On the weekend of September 22-23, 1980, Mass was celebrated Saturday evening in Bliley's Chippenham Chapel and Sunday Masses were held at the Bishop Ireton Center on Courthouse Road, owned by the Knights of Columbus. Parish registration in-

creased rapidly and soon the parish was meeting in Monacan High School for Sunday Masses. Saturday evening liturgy continued at Bliley's Chippenham Chapel.

Religious education began in neighborhood family groups under the direction of Dr. Joseph Ionnone and Sister Anita Sherwood, O.S.B. After the first year, the parish included 613 families. The architect, Glenn German of Midlothian, and the contractor, J. E. Jamerson & Sons of Appomattox, began work in October of 1981 to build the new church.

The Dedication liturgy for the Church of the Epiphany was held on November 7, 1982, Bishop Walter Sullivan presiding.

Within a few short years, the parish had grown to over a thousand families, with 900 children in religious education. The Church of the Epiphany made plans to build an education wing and hired the architect Balzer and Associates of Richmond to design classrooms, a nursery, offices, and all purpose room and restrooms in a 15,000 square foot building. The new wing was dedicated by Bishop Sullivan on September 24, 1989, at a celebration of the parish's 10th anniversary.

The projection was that the parish would continue to grow as more people moved into Richmond and settled in the neighborhoods built around the Church. As this came to fruition with the expansion of western Chesterfield County and with the large number of families attending the southside Richmond parishes, the Catholic Diocese of Richmond developed a plan to open a new parish, Saint Gabriel, which began in 1997 with many families from Church of the Epiphany.

Epiphany continues to flourish in Liturgy, community life, christian formation and human concerns ministries, with parishioners offering outreach to the people of Chesterfield County and beyond. First Wednesday dinners gather our families each month for fellowship. And Human Concerns Ministries help our neighbors near, Epiphany Food Pantry, and far, Saint Teresa Education Center in Kassunga, Uganda.

Saint Joseph

Saint Joseph Catholic Church started with just two or three families gathering in people's homes in 1958, the year the Glenmary Home Missioners settled in Dickenson County. Through the years, the parish population remained steady at 65 members, although many families came from and went to other places due to economic downturn in the area.

The church buildings are in excellent condition due to the skills and efforts of parishioners and help from various volunteers who have come to us

through the (now retired) Saint Joseph Housing Repair Program run by the late Sister Jean Korkisch, CSC, a member of the parish.

Despite its small size, Saint Joseph parishioners are actively involved in local community outreach to the schools and library, the Food Bank, and medical clinics. For the last 30 years, Saint Joseph parish has benefited and been blessed with Sister Jean Korkisch CSC, and Sister Bernie Kenny MMM. As members and spiritual leaders, they have guided the parish and shared the joys and

sorrows of the parish community. Sister Bernie was instrumental in the formation of the Health Wagon, which provides compassionate, quality healthcare to the medically underserved people in the mountains of Appalachia.

Today, parish membership is falling as parishioners age. Despite this struggle, Saint Joseph remains confident that, with prayers and good leadership, the community will continue to exist and serve the Lord as He leads.

Saint Mary

The first Roman Catholic Chapel opened on the ground of the Oak Ridge Estate in 1901. Thomas Fortune Ryan asked Bishop Augustine Van de Vyver for permission to celebrate Mass at Our Lady of Lourdes.

Jumping to the 1950s and 1960s, six Catholic families in Nelson County and priests from Holy Cross Catholic Church in Lynchburg came together twice a month to celebrate Mass and the sacraments.

In 1960, the Father Judge Mission Seminary in Monroe, Virginia, opened and the priests-in-residence took over the chapel at Oak Ridge. Father Jerome Hovanec came every Sunday to celebrate Mass. This arrangement lasted about a decade.

Moving into the mid-1970s, priests from Holy Cross Catholic Church came on Thursday evenings to celebrate Mass. Father Robert J. Warren came from Dilwyn, Father Richard Aylward, a Maryknoll missionary, assigned to Saint George Catholic Church in Scottsville stayed for two years before returning to Japan.

From 1975 to 1985, a priest assigned to Holy Comforter in Charlottesville said Mass on Sunday evenings.

In 1983, he helped the parishioners purchase a Methodist Church in Lovingston, and the parish was named Saint Mary Catholic Church.

Next, priests came to Lovingston from Saint George Catholic Church in Scottsville. In 1999, a Spanish Mass was added for the growing Hispanic population in the area. That Mass continues to the present.

Father Daniel Kelly was assigned to Saint Mary Catholic Church in 1999 and served the parish until his retirement in 2015. During his pastorate, a new church was built on Route 29.

Good Samaritan

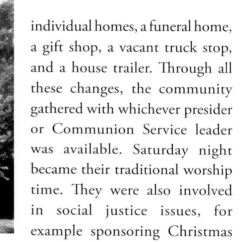

Good Samaritan Catholic Church in Amelia County was forged in faith, flexibility, and perseverance. Its life blood was, and is, the community of parishioners who dreamed of a faith nurtured and guided by the Catholic Church of the Diocese of Richmond.

In 1950, the small, core group who gathered weekly to discuss establishing a Catholic Church in Amelia included Mary and Josef Rudershausen, friends of Bishop Walter Sullivan. As this community grew, they communicated the group's hopes to the Bishop, who encouraged them and eventually named them a diocesan mission parish.

Over the next 30 years, they were known as the Catholic Community of Amelia. This growing group gathered for worship in the Boy Scout House, the basement of the Presbyterian Church, individual homes, a funeral home, a gift shop, a vacant truck stop, and a house trailer. Through all these changes, the community gathered with whichever presider or Communion Service leader was available. Saturday night became their traditional worship time. They were also involved in social justice issues, for example sponsoring Christmas celebrations for families through the Department of Social Services and sponsoring three Cuban refugees, finding them a home and jobs.

The Church, which was initially under the diocesan umbrella, was assigned to the Catholic Church in Blackstone and its pastors. It was Father George Hughes who began serious discussions about building a permanent home for the Amelia church. After each Mass, the community would stay, discuss, and vote on all aspects of the new building project. Bishop Sullivan and dedicated the completed building as Good Samaritan Catholic Church on June 21, 1981.

The church was moved from associations with the Catholic Church in Farmville, to Church of the Epiphany in Richmond, to Saint John Neumann in Powhatan. Through those years, there were periods with no specific leadership, and the parishioners shouldered the responsibilities of maintenance, religious education, etc. Then the community thrived and completed the construction of a new church building and the conversion of the original church into a parish hall in 2002.

When the Spanish-speaking population of the county grew, the English-speaking population of Good Samaritan invited them to share the worship space. That began a meaningful relationship between the two congregations. Sunday late afternoons were, and are, reserved for the Spanish Mass.

Good Samaritan was clustered with Saint Gabriel in 2010. The English and Spanish-speaking communities celebrate bi-lingual Masses on special holidays, joint social celebrations, and joint children's Religious Education.

All the people of Good Samaritan Catholic Church longed for a church home where they could celebrate their faith. They were flexible enough to deal with whatever circumstances arose along that journey, and they continue to persevere in their desire to love God and their neighbors. Good Samaritan is that home.

Saint Theresa
of the Holy Family Parish

— Tazewell • 1980 —

The Catholic faith in Tazewell dates back to before the Civil War when the county had less than 10,000 residents and this town of the same name, only a few hundred people.

The earliest Catholic Church in Tazewell had its beginnings in 1842 and was located in what was then called Jeffersonville, now known as Tazewell. Father Edward Fox of Wytheville traveled on horseback across the mountains on a public trail through Burkes Garden to Jeffersonville to hold Catholic services.

Those first services were held in the "Union Church," which the Methodists made available for use by other Christians. By 1852, however, construction was underway on Marion Street for a Catholic Church. The new church was a simple, single-story, brick building. Among those responsible for helping to establish the church in Jeffersonville were John Warfield Johnson and his wife, Nicolai. They also established a cemetery for Catholic burials.

Just 30 years later, in 1883, a militant anti-Catholic movement led in part to the church ceasing to celebrate Mass in the Town of Tazewell. With fewer Catholics, the Diocese conveyed its lot and church to the elders of a newly forming Disciples of Christ congregation, then the former Catholic property was conveyed to Tazewell County and later was torn down.

In April 1951, the Catholic community in Tazewell began to re-establish itself. The Catholic faithful began to gather for Mass at the home of Mr. and Mrs. J. B. Lynch, on Tazewell Avenue. Fathers Alphonsus Hayes and James Maher traveled from Powhatan, West Virginia, to serve a growing Catholic population in Tazewell. As it grew larger, they began celebrating Mass in a small building, once used as a grocery store, behind the Lynch home, referred to as "the Little Chapel."

It was in that same period the Tazewell Ladies Guild was developed and selected Saint Theresa as the name and patron saint of the church.

Bishop McDonald bought the A.J. Tynes home on Tazewell Avenue in 1960 and for the next several years church services were held in the Tynes home. In April 1967, ground was broken to build the new church. The George Meder family made a sizeable donation for the church through the Catholic Extension Society.

The first Mass in the new church was celebrated just a week before Christmas on December 17, 1967, and the church was formally dedicated on May 27, 1968, with Bishop Joseph to officiate and assist in laying the cornerstone. Father James Walsh was the first pastor of the new church.

In August 1974, the southwest Virginia area was transferred from the Diocese of Wheeling, to the Diocese of Richmond. In late August 1975, Father James Walsh, who had served Saint Theresa and surrounding churches as pastor, returned to his native Ireland.

The original church building was renovated to separate the rectory from the church building and to turn the former rectory area into a commons-fellowship area. A new rectory was built in 2014-2015. In 2010, Saint Theresa was merged with Saint Elizabeth, Saint Mary, and Saint Joseph to form the Holy Family Parish – one parish with four sites, which continues today.

Shepherd of the Hills

The formation of Shepherd of the Hills began in 1979 when a group of Catholic families desired to have a parish in Greene County. Bishop Walter Sullivan granted approval for the parish on January 7, 1980, and the first Mass was celebrated at the old Ruckersville Elementary School on February 17, 1980.

On March 19, 1980, Father Thomas Reardon of Saint George in Scottsville began offering Mass once a month at the school, supported by priests from neighboring parishes. In September 1980, Father Thomas Reardon was appointed pastor and Mass was celebrated on a weekly basis.

The people of the parish choose the name "Shepherd of the Hills" and, in March 1981, the Bishop gave approval. The first Religious Education classes and the first council elections were held in November.

Bishop Sullivan purchased a five-acre lot and house in Quinque on October 1, 1981, for $120,000. The building was converted for use as a church. The parish had 120 registered members at that time. The move into the Parish Center was in January 1982 and Bishop Sullivan celebrated the Rite of Dedication on February 7, 1982. With a growing population, it was necessary to expand the Parish Center in February 1994 to its current size.

The altar and chair were made by Joseph Ference, which started the tradition of using parishioner skills to create what was needed in the church.

In October 1998, the parish decided to build a new church to accommodate more growth. On October 13, 2001, Bishop Sullivan approved the plans for the new church. In April 2002, the groundbreaking ceremony was held for the new building. The architect selected

was parishioner Cliff Walcutt. The new church building was dedicated by Bishop Sullivan on November 2, 2003. The old church now serves as the Parish Center.

We have grown to be the spiritual home for around 80 families and 200 members. With God's Grace, we look forward to many more years of shepherding Greene County to a celebration of Christ's Love.

SPIRITUAL LIFE CENTER OF
SHEPHERD OF THE HILLS
A ROMAN CATHOLIC COMMUNITY
SUNDAYS 8:30 AM
WELCOME
434-985-3929
6562 AMICUS RD. • QUINQUE, VA
WEEKDAY MASS WED 6:00 PM
HOLY ROSARY   SUN 8:00 AM

Saint Joseph

Saint Joseph is a small parish in Woodlawn, located about 30 miles south of Wytheville. In 1981, the current cluster of the parishes was formed. The pastor was a "Circuit Rider" in the hills and mountains of southwestern Virginia, driving from Saint Joseph in Woodlawn, to All Saints in Floyd, to celebrate Mass, and back to Woodlawn after Mass over windy, hilly, two-lane roads. The round trip takes nearly two hours. Sunday morning, a similar commute to Risen Lord in Stuart for 8:30 a.m. Mass takes place, with a return to Saint Joseph in time for 11:00 a.m. Mass.

In 1984, the Diocese of Richmond purchased a house on Joy Ranch Road for a rectory for the pastor and land adjacent to the existing Church

property for future expansion needs. A touching story was told years later by the pastor about how the rectory was repainted when it was needed. One of the parishioner's son who was a Marine at Camp Lejeune came home for the weekend with four of his buddies. They spent all day Saturday painting the outside of the rectory. With another son, there was a total of seven painters. "I had them paint it white with bright blue trim. It only cost us the cost of the paint, about $110. This morning I celebrated Mass for them as a way of thanking them. I will write to their commanding officer and commend them."

In 1997, Saint Joseph in Woodlawn received a $25,000 grant from the Catholic Church Extension Society and a $25,000 donation from the Diocese of Richmond toward building a parish hall addition onto the existing Church. The parish hired a contractor and began building, but snow and rain slowed the progress. It was October of 1998 before the new Parish Center was blessed by Bishop Walter Sullivan. The next year, the parish paved the parking lot and received a generous donation of $4,000 from the Bishop's Appeal to defray the cost.

The pastor began offering Mass in Spanish around 1996, and attendance was so good that by 1999 he offered weekly Mass in Spanish at Saint Joseph in Woodlawn. Because of a generous bequest from a parishioner, Mr. Vernon Brown, of $45,000, Saint Joseph was able

to do major renovations to the Church including a new roof and new HVAC. The longest serving pastor was Father Charles Brickner who was assigned to the three parishes from 1991 to 2012. Reverend David Ssentamu is the current Administrator of Saint Joseph in Woodlawn and Risen Lord in Stuart and All Saints in Floyd. Father Ssentamu is from the Archdiocese of Kampala, Uganda.

Saint Paschal Baylon

— South Boston • 1981 —

The history of Saint Paschal Baylon begins in the homes of South Boston residents. Being few in numbers, Catholics in the area in the 1930's attended Mass in Danville, Virginia, or Roxboro, North Carolina, and from time to time, itinerant priests celebrated Mass in people's homes. Several local businessmen offered space for services as the number of Catholics was slowly increasing. Brooks Funeral Home, Von Patterson's Restaurant, both located on lower Main Street, and Sam Patterson, owner of Little Giant Grocery, offered an adjacent space which became the Catholic Chapel.

Officially, South Boston was a "station" of Sacred Heart Catholic Church in Danville, as listed in 1938 records of the Diocese of Richmond. We were served by Father Joseph Hodges, who later became Bishop of the Diocese of Wheeling-Charleston, West Virginia. The small number of Catholics in the area did not make it feasible to support a parish. Diocesan records indicate that there was no change in status all through the 1940's.

In the early 1950's, the "station's" sponsorship was shifted from Danville to Saint Catherine of Siena in Clarksville, which had been established by the

314

Franciscans in 1947. The "station" was a "mission," the status commonly assigned to geographical areas having small numbers of faithful. Earlier, Saint Catherine of Siena Catholic Church was a "mission" of Emporia, and South Boston was listed as a "station" of Saint Catherine.

In 1953, the Franciscan Order of Friars Minor came south to Clarksville. They assisted the local Catholics in construction of Saint Paschal Baylon Catholic Church and the first Franciscan pastor was Father Pancratius Halstrom, OFM. For twenty-five years, the Franciscans furnished priests and paid for their cars and for their expenses. The priests lived at the Friary in Clarksville. By 1954, Father Gordon F. Schneider, assistant to Father Halstrom, was the first recorded Franciscan to be assigned to live and work at Saint Paschal. Father Brendan Pyle, OFM, received a grant for this "mission" and the funds were used to build an addition on the rear of the church, which became the priest's office and living quarters.

When the Diocese of Richmond split in 1974, a new experiment of service was begun, named Team Ministry, along the Route 58 corridor. Two priests would work the corridor from Emporia to South Boston and they would reside in South Hill and South Boston. The parishioners bid farewell to the Franciscans who had become family and had served the church for over twenty-five years.

Over the years, parish children received the gifts of time and talent from the Sisters - Mission Helpers of the Sacred Heart who drove here each week from Crewe, while the Sisters of Mercy from Sacred Heart Church in Danville prepared the children for the reception of the sacraments for several years.

By 1980 Saint Paschal Baylon Catholic Church was officially declared a parish and many changes were made, including building the Commons area.

In 2009, the Diocese of Richmond made the decision to cluster the parish with Saint Catherine in Clarksville and Good Shepherd in South Hill.

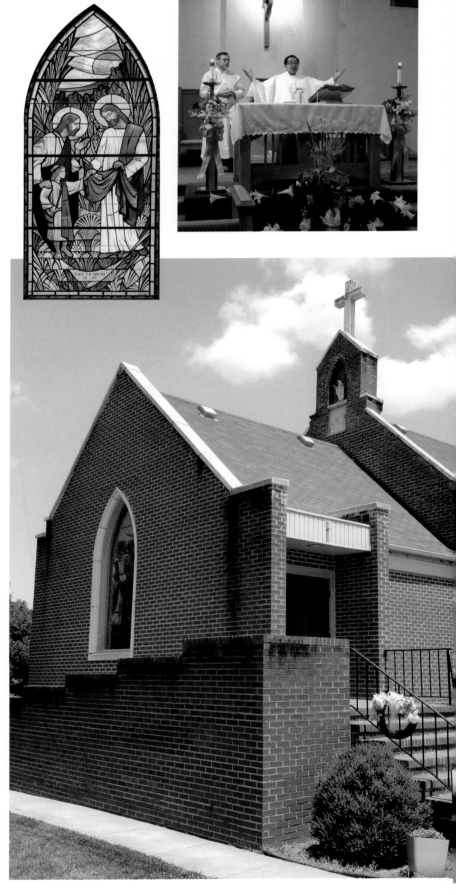

Our Lady of Peace

— Appomattox • 1982 —

We gather in the name of Jesus Christ, who is the Prince of Peace. How apropos, given that one of the two land wars in our great country ended in Appomattox County. Mary, the Mother of Jesus, is the Queen of Peace -- our faith community is named for her. As Mary brought peace to the world, may we bring the peace of Christ to everyone we meet.

Located approximately one mile from historic Appomattox Court House, our vision of Our Lady of Peace began in 1973, as outdoor Masses were celebrated at Graf's Farm in Concord. Three years later, the first parish council was formed, and plans were established to start our church. On August 29th, 1979, with a liturgy celebrated by Bishop Walter Sullivan, the groundbreaking took place. On March 21, 1982, the dedication of Our Lady of Peace Church took place; after nine long years, our Catholic faith community finally had a permanent home.

From the beginning, as our refugee committee provided financial assistance to Cambodian refugee families, to the present, as Mac's Kitchen provides weekly meals and fresh produce to families and individuals in need, our faith community has endeavored to follow our theme song which proclaims: "All Our Welcome in This Place."

As we celebrate our 35th year and reflect over this passing of time, we have worked hard to improve our church home. Located on the beautiful and peaceful church grounds, Our Lady of Peace established a cemetery in 2005. In 2012, the parish added an addition to the worship space which includes: a fellowship area (Corter Hall), pastor's office, and religious education classrooms. In addition, a memorial floral garden and children's play area were added and are maintained by our parishioners. Recently, in 2016, our parking area was paved.

Currently, our parish ministries include committees of: Liturgy and Worship, Christian Formation, Justice and Peace, and Community Life/Parish Social. A sampling of the many missions and activities our faith community support include: our long-standing Prison Ministry (Kairos), CCD Classes (Grades kindergarten through high school),

Summer Vacation Bible School, Saint Ann's Clothing Exchange and Food-bank, Mac's Kitchen (our soup kitchen), Christmas Angel Tree, and our Appalachia Project. In addition, our faith community encourages fellowship through covered dish suppers and monthly breakfasts, Halloween Trunk or Treat, Christmas Grand Illumination and Children's Christmas Programs, Saint Patrick and Saint Valentine parties, church picnics, and swim parties.

Throughout the years, Our Lady of Peace parishioners have been blessed with enlightenment, encouragement, and entertainment from our 17 parish pastors. From Father Pereira, who came to build a church, to our current pastor, Father Jim Gallagher, our pastors, have given much of themselves to help grow our parish community.

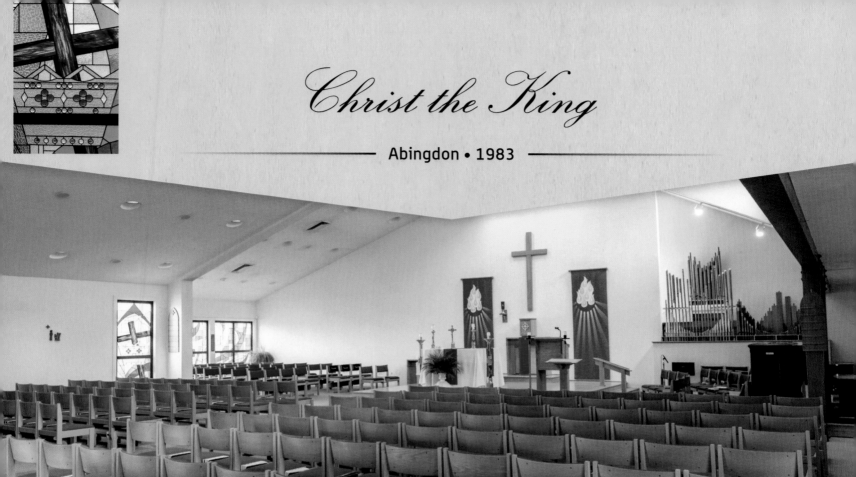

Christ the King

Christ the King Parish began when a group of Catholics living in Abingdon, who had been attending Mass in Marion or Bristol, met in mid-1974 to organize. Bishop Walter Sullivan allowed these Catholics mission status to Bristol's Saint Anne Catholic Church. Father John Fahey of Saint Anne said the first Mass in Abingdon on September 8, 1974, at Saint Thomas Episcopal Church. In December 1974, Abingdon became a mission church to Saint John the Evangelist in Marion.

By April of 1975, this Catholic community chose the name Christ the King and began to meet at Saint John Lutheran Church, as the space at Saint Thomas Episcopal was being outgrown. To this day, Christ the King maintains a long-standing spirit of cooperation and friendship with these two churches.

The Catholic community continued to grow, and the parishioners determined the need to construct their own facility. A building fund pledge drive was initiated in 1980, and the parishioners responded by raising twice the amount Bishop Walter Sullivan requested prior to building. Groundbreaking was held in August 1982, and construction began on September 7, 1982. The dedication of the new church was held on May 7, 1983.

In the 1990s, it was determined there was need for additional space, especially for religious education. This expansion included a larger worship space, kitchen, classrooms and a new fellowship hall. Another pledge drive was initiated and, again, parishioner response was overwhelming. This new space was dedicated June 12, 1994, with Bishop Sullivan presiding.

Of special significance was the legacy of Charles Seger, longtime treasurer of Christ the King Church and one of the most beloved and devoted founding members. Because of his leadership, and because of a substantial bequest to Christ the King at his death, the building committee and pastoral council named the facility Seger Hall in his honor.

Recently, the worship space was re-invigorated, and a beautiful pipe organ put in place. Our parish thrives because of the time, generosity, and talent of its parishioners. A vibrant parish pastoral council oversees the multifaceted ministries and committees that serve Christ the King: Community Outreach plans, evaluates, and implements social justice efforts in our community and as far as Haiti; Parish Life connects us to each other in the celebration of sacramental, liturgical, and traditional events; Adult and Youth Faith Formation guide parishioners in religious education as it relates to the secular world; and the Worship Committee weaves together myriad roles to create a wonderful tapestry of faith community.

Christ the King, Abingdon, has been blessed in many ways. A beautiful worship center stands on a hill as a symbol of a close-knit community called to reach out to its neighbors and the world to share its gifts.

Church of the Vietnamese Martyrs

Many Vietnamese Catholics left Vietnam when the communist forces took over the country in late April 1975. A fair portion of these Vietnamese refugees resettled in Richmond due to the moderate weather, decent jobs, proximity to the ocean and to Washington, D.C.

Under the leadership of Rev. John Trong Tran, the Vietnamese Catholic community in Richmond was established during the Christmas 1977 celebration. Bishop Walter Sullivan expressed his love and support to our newly formed community, allowing us the use of facilities at Saint Joseph's Villa.

By 1983, the Vietnamese Catholic population in Richmond increased to 500 people. In May of that same year, Bishop Sullivan issued a directive to establish the Vietnamese Martyrs Parish in Richmond, appointing Rev. Joseph Chin Dang as the pastor. The Diocese of Richmond provided two buildings located on West Clopton Street in Richmond for use as a church and rectory. Finally having a church of their own, many volunteers dedicated their time, materials, and efforts to renovate the old building into a respectable place of worship.

From 1989 to 1999, the number of parishioners doubled and the need for new church facilities was recognized. In May 1998, the Diocese granted the parish a large parcel of land on Patterson Avenue, to construct a new church, parish hall, and rectory. On Thanksgiving Day 1999, the parishioners of the Church of the Vietnamese Martyrs held their first Mass in the new facilities. The parish had a Eucharistic Youth Group where the youth were able to participate at Mass and in youth activities.

A small house was built in the rear of the church and was blessed in August 2005.

In 2010, the parish established the Vinh Son Liem Sunday Religious and Vietnamese Language school. As the religious education and Vietnamese language programs continued to flourish, the homily in the second Sunday Masses were given in both English and Vietnamese, helping the children understand and become more engaged with the message of God.

Our parish is blessed with great support from the Diocese, strong spiritual leaders over the years, and many dedicated volunteers performing countless tasks. Significant changes have been made over the years to improve the religious, Vietnamese language education, liturgy services, development of faith, and

parish facilities, resulting in the number of registered families to increase to 310. The fruits of hard work and dedication are evident in every aspect of our parish, and we are committed to continuing our growth in catechism, community fellowship, and sustaining our Vietnamese culture and tradition.

Church of Francis de Sales

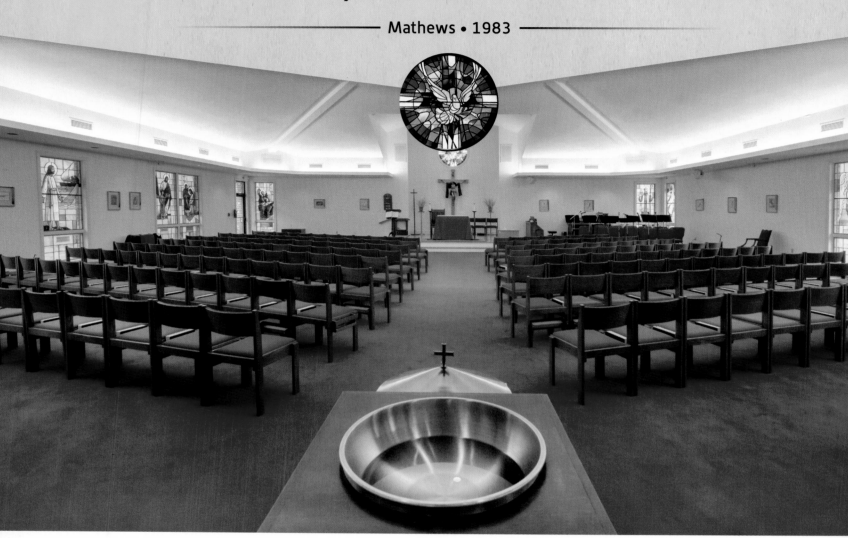

The establishment of a Catholic Community in rural Mathews, Virginia, was always a dream of Catholic residents. In 1980, Father John Dougher, an Oblate of Francis de Sales, was assigned as associate pastor at Saint Therese Catholic Church in Gloucester and was given the task of missionary outreach to Catholics in Middlesex and Mathews.

On December 13, 1980, Father Dougher celebrated the first Mass for Mathews Catholics at Salem Methodist Church. The seeds for a future Mathews parish were sown. The desire for a mission parish in Mathews was seen, but it would have to wait until a location could be found.

In the meantime, Father Dougher encouraged a weekly prayer group, he believed it would lead the way to a parish formation.

The weekly prayer group met for a year. On May 23, 1982, after obtaining a list of Catholics in Mathews, the prayer group sponsored a picnic and people shared that they would like a Mass. Soon after, monthly Mass in Mathews began and was held at Kingston Episcopal parish hall.

In 1983, a meeting was held; those attending the meeting indicated a willingness to start a Parish in Mathews. With permission of

Saint Therese's council Mathews County Catholics sought the approval of Bishop Walter Sullivan. There was enough evidence that Mathews should be established as a Mission. On July 2, 1983, the first Mass of Mathews Catholic Mission was held.

Bishop Sullivan visited the mission on September 3, 1983, and he recognized the need for a permanent building site. That same month the pastor of Kingston Parish offered the use of Trinity Church. The first Mass at Trinity Church was celebrated on Saturday, November 5, 1983.

Soon many activities began at the Mission; a fundraising booth at the local market, a bloodmobile for the Red Cross, home delivered meals, a homebound religious education program.

Bishop Sullivan dedicated the new Sanctuary on January 24, 1988. Thirty years later, the Church of Francis de Sales continues to grow with new renovations and activities and is home to more than 150 families. Through the years, the parishioners have been steadfast in their resolve to build their faith as they build their church.

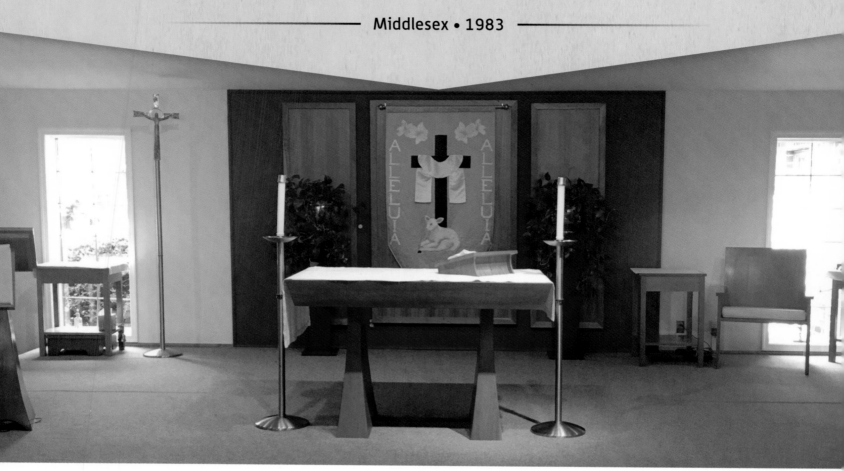

Church of the Visitation

The Church of the Visitation was named by Bishop Walter Sullivan at the July 1, 1983, at a meeting that designated the Middlesex Catholic Community a parish. The scattered group of Catholics in this rural county had been rounded up by a Panama hat-clad priest on a moped in the early 1980s. Parish founder Father John Dougher, an assistant at Saint Therese in Gloucester, had gathered the group at local churches and at the rented Freeshade Community Center for several years. Now the committed mission group promised their own skilled labor, fundraising, and oyster stew for Bishop Sullivan, in return for a church of their own. Two years later, on September 8, 1985, the dedication Mass was celebrated by Bishop Sullivan in the little church near the Chesapeake Bay.

At the time of the church's 20th anniversary in September of 2005, the parish had grown from an original forty families to 165. Changes already included a classroom wing, rectory, and the development of a Catholic cemetery to serve Middlesex, Gloucester, and Mathews counties. After bursting the seams of our multi-purpose worship space, the church embarked on a building campaign that resulted in an enlarged worship space and a new administrative area. The addition was dedicated by Bishop Sullivan, now Bishop Emeritus, on September 21, 2008, on our Silver Jubilee. Future plans include a new Sanctuary and conversion of the present space into a fellowship hall.

God has truly blessed our growing community through the years. Each new parishioner came with his or her own special talent, which was always just what the young parish needed at that time. Over the years, ministries have changed as our rural parish has changed. We have traveled with our youth to Haiti, worked locally with the needy, knitted for prayer and friendship, held a community yard sale, established fundraising memorials for Father Boddie, and feasted with the Knights of Columbus. We will continue to adapt and expand our community outreach.

The unwavering faith of the Catholic population in Middlesex County in the early 1980s led to the establishment of a vibrant and dynamic Roman Catholic community that eagerly seeks to grow and flourish into the future. The spirit which built the Church of the Visitation continues today.

Church of the Resurrection

In 1977, eight couples who had moved to Smith Mountain Lake started having Mass in the home of Pat and Harry Marlar. As the Catholic population grew to 70 families, they moved the Mass to the Moneta Elementary School. In 1984, the parish was given the name Church of the Resurrection by Bishop Walter Sullivan. As they continued to grow, Bethlehem Methodist Church offered the use of their Sanctuary on Saturday nights.

The year 1985 saw 65 registered families and 25 part-time parishioners. In May 1987, the parish broke ground for the first church for Resurrection. In seven years, they had finished paying the mortgage.

The parish was then able to return the favor done for them and serve as a temporary home to the new Trinity Ecumenical Parish from 1988 - 1997.

The ever-growing Catholic population brought the need for expansion. On November 23, 1997, the larger addition to the sanctuary, a new social hall, and several classrooms for a Religious Education Program were dedicated by Bishop Sullivan.

The Parish of Resurrection continues to be a strong presence in the Smith Mountain Lake area which includes three counties in Virginia: Franklin, Bedford, and Pittsylvania. Church of the Resurrection now includes a lovely cemetery and a Labyrinth garden.

Saint Francis of Assisi

Rocky Mount • 1984

The Catholic population in the foothills of the Blue Ridge Mountains was sparse until after World War II. In the 1950's, there were enough Catholics to necessitate sending "Saint Mary of the Highways," the traveling missionary priests, to administer the sacraments and to minister in Franklin County. Mass was celebrated in parking lots from a mobile chapel serving as a temporary altar. Confessions were heard, and babies were baptized.

In the 1960's, priests from neighboring counties would celebrate Masses from time to time at various locations in Rocky Mount. In 1978, a small group of Catholics gathered monthly in local homes for Masses celebrated by priests from Our Lady of Nazareth parish in Roanoke.

With continued growth, a parish community was established in 1984 administered by Sisters Mary Heyser and Eveline Murray, both Religious Sisters of the Sacred Heart of Mary. At that time, Mass was celebrated on Saturday evenings at Trinity Church in Rocky Mount with priests from parishes in the Roanoke area and Saint Joseph's in Martinsville. Parishioners' eventually located land in Rocky Mount and purchased property for the parish church on Glennwood Drive. On February 22, 1987, the Feast of the Chair of Saint Peter, the partially finished structure was solemnly dedicated to Saint Francis of Assisi by Bishop David Foley, Auxiliary Bishop of Richmond. Priests at Saint Joseph's in Martinsville served as non-resident pastors.

The Catholic population continued to grow throughout the 1990's and many Spanish-speaking families joined the parish. As the parish outgrew the existing facility, it was decided to expand the church to its current size. The new fellowship hall, the current nave, and apse were constructed and dedicated in May of 1998 by Bishop Sullivan. In 1999, the parish purchased the rectory on Orchard Avenue in Rocky Mount. The parish grotto was blessed and dedicated to the Blessed Virgin Mary. In the early part of the new century, the parish completed the existing basement fellowship hall, converted part of it to classrooms for religious education and added a professional kitchen. During this period the parish was able to sponsor a parish Knights of Columbus Saint Francis of Assisi Council #14509.

Saint Francis parishioners participate in the Rocky Mount Soup Kitchen, the Roanoke area Gift of Life Committee, and have a giving tree apostolate during the holidays and for back-to-school. The parish twins with Saint Anne in Trianon, Haiti, and the Followers of Francis apostolate works diligently to raise funds for various parish and community needs.

Updates were recently made to the commons and pastor's office, and some modifications were made to the apse area. Through the sacrificial gifts of parishioners in the "Living Our Mission" campaign, the parish was able to update the nave and apse with a wooden floor, marble altar area, the installation of pews, and beautiful images of the Sacred Heart, Our Lady of Grace, Saint Joseph, and Our Lady of Guadalupe as well as a large Christmas crèche. Saint Francis of Assisi has continued to grow in numbers and in its diversity in recent years and looks forward to another century of faith and outreach to the community.

Saint Kim Taegon

Richmond • 1986

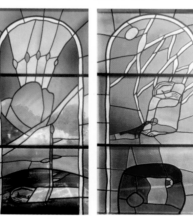

Saint Kim Taegon Church is a Korean Catholic parish located in Richmond, Virginia. Its history dates back forty years. On December 25th, 1977, four Korean families from Saint Elizabeth Catholic Church joined together and decided to form a community that would allow Korean Catholics to meet one another, share a common culture and language, and most importantly, come together to grow their faith. Thanks to these families, who hoped for such a gathering, the Korean Catholic Community was established.

Father Dennis Karamitis kindly joined these families once a month to provide and celebrate Sunday Mass. By August 1978, this small yet dedicated community grew as twelve new members were baptized. Then in September of the same year, the location of Sunday Mass moved to Saint Peter Catholic Church. In June, 1983, the Korean Catholic Community was gifted with a wonderful blessing. A Korean priest, Father Jong Chul Lee, arrived. With Father Lee, by November 1983, eight new members were baptized. They were the first to be baptized in their native language.

Finally, after almost 10 years since the start of their gathering, the Korean Catholic Community found their newly established parish on Logandale Avenue in Richmond. The church was named Saint Kim Taegon Korean Church after the first

Korean Catholic priest in Korea, and to this day, it is the home and loving parish of many Korean American Catholic families within the tri-city area and surrounding counties of Richmond.

Since then, all members of Saint Kim Taegon join for not only Sunday Mass, but daily Mass as well, to celebrate their faith during Mass in their native Korean language. For the students and children of Saint Kim who may be more proficient in the English language, English readings are also provided allowing them to be able to embrace the culture and language of their families and faith simultaneously. Being in

Richmond City, international Catholic students from Korea studying and attending Virginia Commonwealth University (VCU) are welcomed and able to attend weekly Mass. The members of the parish are always working together to ensure that these students are given the best environment to continue practicing their faith even while abroad and to have a home away from home. Today, all at Saint Kim Taegon Korean Catholic Church are forever thankful to be able to come together to celebrate not only their shared culture and language but also their Christian faith.

Saint Luke

Saint Luke had its humble beginnings in May 1986 when Bishop Walter Sullivan approved a new church to be known as Saint Luke in southern Virginia Beach. The first Mass was celebrated on June 29, 1986, at Indian Lakes School with about 35 families. In July 1986, the Diocese of Richmond purchased three acres of land with a house on Salem Road. The house became the parish house and rectory where religious education classes and parish meetings were held. The first Confirmation and First Communion candidates received the sacraments in April and May of 1987 respectively.

In July 1988, Bishop Sullivan bought a nine-acre property adjacent to the parish house and rectory to build a church. The need to have a bigger

space for a growing parish caused the parish to move to the Rosemont Forest School in 1989 and again to the Glenwood School cafeteria until the summer of 1993. On Sunday, there were two Masses and religious education classes for 247 children. However, Saturday Vigil Mass, faith formation classes, and parish meetings were still held in the parish house and rectory.

In 1992, a ground-breaking ceremony marked the start of building a church. The cornerstone was blessed by Bishop Sullivan in February 1993, and on July 11, the Bishop dedicated the new church. In October 1998, the Hispanic Apostolate of Cristo Rey joined Saint Luke with a Spanish Mass each Sunday that further enriched the cultural diversity of the parish.

Several improvements were made. Chairs with kneelers replaced the metal chairs. Daily Mass was celebrated, and a monthly Filipino Mass was added. First Friday Mass was introduced, and Christmas Eve Mass became a trilingual event. In 2005, several dedicated parishioners began Eucharistic Adoration. The Adoration reached a peak of seventy hours per week with overnight adoration for two nights, concluding with Benediction on Saturday morning.

The success of Eucharistic Adoration initiated a renovation of an existing small chapel and storage space into a larger Eucharistic Chapel in 2006. The same year saw the formation of the John Paul the Great Council of the Knights of Columbus and the Ladies Auxiliary at Saint Luke, as well as a revival of the youth ministry.

In 2009, two trailers were acquired for the office and religious education

spaces. The sacristy was renovated, storage was added, and exterior lights were installed around the property. Saint Luke celebrated its Silver Jubilee in May 2011, with a multilingual Mass, which has continued as our custom for holidays, Holy Days and other devotions such as the Stations of the Cross.

The initial approval for the proposed expansion and renovation of the church building was given in February 2017. Saint Luke, currently with over 600 families, maintains the "people orientation" ethos. Saint Luke's logo of three bodies under the Cross are the pillars of our strength - faith, hope, and charity. The Holy Spirit helps us to put our faith into action, echoing an invitation to everyone to join us at the Altar of the Lord as we give thanks and praise to God through Jesus Christ our Lord.

Saint John the Apostle

Virginia Beach • 1989

Although the parish of Saint John the Apostle was formally established by Bishop Walter Sullivan on May 30, 1989, its roots reach back to 1967 when some Catholic residents were given permission to have weekly Mass at a home in Sandbridge Beach. In 1973, with the number of participants increasing, celebration of Mass was relocated to Saint Simon by the Sea Episcopal Chapel.

In 1987, Star of the Sea Catholic Church was asked by Bishop Sullivan to organize a committee to research the logistics of a new parish in the southern portions of Star of the Sea boundaries. Based on the committee's conclusions, a site was selected at Painter Lane and Sandbridge Road. The following year, celebration of a Saturday evening Mass was started at Tabernacle United Methodist Church, and Bishop Sullivan formally named this community "The Catholic Community of Southeast Virginia," established as a mission of Star of the Sea.

When the parish was formally established in 1989, Bishop Sullivan assigned the name "Saint John the Apostle" to complement the other

three parishes in Virginia Beach, which bore the names of the other three Evangelists. The present church was blessed by Bishop Sullivan on June 24, 1995.

Saint John the Apostle School opened on August 19, 2002. The school facility would provide classroom space for the religious education program, as well as providing space for other parish activities.

Over the years, the number of registered families has increased, and further expansion and renovation of the church sanctuary and facility have become necessary. Two side wings were dedicated by Bishop DiLorenzo on January 15, 2005. Phase One of our Parish expansion plan was accomplished in 2011 when the parish office, which had previously been located on the first floor of the rectory, was moved over to the church, the church Commons was expanded, and new meeting rooms were built. Phase Two took place over the summer of 2015, with a $2 million renovation of the church sanctuary. A new parish assembly hall will be built in the years to come, which will be Phase Three.

From the humble beginnings, back in 1967, to its establishment as the latest parish in Virginia Beach, Saint John the Apostle now supports a parish community of 3,000 families. The Parish continues to minister to this growing community, and to take on the challenges of bringing the message of Jesus Christ and His Church to a new generation.

Prior to 1984, Catholic families of the Isle of Wight County traveled to Newport News, Hampton, Suffolk or Portsmouth to attend Mass. In March of 1984, a meeting was held with area priests and about eighty Catholics and plans for the first Catholic Church in Smithfield were set. The Catholic community of Smithfield was a mission of Saint Mary of the Presentation in Suffolk, Virginia.

Mass was originally celebrated on Saturday at the Christ Episcopal Church with the first Mass on July 21, 1984, celebrated by Reverend Chris Haydinger. Approximately fifty families attended. Religious education classes were held in parishioners' homes. The parish's name, "Church of the Good Shepherd," was chosen. Groundbreaking for the new church took place in February of 1992 for the first phase of construction of the first building. On September

27, 1992, the new church was consecrated at a Mass presided by Bishop Walter Sullivan. Finally, the Isle of Wight had its first Catholic Church.

By June 2000, the church community had grown to almost 200 families and was ready to begin the second phase of building. Groundbreaking took place on June 18, 2004, and the new sanctuary was dedicated on June 26, 2005. The new building, an extension of the original, has seating capacity for 560, and a daily Mass chapel for 50.

With 250 active families in the parish, religious education programs are offered for all ages. The parish has a twinning program with Saint Anthony of Padua in Haiti. The Mission of Hope ministry houses individuals in need and parishioners assist through the Christian Outreach Program. The parish also partners with United Christian Ministries to provide financial support for those in Isle of Wight County who need

housing, utilities and other assistance. In 2013, the rectory was purchased for the resident pastor. As a Catholic community in Smithfield, the Church of the Good Shepherd continues to grow in faith and to share its gifts as they welcome everyone through its doors.

Saint Elizabeth Ann Seton

— Quinton • 1986 —

In early 1986, a small group of Catholics living in New Kent came together to organize an effort to have a Catholic Mission established in the county. At a meeting with Reverend J. Scott Duarte, pastor of Our Lady of the Blessed Sacrament Parish, comprised of King William, King and Queen and New Kent Counties, they presented the needs of the Catholic community and the desire to establish a new parish in New Kent. Bishop Walter Sullivan established the New Kent County Catholic Mission which was given the name Saint Elizabeth Ann Seton Catholic Mission in late 1986. Father Duarte served as pastor of the Catholic community, along with two Trinitarian Sisters, Sister Mary Alma Jankowski and Sister Mary Agnes Nagle during the first year.

The group obtained permission from New Kent County to use the auditorium of George W. Watkins Elementary School for Sunday Mass. Every Sunday and Holy Day, vestments and supplies needed for Mass were brought to the school and an "altar" was set up on the stage of the auditorium. Father Duarte would drive the 20 miles from West Point to the school to celebrate Sunday Mass.

Benedictine Priory in Richmond and other priests came weekly to New Kent County to celebrate Sunday Mass. The joyful enthusiasm of the small Catholic community supported a regular Wednesday evening Mass and fellowship which was held in a member's home. An active Religious Education program made it possible for the children to receive First Reconciliation and First Holy Communion as well as Confirmation. The Saint Elizabeth Ann Seton Mission congregation was able to meet at Watkins School for a few years but then needed to find another location for Sunday services. A converted barbershop in Quinton was the meeting place for three months until the pastor of Kentwood Heights Baptist Church offered the use of their new sanctuary on Saturday evenings for Mass. This generous ecumenical agreement lasted until the Saint Elizabeth Ann Seton Mission grew and was able to purchase the current property on Pocahontas Trail near Bottom's Bridge.

The church property was dedicated on September 7, 1991. A multi-purpose building and an open pavilion were the first buildings on the property. Saint Elizabeth Ann Seton Catholic Mission was elevated to parish status.

In 2008, Fr. Duarte returned and the parish grew by almost seventy-five percent, so the multi-purpose building has been renovated to serve the parish as a church, and the open pavilion was enclosed and turned into a social hall. A Religious Education building has been erected, and a parish rectory has been purchased. Saint Elizabeth Ann Seton offers three Masses each weekend. Plans are now underway for a new church building that will accommodate the needs of the parish into the future.

Saint Elizabeth Ann Seton Parish looks forward to the day when our new church will stand proudly as a visible Catholic presence for the counties of New Kent and Charles City.

Saint Kateri Tekakwitha

On Sept 7, 2016, Saint Kateri Tekakwitha Catholic Community joyfully celebrated its 30th anniversary of service and ministry. Bishop Walter Sullivan, in May 1986, established a parish in Poquoson and Tabb. The first Mass was held on June 1, 1986, in a private home and eventually moved to Poquoson High School where Sunday Mass was celebrated for 10 years. Parishioners voted to name the parish Blessed Kateri Tekakwitha to show a historical connection to the local Native American population, and in recognition of the first Native American candidate for Canonization. At the Mass for the official founding of the parish on Sept. 7, 1986, Bishop Sullivan challenged the approximately 90 charter families to become "a parish family following in the footsteps of Jesus." The charter members chose to institute a Biblical tithing model, pledging 5% of our income to the parish and 5% to other causes of our choice. Our tithing calls for a definite decision regarding our stewardship of the gifts we have received from God.

In the spirit of service to those around us, ministry has been one of the fundamental tenets at Saint Kateri. Today parishioners are challenged to support and participate in ministries which include Social Justice, the twinning relationship with our sister parish in Haiti, St. Michel in Hinche; the Thrift Shop / Food Pantry; PORT (feeding the homeless); and the prison ministry, Kairos. Our faith formation programs offer learning opportunities through bible study groups, RCIA, and House Church. Religious education for grades PK-4 through 12 includes regular classes and sacramental preparation. There are ministry opportunities in liturgy, administration and hospitality.

The commitment to ministry was evident in the acquisition and selection of facilities. In September of 1987, a Thrift Shop and Food Pantry was established in Poquoson. The initial facility purchased was large enough to house the outreach ministry and the church offices. While providing support to the community, the offices were used for the planning and construction of our current worship/multi-purpose space. Saint Kateri Tekakwitha Catholic Church was dedicated on March 27, 1996.

The parish also offers events for community growth including: Catholic Heart Workcamp for teens, an annual talent show, a community pancake supper, Saint Nicholas Breakfast, Men's prayer breakfast, Mom's group, and the Pentecost Pot Luck picnic.

Through 30 years this community has continued to remain true to its founding principles. As challenged by Bishop Sullivan 30 years ago, "We are a parish family following in the footsteps of Jesus."

Saints Peter and Paul

— Palmyra • 1986 —

From humble beginnings in 1983, Saints Peter and Paul Catholic Church has become a vibrant and growing community in Fluvanna County. Father John Cummings was named pastor of Saint Joseph (parent parish of Saints Peter and Paul Mission church) in Columbia, and Saint George in Scottsville. In January of 1985, he celebrated the first Mass for Lake Monticello families in a parishioner's home and, as numbers increased, they were invited to hold Saturday evening Mass at Effort Baptist Church. In September, the first "Town Hall" meeting was held for the Catholic Community of Fluvanna.

Bishop Walter Sullivan visited the mission in June of 1986, celebrated Mass on the Feast Day of Saints Peter and Paul, met with the Parish Council after Mass, and named the mission church Saints

Peter and Paul. Parishioners were notified that Father Cummings had bequeathed a significant amount from his estate to build a chapel. A land search was initiated and, in Spring of 1987, land on Route 53 was located that would meet the needs for building the first church.

The land purchase was approved by the Diocese, and a two-year process for building a church began. In 1990, the groundbreaking took place, and in October, Bishop Sullivan dedicated the new Saints Peter and Paul Catholic Church for 100 registered families.

Since its founding, Saints Peter and Paul has experienced phenomenal growth, and the local community expressed a real need for a Parish Center and Educational Building to support that growth. Saints Peter and Paul initiated a Capital Campaign, "Building Our Future, United in Christ" in 2013, broke ground and began construction of a new Parish Hall and Learning Center. Named Saint Francis Center to honor Francis, our Pope, our Bishop and our Pastor, Father Gerald Francis Musuubire, the grand hall provides more seating, a full commercial kitchen, stage and sound system, ample parking and is available for community functions and events. The Saint Nicholas Learning Center complete with 11 classrooms offers full and half day, year-round programs for Pre-K and Kindergarten children. The formal dedication was celebrated in May of 2015 by Bishop Francis X. DiLorenzo.

The parish's newest addition is a Cemetery, Columbarium and Resurrection Garden located on the church property. The road leading to the Cemetery is lined with the Stations of the Cross. Dedication was held in May of 2016.

More than 500 families are members of this faith community today who have dedicated themselves to praising God through liturgical, educational and social service ministries.

This vibrant parish community currently supports more than 37 ministries providing both education and pastoral ministry services to children, youth and adults and conducting a vigorous social ministry outreach program both locally and internationally.

Church of the Transfiguration

— Fincastle • 1989 —

The first Catholic Mass celebrated in Botetourt County occurred on August 5, 1981, at the home of Richard and Rosalie Sloan. Father Scott Duarte, an associate pastor of Saint Andrew Catholic Church in Roanoke, led the service. Masses continued at Rader Funeral Home in Troutville until October 1981.

In February 1988, regular monthly meetings began at Rader Funeral Home to spur interest in a Catholic Church community in Botetourt County. In May of that year, Saint Mark United Methodist Church in Daleville opened its doors to the new Catholic community for worship, fellowship, and subsequently, religious education. On October 1, 1988, Bishop Walter Sullivan celebrated Mass and declared the site a Mass Station of Saint Andrew. Father William O'Brien served as pastor and Father John Abe served as facilitator of the Mass Station.

In May of 1989, Bishop Sullivan elevated the Mass Station to a Mission Church. On August 5, 1989, Bishop Sullivan established a new Catholic parish in Botetourt County – Church of the Transfiguration. Sister M. Madeline Abdelnour

became our first pastoral coordinator. Mass moved from Saint Mark United Methodist to Fincastle United Methodist Church. In August of 1991, Sister Madeline retired and was succeeded in January 1992 by Sister Eveline Murray. Plans for a permanent home for the congregation began.

Over four acres of land along US 220, just south of Fincastle, were purchased in September 1992, and construction of a permanent church began. On October 2, 1994, the Church of the Transfiguration sanctuary was dedicated. In 1999, a 14-room education wing was built.

In May 2004, Father Ken Shuping became Transfiguration's first resident pastor, followed in 2008 by Father Rene Castillo as pastor of both Transfiguration and Saint John the Evangelist in New Castle while also continuing his duties as pastor of Saint Gerard in Roanoke.

Our second resident pastor, Father Steve McNally arrived in July 2009. Father McNally continues to serve as pastor for Transfiguration as well as Saint John the Evangelist in New Castle. Father McNally has celebrated both his 25th and 30th anniversaries of priesthood here at Transfiguration.

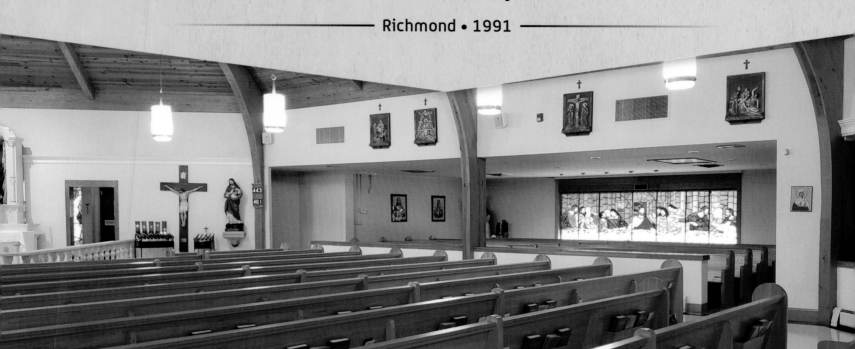

Saint Joseph

One of many treasures of the Catholic Church is the Traditional Latin Mass. In the last years of the 20th century, two men, Charles Furlough and Michael Reardon, requested a place to celebrate the "Extraordinary Form of the Roman Rite" from Bishop Walter Sullivan. Bishop gave his approval with the understanding that this new group would be a ministry of Saint Benedict Parish. Father Adrian Harmening, O.S.B., the recently retired principal of Benedictine High School, agreed to be its chaplain. On May 12, 1991, about 35 people gathered in the chapel at the old orphanage, Saint Joseph Villa, and assisted Bishop Sullivan in offering the inaugural Mass.

The community was the first of its kind in the U.S. and received some national attention. The chapel became a destination for Catholics seeking this liturgy, where Latin and Gregorian Chant had pride of place. Attendance soon grew to a consistent 200 faithful. For 10 years the community flourished, especially with the help of many dedicated volunteers. Notably, two vocations were fostered at this time: Hélène Fabiato (Sister Marie-Hélène) made vows with the Sisters of the Visitation at Monte Maria Monastery in Rockville, Virginia in May, 2001; Neal Nichols was ordained a priest for the Fraternity of Saint Peter in June, 2001.

In 2001, the time had come for the community to find its own property. With Bishop Sullivan's approval, the community acquired a church building in Bon Air. The former Pentecostal church required renovations. The whole direction of the church was reversed, and a Catholic altar, altar steps and communion rail were added. On November 3, 2002, Bishop Sullivan presided

at the Mass of Dedication. In a surprise move, he elevated the community to a canonical Catholic parish, saying: "Why did I say yes? I aid yes because the church and specifically Pope John Paul II said yes ... we are all equal in God's eyes... And so today this church is a visible sign that you have a permanent home and that you – Saint Joseph's Church – is here to stay."

The new Saint Joseph Parish of Bon Air experienced a period of exciting growth. Being master of its own house meant that daily Masses, classes and social events were convened with greater freedom. Eventually, another Benedictine, Father Joseph Mary Lukyamuzi came on to help Father Adrian. The Parish hired a Religious Education coordinator, organized a Catholic lending library and designated a permanent room to sell religious goods. A renovation committee continued to make improvements, such as a beautiful daily Mass chapel and grand vestibule.

After 20 years of faithful service, the founding pastor retired. Bishop DiLorenzo, "In order to ensure continuity in ministry for the future," invited the Priestly Fraternity of Saint Peter, a society which specializes in the Extraordinary Form, to serve the parish. Since July 2011, the Fraternity has supplied two priests to staff the parish.

As testimony to God's grace, the parish is now home to 300 families and new vocations are continuing to be nourished. Another blessing came in the form of the parish's Silver Jubilee. To mark the occasion, several renovations were completed, including a new entry way, new offices, and an expanded social hall which was named after the parish's founding pastor. The hall was dedicated with great joy on January 15, 2017.

Saint Joseph Parish has abundant reasons to give glory to God: the blessings of the past, the security of the present moment, and the hope for the future.

Saint Benedict

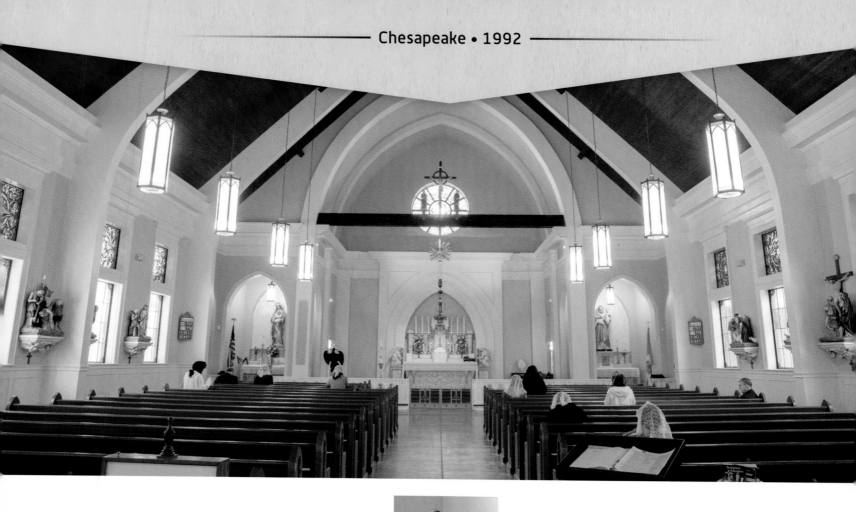

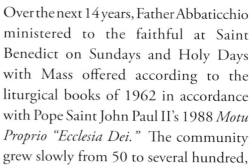

Chesapeake's Saint Benedict Chapel was founded in 1992 as a mission of Saint Gregory the Great Church in Virginia Beach. Formerly named Our Lady of the Rosary, the chapel had been established on private land by a group of lay Catholics devoted to the Tridentine Rite and was regularized with the approval of Bishop Walter Sullivan. Father Damian Abbaticchio, O.S.B., a Benedictine monk of Saint Vincent Archabbey, who had retired in residence at Saint Gregory's, agreed to serve as Chaplain at the Bishop's behest. At this point, Saint Benedict was one of only two chapels in the United States where the Tridentine Rite was in exclusive use.

Over the next 14 years, Father Abbaticchio ministered to the faithful at Saint Benedict on Sundays and Holy Days with Mass offered according to the liturgical books of 1962 in accordance with Pope Saint John Paul II's 1988 *Motu Proprio "Ecclesia Dei."* The community grew slowly from 50 to several hundred, combining the original core group of traditionally minded Catholics with a substantial Filipino contingent and sizeable number of transient military personnel from nearby bases.

In late 2005, the Richmond Diocese requested the Priestly Fraternity of Saint Peter (F.S.S.P.) to assume responsibility for the Chapel. During this time, the Chapel began the construction of a new and larger church, designed by Franck & Lohsen Architects of Washington, D.C.

In 2008, Father Neal Nichols, F.S.S.P., assumed responsibility for the community. The new church was dedicated on March 5, 2011, by Bishop Francis X. DiLorenzo. He subsequently made Saint Benedict Catholic Church a personal parish on January 1, 2012, releasing it for the first time from the oversight of Saint Gregory the Great. Saint Benedict installed a magnificent Berghaus Organ in 2014, providing fitting accompaniment to the beautiful liturgy.

Spurred by the construction of the large new church, Saint Benedict has grown steadily to a parish of 261 families including many young children. Saint Benedict has a special charism to promote the spiritual growth and development of its parishioners dedicated to the preservation of the Holy Mass, Sacraments, and traditional devotions in the Extraordinary Form in cooperation with and in obedience to the Bishop of Richmond. All-day Eucharistic Adoration is held every Wednesday.

Highlights of the year at Saint Benedict include: The Feast of Our Lady of the Rosary of La Naval each October; a special "Triduum of Feasts" on Laetare Sunday each Lent

honoring our patron Saint Benedict as well as Saints Patrick and Joseph; and regular "Family Fun Days" following Sunday Mass during the warmer months. Additionally, the parish sends a sizeable contingent to the Annual Eucharistic Procession on the Virginia Beach Boardwalk each Fall. All are welcome to join our community!

Saint Michael

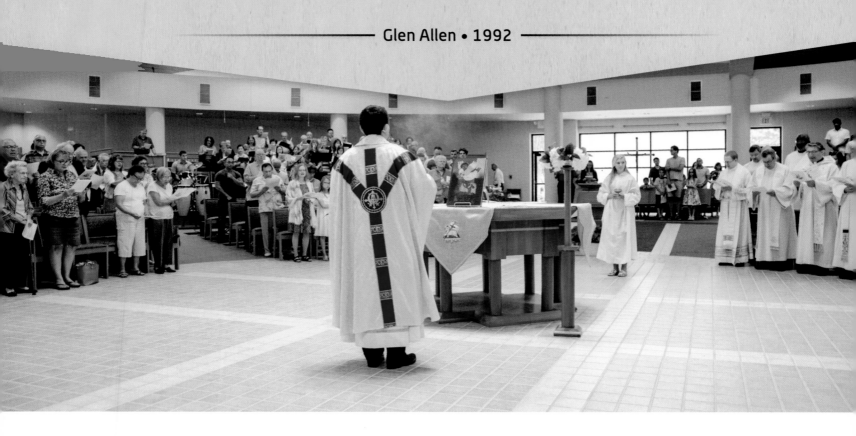

Saint Michael parish came into being in December 1991, when Bishop Walter Sullivan began the process of forming a new parish, to be located on property owned by the Diocese of Richmond on Springfield Road. An initial group of 150 families from surrounding parishes undertook the creation of the new faith community and, with the Bishop's approval, chose the name Saint Michael the Archangel.

The Diocese provided startup funds and Saint Michael held its first Mass in May 1992. From 1992 until 1996, the parish operated in space borrowed from other churches in the area, Short Pump Middle School, and Bennet Funeral Home. In 1996, Saint Michael had 1,000 registered families and celebrated completion of its first building on the Springfield Road property.

The new building included a multi-purpose room large enough to accommodate 600 chairs when used as a worship space, a Blessed Sacrament Chapel,

Commons area, and adjacent classroom and meeting rooms. In 2002, a second building project was completed, giving the parish a permanent worship space and freeing the multi-purpose area for other activities.

As the parish has continued grow, two subsequent expansions have taken place. In 2013, expansion and renovation of existing space was completed to accommodate faith formation programs, create additional meeting space for parish groups, and enlarge staff and administrative areas.

In 2016, Saint Michael ran its own capital campaign in conjunction with the Diocesan Living Our Mission campaign. The parish quickly met its initial goal of $3,300,000, and went on to exceed its challenge goal of $4,000,000. This money made possible the construction of a community building to provide space for parish youth programs, the Knights of Columbus, and a range of activities that can no longer be accommodated in the existing building. Completion of that facility, named the Lake House, took place and was dedicated on June

30, 2018, by Bishop Barry C. Knestout, Thirteenth Bishop of Richmond.

Father Dan Brady has led the parish through two successful capital campaigns in over 12 years as pastor. Today, Saint Michael is a parish of 3,000 registered households with a full and part-time staff of more than 20 individuals. It has become more diverse, with parishioners from all over the world, including a sizeable Indian community. Its faith formation program now has a staff of six and its classes extend from preschool through the Rite of Christian Initiation for Adults. Its Human Concerns programs include twinning relationships with Holy Family Parish in the Appalachian region of Virginia, Saint John the Baptist Parish in Dos Palais, Haiti, and Saint Elizabeth Parish in Richmond. Its Job Assistance Ministry, begun during the recession of 2008-2009, continues to offer services to those seeking employment.

As Saint Michael Catholic Church celebrated its 25th anniversary, it is a vibrant and still growing community.

Saint Olaf

Bishop Walter Sullivan began to consider a new Catholic community in the Williamsburg area in 1986. With the rapid growth of the Catholic population, Saint Bede, the only Catholic Church in Williamsburg, had grown beyond its existing capacity. In the summer of 1989, Bishop Sullivan established a new faith community, to be called Saint Bede's Norge Mission and directed the Diocese to purchase a plot of land adjacent to Route 60 (Richmond Road).

On Saturday, September 16, 1989, the first Mass was celebrated in Our Saviour Lutheran Church. Reverend George Zahn, pastor of Saint Bede, presided over the new mission which consisted of about 40 families. In 1992, with 100 households, Bishop Sullivan announced that a new parish would be designated with priests from Saint Bede continuing to administer the sacraments, and named the new parish Saint Olaf, Patron of Norway, Catholic Church. Donna Young

Whitley was appointed as Pastoral Coordinator. To aid in the establishment of the parish, a generous monetary gift, a tabernacle, a chalice, and religious education books for all grades were given by the parishioners of Holy Redeemer by the Sea in Kill Devil Hills, North Carolina.

During the years from 1992-1995, Mass was celebrated at Our Saviour Lutheran Church, then Norge Elementary School, and later at Toano Women's Club. A house was purchased adjacent to the land that had already been purchased to use as office, meeting space and the Food Pantry. In 1994, a groundbreaking ceremony was celebrated in anticipation of the first building and on July 29, 1995, the Feast of Saint Olaf,

Bishop Sullivan dedicated the Saint Olaf Worship and Fellowship Center. Saint Olaf was a thriving Catholic community of more than 200 families. After the last Mass held at the Toano Women's Club, the Blessed Sacrament was brought in procession from the Club to the new church and placed in the tabernacle. At the dedication of the church, the parish adopted the words by which our parish continues to live: "All Are Welcome." Embodying those words, ministers were present for the dedication from the Lutheran, Episcopal, Methodist, Mennonite, Christian Scientist, Presbyterian, and Byzantine Churches and the Jewish Synagogue along with Bishop Sullivan, parishioners of Saint Olaf and the priests of Saint Bede.

In 1999, Reverend John Ridgell was named the first pastor of Saint Olaf. The parish had grown to 400 families by that time. During his tenure, the Food Pantry was expanded, participation in lay ministry increased and, in 2003, the debt for

building the church was retired. In 2006, the parish welcomed Reverend Peter Creed as pastor and during his leadership at Saint Olaf, our faith community grew to 600 families. The building was enlarged to accommodate increased seating and included a new Commons for fellowship.

In 2012, Reverend Thomas Mattingly became pastor, just in time to celebrate our 20th anniversary as a parish. Under his leadership, the debt for the expansion was retired, allowing planning to move ahead for our long-awaited church. The parish celebrated groundbreaking on April 8, 2016, and the building was dedicated by Bishop DiLorenzo one year later.

As of this day, the faith community has grown to over 1000 families, with the growth of the population of the area. The parish continues to emphasize the importance of faith, hospitality and community, outreach and ecumenical cooperation.

Holy Spirit

O n June 11, 1994, the determined residents of Christiansburg, Virginia, gathered at the local Knights of Columbus Hall for Mass. The Diocese of Richmond, with Bishop Walter Sullivan's approval, allowed a small group of Catholics to hold Mass and determine the level of interest in a permanent church in the town of Christiansburg. After only a few short months, it was decided that there was indeed a great deal of interest and attendance, and the "Catholic Community of Christiansburg" was assigned its own priest, Reverend Louis Benoit. Holy Spirit began with Mass celebrated weekly on Saturday evenings at a very kind and generous Lutheran church. Religious education thrived with our first children celebrating First Holy Communion in 1995.

Bishop Sullivan granted us our name, Holy Spirit Catholic Church, in September 1995. With only a small number of parishioners, we knew each other by name and participation. Everyone accepted the responsibility of building a house for

God in our community. Our faith carried us through to 1997 when Bishop Sullivan purchased land for the site of our building. Every fundraiser you can imagine was held and everyone worked to make the building of our church home a reality. Our church family grew, not only in numbers but in dedication to each other to complete this gift for God.

An official groundbreaking ceremony was held in November 2002. The day was beautiful; all the church family gathered under tents assembled for the Mass and the wind blew and blew as we celebrated the gift of having land to build our church for God. The work was only beginning and we all dug in to do our part.

In June of 1998, Reverend John Prinelli was assigned to Holy Spirit and his goal was clear – to erect a home for the Holy Spirit family under his guidance and direction, and in August of 2004, we had accomplished the first phase. We celebrated with the dedication of Holy Spirit Catholic Church by Bishop Francis DiLorenzo.

Following the death of Father Prinelli in 2012, Holy Spirit was assigned several inspiring priests who left

us with a renewed dedication to each other and the determination to bring our Catholic faith to others. No longer a Saturday evening, one Mass only parish, we now offer weekday Masses, Adoration of the Blessed Sacrament, three weekend Masses and religious education classes for almost 100 children. An Hispanic community doubling the size of the parish has brought a new diversity to our celebrations.

In July 2015, Fr. Anthony O. Senyah came to our parish and, along with our newly assigned Deacon, Jose Melendez, new ministries to all our parishioners are offered with the hope for continuing our future as a diverse and faithfully prospering Catholic parish.

Our Lady of Lavang - Vietnam

Our Lady of Lavang, Norfolk

Our Lady of Lavang Vietnam is a popular parish. It has two separate communities with two churches. The church in Hampton was named "Our Lady of Vietnam Chapel." The church in Norfolk was known as "Our Lady of Lavang." Father Joseph Nguyen is pastor at both locations.

After the fall of South Vietnam in April 1975, the community of Hampton Roads had Vietnamese families come to live in the area. At first, they attended the churches in their local neighborhoods, but later they joined together under the guidance of Father Joseph Huan Tran to celebrate Sunday Mass in the Vietnamese language. These first Vietnamese immigrants to the United State after the fall of South Vietnam were well-educated and wealthy. Later, Vietnamese immigrants who came to Hampton Roads were those who escaped from their country by boats.

At this time, the community of Vietnamese Catholics grew quickly. They looked for a church to gather together on Sunday for Mass. Saint Rose of Lima opened their doors to them. They stayed at Saint Rose of Lima in Hampton for some years, and then moved to Holy Trinity in Norfolk. In 1989, the group moved to Saint Pius X in Norfolk for Sunday Liturgy, and then they went to Christ the King in Norfolk for a short time. By then, the congregation had grown greatly.

Around 1993, Bishop Walter Sullivan helped the Vietnamese Catholic congregation in Hampton Roads to build their own churches. By this time, they were large enough to have two communities: one in Norfolk, south of the Hampton Roads tunnel, and the other in Hampton, north of the tunnel. The end of 1995 marked a historic milestone for the Norfolk community when they purchased a building on the corner of

Our Lady of Vietnam, Hampton

Campostella Road and Filmore Street in Norfolk to become their church. Bishop Walter Sullivan dedicated the church and named it Our Lady of Lavang.

On the 8th day of August in the year 2008, Bishop Francis Xavier DiLorenzo erected the personal parish of Our Lady of Lavang-Vietnam.

In July 2016, the congregation in Hampton purchased the Jewish temple on 318 Whealton Road, and renovated the building to make it their own Catholic Church. This new church was consecrated and dedicated on August 06, 2017, by Bishop Francis Xavier DiLorenzo.

Saint Francis of Assisi

Saint Francis of Assisi in Amherst began on October 1994 as the Catholic Community of Amherst. Many Amherst County Catholics were members of Holy Cross Church in Lynchburg. As part of a Lenten parish program in the early 1980's, several Amherst Catholics came together in the home of Walter and Eileen McDonald to share their faith with Father Joe Lehman, associate pastor at Holy Cross. The group slowly increased in number.

In the early 1990's, an Amherst Catholic contacted Bishop Sullivan about establishing a church in Amherst County, one of the few counties in the Diocese that was lacking a Catholic Church. In 1991, Bishop purchased land in a rural area of the county. While the Amherst group was excited

and appreciative about the purchase, the isolated location was not ideal and expressed such to the Bishop.

On October 31, 1994, Bishop Sullivan celebrated Mass for seventeen Catholics in the local Anglican Church. He told them to call themselves the Catholic Community of Amherst.

Father Ralph Hamlet, pastor at Saint Mary in Lovingston as well as the mission of Saint George in Scottsville, agreed to say Mass on Saturday evenings. Ascension Episcopal Church graciously offered their facilities, and the Catholic Community of Amherst began to grow, officially named Saint Francis of Assisi by Bishop Sullivan on September 19, 1998.

In April of 2000, Bishop purchased the property on South Main Street that was the site of an historic home, Seven Oaks. The property on Main Street was an ideal location. Following demolition, construction began on October 26, 2003. Many retired members of the community were able to assist with construction under the supervision of the general contractor. Initially, they did small jobs, but when a subcontractor was not available to do the framing which would delay the progress of construction, the "over the hill gang" began work in earnest. The retirees worked during the week with periodic assistance from a group of independent construction workers supplied by a parishioner. With their work, the building was completed in Spring of 2004, ahead of schedule and under budget. Bishop Sullivan dedicated the building on May 19, 2004, with a joyful congregation in attendance.

Since the building was completed, other structures have been added to the grounds. Columbaria donated by a parishioner were placed on the north side of the building in a lovely garden setting designed and built by parishioners. A pavilion with storage shed was also built by parishioners behind the church; picnics and other outdoor festivities are held there.

Saint Francis of Assisi remains a small church in a small town. The community continues to be an outpost of the Catholic faith in a rural community. There is a monthly collection that supports two other parishes, one in Virginia and one in South Dakota. A food pantry is also maintained for individuals in need.

The community continues with the original traditions of faith sharing through religious education for both adults and children and community building with regular social opportunities of covered-dish dinners after the Saturday Mass and breakfasts after Sunday morning Mass. Volunteerism is a large part of what built St. Francis and it continues, with volunteers cleaning and maintaining the building and beautiful gardens and organizing the library. All is done for the honor and glory of God.

Saint Peter the Apostle

Saint Peter the Apostle Catholic Church began in 1985 as the dream of one devoted Catholic man. Residents in the Lake Gaston area focused on the need for a Sunday Mass. In 1993, a few vacation property owners and permanent residents of Lake Gaston found an abandoned country store in Valentines, Virginia, and rented it. The William and Mary College Youth Apostolate, as well as members of Saint Richard's, renovated the building. Beginning Memorial Day weekend, weekly Mass was held. Labor Day marked a change in the Mass schedule to once a month. Efforts were now focused on creating a permanent parish at the lake.

In the winter of 1994, Bishop Walter Sullivan authorized the purchase of eight acres of land in Ebony for a future church site. Weekly Mass resumed on a regular basis at the rented building in Valentines, in April 1995. In May 1995, the Richmond Diocese designated Saint Peter the Apostle Catholic Community at Lake Gaston. A Parish Council and a Finance Council were formed. The process began to formulate a plan to develop the property in Ebony and to construct a new church building.

In June 1996, Reverend Leo T. Cervantes became pastor of Saint Richard in Emporia and Saint Peter the Apostle at Lake Gaston. Bishop Sullivan blessed and dedicated the building site near Ebony in May 1997. Construction of the Fellowship Hall, which would be used for Mass until a permanent Church was built, began in August of 1997. The pre-engineered 2,240 square foot building was constructed almost entirely with volunteer labor. Dedication of the Fellowship Hall and the first Mass at the new location took place in March 1998.

Bishop Sullivan recognized the growth taking place at Saint Peter. Through the combined efforts of the parish and the diocese, a residence for the pastor was located and purchased. Many "firsts" followed, including an RCIA class, a Confirmation class, an Ecumenical Thanksgiving, feeding over 300 families, and the celebration of Christmas Eve midnight Mass.

Saint Peter the Apostle Parish continued to grow. It was determined that a larger 250 seat church needed to be built on the existing site. The resilience and hard work of our parishioners enabled us to move forward. Selling the old rectory, renegotiating the mortgage, fundraising, holding a Parish Festival, making pledge commitments, launching a brick sale, and securing a grant from the Catholic Extension Service all took a tremendous amount of time and determination.

The building phase was completed in October 2007. On December 15, 2007, Bishop Francis DiLorenzo presided at the dedication. It should be noted that, with thanks to our parishioners, our debt of more than one million dollars was paid off in just five years.

In July 2012, Reverend Anthony Mpungu from the Archdiocese of Kampala, Uganda, was named Pastor of Saint Peter and Saint Richard. He encouraged parishioners to attend daily Mass, and he reinstituted the tradition of the Blessing of the Boats. In September 2015, Reverend Patrick Baffour-Akoto became Pastor of Saint Peter and Saint Richard. He came to us from Ghana where he was Pastor of a village parish. He spent much of his time visiting the sick, and he continued to encourage daily Mass attendance.

The project to pave the parking lot and to plant shrubbery and crape myrtle trees accomplished significant beautification of the grounds and church during this time.

In August 2016, Reverend Joker "Jong" Bayta became Pastor. Father Bayta served in parishes in Camarines, Sur, Philippines in the Archdiocese of Caceres for over 17 years.

The remodeled Bait Shop which was the New Church for Memorial Day 1994 for the Lake Gaston Catholic Community.

Saint Gabriel

— Chesterfield • 1997 —

In 1997, with the expansion of western Chesterfield County and with the large number of families attending the southside Richmond parishes, the Catholic Diocese of Richmond developed a plan to open a new parish. Bishop Walter Sullivan met with a small group of Epiphany and Saint Edward families who were eager to build a Catholic Church in their own community.

Masses started at Clover Hill Elementary School on August 2, 1997, with about 400 families. Bishop Sullivan, wanting to honor the three Archangels, recommended the names of Saints Gabriel, Raphael, and Michael to the parish community. The parishioners selected Saint Gabriel.

In June 2001, the parish moved to its permanent location on Winterpock Road. Reverend Pasquale "Pat" Apuzzo came to the parish as administrator during Advent of 2002 and became the pastor in March of 2003. In June of 2006, the parish dedicated its Prayer Memorial Garden in front of the church. In September of 2006, the offices were moved from their previous location on Route 360, near the Chesterfield Berry Farm, to the present onsite location behind the church.

In 2009, Father Apuzzo began celebrating monthly Masses in Spanish for a developing Hispanic community within the Parish of Good Samaritan in nearby Amelia County. As the result of diocesan pastoral planning, Saint Gabriel Parish

clustered with Good Samaritan Parish. In March of 2010, Bishop DiLorenzo assigned Father Apuzzo as pastor of Good Samaritan in addition to Saint Gabriel. In 2012, Bishop Emeritus Walter Sullivan generously gifted the parish with new seating within the worship space.

The parish welcomed Reverend Eric Ayers as Pastor of Saint Gabriel and Good Samaritan Parishes on July 1, 2013. Under his direction, the parish continued to provide for the many sacramental needs of the parish, and support a growing and dynamic children, youth, and adult Faith Formation Program, outreach to the surrounding community through many different ministries - feeding the homeless, visiting the imprisoned, and helping the elderly, and ministries to the sick and bereaved.

Staying true to the mission on which Saint Gabriel was founded, parishioners announce the Good News alive today through the commitment to be a parish of welcome and hospitality through the stewardship of their gifts. Through worship, outreach, formation, compassion, and forgiveness, the community is called

to pause and reflect on their relationship with God and one another as they live the Gospel each day of their lives. The call to full and active participation in the life of the parish is at the foundation of our life as a community of faith.

Saint Gabriel has since grown to a parish of nearly 1,100 families in a rapidly developing section of the county and celebrated its 20th anniversary in 2017.

Saint Stephen Martyr

Chesapeake • 1997

Saint Stephen Martyr can be seen and felt throughout the community with its cross-topped bell tower, acts of good work, and deep spiritual commitment. The parish in the southern reaches of Chesapeake is over 20 years old. Its territory was carved from its sister church, Prince of Peace, and first met in Southeastern Elementary School on June 29, 1997. The parish's founding priest, Father James Gordon, wanted to begin with a single Mass to bring everyone together at one time and place. The new parishioners filled every seat and crowded into the aisles and hallway, signaling an immediate need for a full slate of Masses.

Within weeks, ministries were formed. Parishioners visited the sick in hospitals, children began meeting in people's homes for Faith Formation, a pancake breakfast was organized to benefit Habitat for Humanity. Food and gift baskets for the poor were collected and delivered for Christmas in a family-to-family approach.

Liturgies were held at Hickory Middle School and Twiford's Funeral Home, and committees were formed to create a mission statement, start a building campaign, and design a church. Bishop Walter Sullivan dedicated the new church building on Battlefield Boulevard on June 18, 2002.

Saint Stephen Martyr has grown from its initial 150 families to more than 1,600 families. The distinctive cross-topped bell tower was dedicated in October of 2006, and a columbarium, Our Lady Queen of Heaven Mausoleum Garden, was dedicated in August of 2009.

Woven tightly into the church's fabric are the parish social justice efforts, such as fundraising and visits to Maison Fortuné Orphanage in Hinche, Haiti, and a prison ministry that provides fellowship and spiritual development at prisons throughout the region, and a week of housing the homeless every year in an effort that combines faith communities across the region.

Parish nurses conduct health outreach, such as blood pressure checks, blood drives for the Red Cross, and personal support for parish members who are sick and for their caregivers. The parish has a strong Respect Life effort, and recently erected 3,300 crosses on the church grounds in the shape of a flag to represent the number of abortions that occur every day in America.

The parish has a wide array of religious programs to educate people of all ages, with Children's Liturgy of the Word, Blaze, Edge, LifeTeen, Catholics in Action, Adult Faith Formation, RCIA/RCIC, Walking with Purpose, Men of Saint Joseph, Amazing Grays, Cursillo, and more. There's also a very active Knights of Columbus chapter.

Parish community life is rich with such activities as Lenten lessons, Easter Egg hunts, anniversary picnics, annual Christmas in July festivals and various sporting events. There's a wide range of community outreach, such as a homeless housing program called NEST, Advent outreach through three different community programs, and a Samaritan Fund that provides thousands of dollars annually to families in need in our area.

Saint Stephen Martyr continues to grow in the Hickory area of Chesapeake and to bless our community for present and future generations.

Saint John the Evangelist

— New Castle • 2000 —

Saint John the Evangelist Parish was founded in 2000 by the Most Reverend Walter F. Sullivan, Eleventh Bishop of Richmond, for the Catholics of Craig County. The Diocese of Richmond donated $50,000 and the Catholic Church Extension Society donated $50,000 toward the building fund for the new church. Building began in late 2001.

With another grant from the Catholic Church Extension Society for $20,000 in 2002, and $10,000 in 2003, the small parish continued to grow and add to its ministry. Monthly support from the Hampton Roads parish of Immaculate Conception helped this small, rural church continue to minister in the community in the Blue Ridge Mountains. Both Saint John in New Castle and Transfiguration in nearby Fincastle were praying for a priest to be assigned to their parishes. In 2009, Reverend Stephen McNally was made pastor of both parishes.

Bishop Francis X. DiLorenzo

Francis X. DiLorenzo (1942–2017) of Philadelphia was named the twelfth bishop of Richmond in 2004. A priest of the Archdiocese of Philadelphia, DiLorenzo had been an auxiliary bishop in Scranton and then bishop of Honolulu. During his tenure in Richmond, the diocese found new ways to meet persistent and evolving challenges such as the shortage of priests and declining religious practice. After reaching the usual retirement age for a bishop (75), Francis DiLorenzo continued to lead the diocese until his unexpected death (2017).

Restructuring and New Initiatives
(2004-2017)

In response to the aging of priests and scant ordinations in previous decades (ca. 1980–ca. 2005), the diocese began to recruit more seminarians, an effort that yielded a modest increase of priests.[1] But with retirements outstripping ordinations, still more priests were needed. To alleviate the shortage, the Richmond Diocese negotiated agreements with dioceses in Africa, the Philippines, and Latin America to bring priests from those places to temporarily staff parishes (2004). These arrangements marked a historic role reversal as some regions supplying priests had once been missionary territories themselves. The clergy of the Diocese of Richmond consequently became more diverse, as eventually thirty-five percent of its priests originated from other countries.[2]

Moreover, some priests were assigned to multiple churches as part of several parish "clusters" (beginning in 2005). These structures hearkened back to an earlier period in diocesan history and reflected the longstanding practice in southwest Virginia. Finally, more permanent deacons were ordained (starting in 2011), who provided ministerial support at both the parish and diocesan level.[3]

Education and Catholic identity were distinguishing features of DiLorenzo's episcopate. New funding, a systematic outreach to Hispanics (Segura Initiative, 2010), and greater oversight made Catholic schools more affordable, accessible, and effective throughout the diocese. In another initiative, the Lay Ecclesial Ministry Institute (2010) began to train professional men and women for various roles in parishes, schools, and campus ministries. Bishop DiLorenzo, together with the bishop of Arlington, also established the Virginia Catholic Conference (2004) to advocate for Catholic values in the Virginia General Assembly and with the governor of the commonwealth.[4]

Catholics in the Diocese of Richmond, as in the rest of the United States and other parts of the world, lived in an increasingly secular

Leaders of the Virginia Catholic Conference

Bishop DiLorenzo with priests from Africa

Ordination of permanent deacons

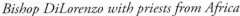

Bishop DiLorenzo with Catholic school children

society. One effect was the continuing ebb in Mass attendance and reception of the sacraments among English-speakers. Religious practice held steadier in ethnic communities where culture was more closely tied to faith, notably among Hispanics and Filipinos, although even there some erosion was evident.

Lay Ecclesial Ministry Institute

Beyond the Church, there were signs that American culture was becoming more skeptical of institutional religion and hostile toward its values. By way of example, the Supreme Court legalized same-sex marriage (2015) less than a decade after Virginia adopted an amendment to the state constitution outlawing the practice (2007). The Dioceses of Richmond and Arlington had strongly supported this measure as part of the referendum. In another trend, more Americans, particularly those belonging to the "millennial" generation (who were born ca. 1982–ca. 2004), were affiliating with no organized religion, while often still seeking spiritual experience.[5]

In response to these trends, the diocese reorganized its staff to form an Office for Evangelization (2011), which encompassed ministry to young people (ages 12–17), college students (ages 18–22), and young adults (ages 18–30). This decision reflected an awareness of the many universities and colleges (sixty-eight) within the territory of the diocese. Faced with a changing religious landscape, parishes and campus ministries made greater efforts to reach non-practicing Catholics and to bolster the commitment of those already in the pews.

These were stirrings of the "New Evangelization," Pope St. John Paul II's initiative (1983) to rouse the growing numbers of inactive members of the Church in historically Catholic areas (namely, the Americas and Western Europe).[6] By way of background, Vatican II[7] (1962–1965) and Pope Paul VI[8] (1963–1978) had recognized the change in religious attitudes. More recently, John Paul II's successors[9] have renewed his call for a large-scale evangelizing campaign within the Church.

The newness of this project entailed a paradigm shift in Catholic practice: the full involvement of the laity, emphasis on dialogue and mercy rather than on condemnation, a focus on one's personal relationship with God, giving testimony to one's faith, and developing a missionary outlook on ordinary life.[10] Throughout the history of the Diocese of Richmond, Catholics lived in a missionary territory because they were outnumbered by Protestants. While that disparity continued, Catholics were now a religious minority in another sense: the surrounding culture and population were becoming less religious.

The Diocesan Youth Conference, one of several activities intended to evangelize young people during Bishop DiLorenzo's tenure

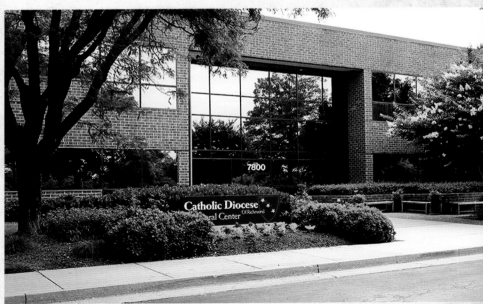

Saint Rose of Lima and Korean Martyrs

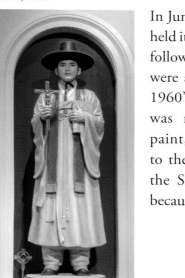

In May of 1948, Bishop Peter Ireton created a new parish in the Wythe Section of Hampton formed from parts of the existing Saint Mary Star of the Sea and Saint Vincent de Paul. The new parish was named Saint Rose of Lima in honor of his sister, Rose. The first Mass was offered on July 31, 1948 in a former government building converted into the chapel. Another building was made into the parish rectory. Adjoining land was purchased, and a parish hall was built. Bishop Ireton donated a statue of the parish patron saint, in memory of his sister.

The Parish established an Altar and Sanctuary Society for women and the Holy Name Society for men. The parish school opened its doors on September 8, 1949, staffed by Benedictine Sisters from Bristow,

Virginia. Members formed the Catholic War Veterans and the Ladies Auxiliary. As the Parish continued to grow the parish hall was no longer large enough for Sunday Mass attendance. Ground was broken on Easter Sunday, April 18, 1952, for the new structure. On December 21, 1952, the newly ordained Auxiliary Bishop Joseph H. Hodges laid the cornerstone and blessed the new Church.

In June of 1955, Saint Rose's School held its first graduation exercises. The following year, two more classrooms were added to the building. In the 1960's, the interior of the Church was renovated with new wood, paint, and other improvements to the appearance. After 18 years, the Saint Rose School was closed because the Benedictine Sisters were

unable to continue staffing it. Students continued at Saint Vincent in Newport News or Saint Mary at Old Point. Saint Rose Parish was consolidated with Saint Mary Star of the Sea at Old Point. Construction of a new parish center was begun in 1971 on Cunningham Drive in Hampton.

In 2012 a proposal for the suppression of St. Rose of Lima Parish, Hampton VA, and the erection of the Parish of St. Rose of Lima and the Korean Martyrs was introduced. Since the number of non-

Korean parishioners and the growth of the Catholic Community of the Korean Martyrs which has been worshipping at St. Rose of Lima Church since at least 1997, and for other practical reasons, it was proposed by Bishop Francis DiLorenzo, that the Parish of St. Rose of Lima be suppressed; that the Catholic Community of the Korean Martyrs, operating as a quasi-parish, also be suppressed; that the assets and debts of both communities, be assumed by a newly erected parish, The Parish of St. Rose of Lima and the Korean Martyrs. The territorial boundaries of the new Parish are the same as those of the suppressed St. Rose of Lima Parish. In consultation with the Diocesan Council of Priests held on September 19, 2012, the proposal was adopted.

Crozet Catholic Community

Crozet • 2017

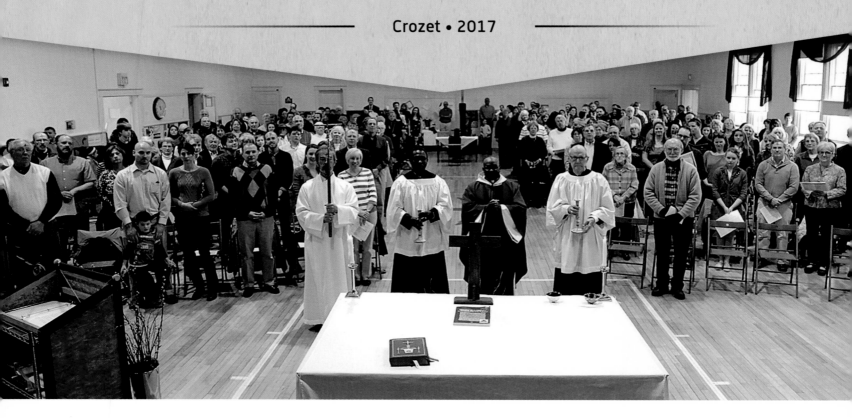

Bishop Francis X. DiLorenzo, Twelfth Bishop of Richmond, originally gave permission for a representative group of Catholics in Crozet, once a largely rural community 15 miles west of Charlottesville, to have Mass once a month beginning in January 2014. He named Father Joseph Mary Lukyamuzi, as priest-chaplain for the group. Local Catholics formed the Crozet Mass Committee and scheduled Mass to be held monthly at the Field School on the second Sunday of the month beginning in March 2014. The Field School, built in 1924 by the Albemarle County government as an elementary school, is now a private middle school for boys. It is leased to the private school by the county. The first Mass in 2014 attracted 250 people.

In 2016, Bishop DiLorenzo gave approval for the Crozet Catholic Community to take steps to become an official mission parish of the Diocese of Richmond after meeting with Father Joseph Mary Lukyamuzi, pastor of Holy Comforter in Charlottesville, Father Gregory Kandt, pastor of Church of the Incarnation in Charlottesville and two lay representatives of the Catholic Community. The meeting was held December 15, 2016, at the Diocesan Pastoral Center and included Monsignor Mark Richard Lane, Vicar General, and Monsignor R. Francis Muench, Judicial Vicar.

With mission status, the Crozet Catholic Community (its official name) can begin to hold

weekly Mass, offer the sacraments and begin a religious education program. In addition, the community will begin a search for a site on which to build a church.

Holy Comforter will continue to serve the people until the community becomes independent as a separate parish. Michael Marshall, chair of the Crozet Mass Committee, said that there are 249 registered households which have 689 people and include 233 school-age children. There are 20 people of college age.

It is estimated that the current population of 7,500 in Crozet will likely rise to 10,000 by 2020. Approximately 100 houses a year are being built.

Mr. Marshall, who is editor and publisher of the Crozet Gazette, had written to Bishop DiLorenzo to invite him to celebrate Mass and to meet the Crozet Catholic community.

As part of its outreach to the local community, Crozet Catholics regularly help needy families by bringing canned goods and other food items to Mass which are then delivered to the Food Bank operated by Crozet United Methodist Church and to Holy Comforter which has a large community outreach. "The Protestant churches have been very encouraging and supportive to us," Mr. Marshall said. "They see establishment of a Catholic church as a positive sign in the community."

Mass is now offered in Crozet at The Field School every Sunday. Our celebrants include Fr. Joseph Mary Lukyamuzi, pastor of our sponsoring parish, Holy Comforter, as well as visiting priests.

Chapter XIV

Bishop Barry C. Knestout

Barry C. Knestout (b. 1962) of Cheverly, Maryland—a priest and auxiliary bishop of Washington, DC—became the thirteenth bishop of Richmond in 2018. A monumental anniversary for the diocese lay on the horizon.

Preparing for the Diocesan Bicentennial (2018-2019)

Installation as the thirteenth bishop of Richmond (2018)

The new bishop began his tenure by crisscrossing the vast territory of the Richmond Diocese to learn about its people, parishes, and other institutions. The various regions of the diocese were subsequently reorganized into deaneries (groups of parishes) in order to foster priestly fraternity and to aid the bishop in his task of governing (2018).[1]

As the bicentennial of the local Church approached, a commemoration was planned to strengthen the bonds of fellowship within it and to revitalize its evangelizing mission, inspired by the exhortation of St. Paul: "Shine like stars in the world, as you hold fast to the word of life" (Phil. 2:15–16). Numerous bicentennial activities were organized: a year-long program of spiritual preparation; Masses in historic churches to recognize key events in diocesan history; pilgrimages; service projects; and, as the culmination, a Eucharistic Congress in Richmond.

Greeting Catholic students during an initial visit to the diocese (2018)

The clerical abuse scandal reemerged six months into Knestout's tenure (2018). It had become international in scope and involved the personal and professional malfeasance of bishops. Knestout responded to the crisis by meeting with victims of abuse (2018).[2] He also wrote a pastoral letter on the calamity (2018);[3] he celebrated Masses of atonement and conducted listening sessions throughout the diocese (2018); and, like other bishops in the United States, he published a list of all priests in the diocese against whom a credible and substantiated accusation of sexual abuse of a minor had been made (2019).[4] These were steps toward rebuilding trust in the Church.

Meeting parishioners

Celebrating Mass in southwest Virginia

Ordination of priests
(2018)

Reaping the Fruit: The Diocese Marks Its Bicentennial (2020)

With advances and setbacks, the Catholic Church in Virginia spread gradually across an expansive, uneven terrain. The two-hundredth anniversary of the Diocese of Richmond (July 11, 2020) is a vantage point from which to survey how Catholics in this commonwealth have practiced and transmitted their faith over that period. The Church has grown since the arrival of the first missionaries. There are now two hundred thousand Catholics in the Richmond Diocese, who make up five percent of the total population. The diocese has 191 priests, 161 deacons, 139 parishes, and 30 schools.

An assessment of the prospects of the Church in Virginia, written around the time of the first Catholic mission (1570–1571), is instructive. Six months after the martyrdom of his fellow Spanish Jesuits, Father Juan Rogel sensed the challenges that the Church would face in this land: "I truly fear that there will be the same hardness in them [the indigenous people] regarding conversion as in the other places we have been; and if there is to be any fruit, it will come about over time, as when they are softened by water dripping on rock."[5]

Perseverance has borne fruit over time, as the Catholic Church cultivated the Gospel in all types of Virginia soil, ranging from barren to fertile (Matt. 13:19–23). That story of struggle, failure, and modest growth is the parable of the grain of wheat: "Unless a grain of wheat falls to the ground and dies, it remains just a grain of wheat; but if it dies, it produces much fruit" (John 12:24). Catholics in Virginia have overcome adversity, they have committed errors, and they have bettered society in their continuing effort to serve God.

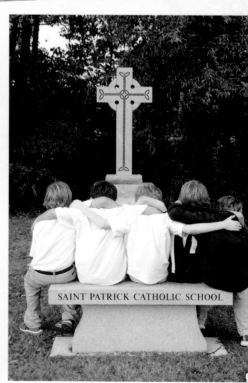

SAINT PATRICK CATHOLIC SCHOOL

Catholic Schools

The 30 Catholic schools within the Diocese of Richmond meet the spiritual and academic needs of almost 9,000 students across Virginia. Fourteen of these schools have been awarded the status of Blue Ribbon Schools by the U.S. Department of Education. It recognizes elementary, middle, and high schools based on their overall academic excellence or their progress in closing achievement gaps among student subgroups. High schools in the diocese have a 100-percent graduation rate.

Eastern Vicariate
- Catholic High School – Virginia Beach
- Christ the King Catholic School – Norfolk
- Our Lady of Mt. Carmel Catholic School – Newport News
- Peninsula Catholic High School – Newport News
- Portsmouth Catholic Regional School – Portsmouth
- Saint Gregory the Great Catholic School – Virginia Beach
- Saint John the Apostle Catholic School – Virginia Beach
- Saint Mary Star of the Sea Catholic School – Hampton
- Saint Matthew's Catholic School – Virginia Beach
- Saint Patrick Catholic School – Norfolk
- Saint Pius X Catholic School – Norfolk
- Star of the Sea Catholic School – Virginia Beach
- Walsingham Academy – Williamsburg

Central Vicariate
- All Saints Catholic School – Richmond
- Benedictine College Preparatory – Goochland
- Blessed Sacrament Huguenot Catholic School – Powhatan
- Cristo Rey Richmond High School - Richmond
- Our Lady of Lourdes Catholic School – Henrico
- Saint Benedict Catholic School – Richmond
- Saint Bridget Catholic School – Richmond
- Saint Edward-Epiphany Catholic School – Richmond
- Saint Gertrude High School – Richmond
- Saint Joseph Catholic School – Petersburg
- Saint Mary Catholic School – Henrico

Western Vicariate
- Charlottesville Catholic School – Charlottesville
- Holy Cross Catholic School – Lynchburg
- Roanoke Catholic School – Roanoke
- Sacred Heart Catholic School – Danville
- Saint Anne Catholic School – Bristol
- Saint John Neumann Academy – Blacksburg

Women Religious in the Diocese

Before the Diocese of Richmond existed, three sisters from Mother Seton's Sisters of Charity of Saint Joseph began teaching classes in what became Virginia's first Catholic school. Sisters Margaret George, Editha Barry, and Ann Catherine Reilly opened Saint Joseph's Orphan Asylum and Free School in Richmond on November 25, 1834. They were the first women religious in the diocese. In 1850, the order became known as the Daughters of Charity of Saint Vincent de Paul.

In their ministry in the Diocese of Richmond, the Daughters of Charity set the high standard for Catholic Schools in Virginia. On January 17, 1876, they opened Saint Joseph School on Market Street in Petersburg. In 1878, the Daughters of Charity were asked to take over teaching duties at Saint Francis School in Staunton. They would go to Harrisonburg, Waynesboro and Lexington for Sunday School, as well as Western State to visit patients once a week. Daughters of Charity lived in a convent in Lynchburg, next door to the old parish building that was converted into Holy Cross Academy in 1879.

In addition to their services educating the poor, the Daughters of Charity were committed to tending the sick and those in need. During the Civil War years, this pioneering group of nuns with a habit that featured a wide white cornet became known as battlefield "angels." They treated the wounded of the Confederacy with  devotion and care. The Sisters served in Richmond at Saint Francis de Sales Infirmary, The Richmond General Hospital, and Saint Ann's Military Hospital. Sister Juliana Chatard (1833-1917) penned a description of the situation in Richmond at Saint Ann's Military Hospital during the war in which she recounted a battle that raged for seven days. The streets were filled with ambulances bringing the wounded to the city hospitals. Supplies and food were scarce. In Sister Juliana's account, it was difficult to describe the routine at the military hospital because "to lay the scene truly before you is beyond any human pen. All kinds of misery lay outstretched before us."

Sister Euphemia Blenkinsop (1816-1887) operated in the Confederacy as a representative of her superiors in the North. She relayed the bravery of the sisters who served on the battlefields in Virginia, especially in Norfolk and Richmond, "our poor sisters, though the shells were flying around them, did not even interrupt their duties."

The Sisters of Charity were the first religious women in the Diocese of Richmond, but their courageous beginning was followed by hundreds of women religious who contributed to the parishes, schools, hospitals, and charities of Virginia, and continue to this day.

- Daughters of Charity (1834)
- Sisters of the Visitation of Holy Mary (1866)
- School Sisters of Notre Dame (1867)
- Benedictine Sisters of Virginia (1868)
- Franciscan Sisters of Mill Hill (1889)
- Little Sisters of the Poor (1889)
- Sisters of Notre Dame (1889)
- Sisters of the Holy Cross (1889)
- Sisters of Charity of Nazareth (1893)
- Sisters of the Blessed Sacrament (1895)
- Dominican Sisters of Nashville (1923)
- Sisters of Mercy of the Union (1935)
- Daughters of Wisdom (1945)
- Poor Servants of the Mother of God (1949)
- Religious of the Sacred Heart of Mary (1950)
- Dominican Sisters of Adrian, MI (1951)
- Missionary Sisters of Verona / Comboni Missionary Sisters (1953)

  - Poor Clares (1956)
  - Trinitarian Sisters of Rome (1956)
  - Bernardine Sisters of the Third Order of St. Francis (1959)
  - Mission Helpers of the Sacred Heart (1959)
  - Sisters of Bon Secours (1959)
  - Sisters of the Holy Names of Jesus and Mary (1959)
  - Sisters of Mercy (1959)
  - Sisters of Notre Dame de Namur (1959)
  - Sisters, Servants of the Immaculate Heart of Mary (1959)
  - Missionary Servants of the Most Blessed Trinity (1971)
  - Felician Sisters (1973)
  - Madonna House Apostolate (1973)
  - Poor Sisters of St. Joseph (1973)
  - Sisters of Charity of Seton Hill (1974)
  - Sisters for Christian Community (1974)
  - Medical Missionaries of Mary (1980)
  - Congregation of Divine Providence (1982)
  - Trappistine Sisters (1987)
  - Little Sisters of Saint Francis of Assisi (1996)
  - Franciscan Sisters of Saint Joseph (2000)
  - Sisters of the Daughters of the Mary Immaculate Congregation (2005)

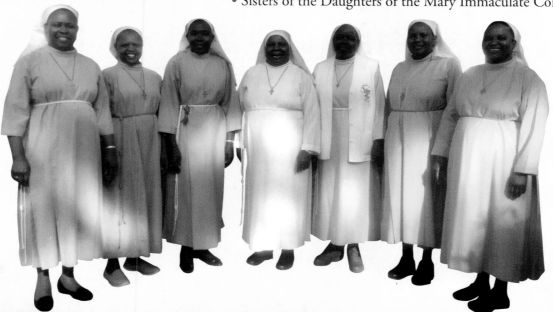

Index: Bishops and Parishes

Chapter VIII

Chapter IX

Chapter X

Chapter XI

Chapter XII

Chapter XIII

Chapter XIV

Notes

Introduction

1 - Juan Rogel, SJ to Francis Borgia, SJ, Bay of the Mother of God, August 28, 1572, in Clifford M. Lewis, SJ, and Albert J. Loomie, SJ, *Spanish Jesuit Mission in Virginia: 1570–1572* (Chapel Hill: University of North Carolina Press, 1953), 103. The author made the translation from the original document. Used with the permission of the Virginia Historical Society.

Chapter I

1 - Lewis and Loomie, *Spanish Jesuit Mission in Virginia*, 3–64.

2 - Gerald P. Fogarty, SJ, *Commonwealth Catholicism: A History of the Catholic Church in Virginia* (Notre Dame, IN: University of Notre Dame Press, 2001), 8–10.

3 - Christopher M. B. Allison, "Jamestown's Relics: Sacred Presence in the English New World," *Conversations: An Online Journal of the Center for the Study of Material and Visual Cultures of Religion* (2016), https://doi:10.22332/ con.ess.2016.2

4 - Fogarty, *Commonwealth Catholicism*, 10.

5 - Hugh Thomas, *The Slave Trade: The Story of the African Slave Trade: 1440–1870* (New York: Simon and Schuster, 1997), 398; John Thornton, "The African Experience of the '20. and Odd Negroes' Arriving in Virginia, August 1619," *The William and Mary Quarterly* 55, no. 3 (July 1998): 434.

6 - Engel Sluiter, "New Light on the '20. and Odd Negroes' Arriving in Virginia, August 1619," *The William and Mary Quarterly* 54, no. 2 (April 1997): 395–98.

7 - Margaret McCartney, "Virginia's First Africans," in *Encyclopedia Virginia*, accessed February 11, 2019, https://www.encyclopediavirginia.org/Virginia_s_First_Africans

8 - Fogarty, *Commonwealth Catholicism*, 14–18.

9 - Fogarty, 13–14, 16, 22; Robert Emmett Curran, *Papist Devils: Catholics in British America, 1574–1783* (Washington, DC: Catholic University of America Press, 2014), 65, 71, 133.

10 - Fogarty, *Commonwealth Catholicism*, 20, 22.

11 - Fogarty, 17, 28–29, 33.

12 - Fogarty, 33–37.

13 - Fogarty, 54.

14 - Fogarty, 39–41.

15 - Fogarty, 41–43, 45.

16 - Fogarty, 42–45.

17 - Fogarty, 45–47.

Chapter II

1 - Fogarty, 40, 45.

2 - Fogarty, 45–50, 52.

3 - Fogarty, 52–54.

4 - Fogarty, 62–70, 79, 104–108.

5 - Fogarty, 67–68.

Chapter III

1 - Fogarty, 94.

2 - There is no extant decree, if one ever existed, declaring St. Vincent de Paul to be the patron of the Diocese of Richmond. The first mention occurs during Whelan's tenure in Richmond, when the saint's patronage was already recognized. In 1843, Whelan asked *Propaganda Fide* which readings should be used in the Breviary (Divine Office) for the feast of St. Vincent de Paul, patron of the Diocese of Richmond. *Udienze di N.S.,* March 17, 1843, in *United States Documents in the Propaganda Fide Archives: A Calendar,* 1ˢᵗ ser., ed. Finbar Kenneally (Washington, DC: Academy of American Franciscan History, 1977), vol. 7, no. 571.

That same year, Whelan also received permission to celebrate the feast of the diocesan patron in the manner of the Vincentian order. Pope Gregory XVI, *Facultates extraordinariae,* May 14, 1843, in *United States Documents in the Propaganda Fide Archives: A Calendar,* 1ˢᵗ ser., ed. Finbar Kenneally (Washington, DC: Academy of American Franciscan History, 1975), vol. 6, no. 1639e.

In 1853, Pope Pius IX, in response to a request from Whelan's successor, John McGill, declared that Vincent de Paul remained the patron of the Diocese of Richmond even after the Diocese of Wheeling had been created from it (1850). *Udienze di N.S.,* January 2, 1853, in *United States Documents in the Propaganda Fide Archives,* vol. 7, no. 1068; see also McGill's request: Udienze di N.S., December 13, 1852 in *United States Documents in the Propaganda Fide Archives,* vol. 7, no. 1069.

3 - Fogarty, *Commonwealth Catholicism*, 81–83.

4 - Fogarty, 88–90.

5 - Fogarty, 91, 98, 100.

Chapter IV

1 - Fogarty, 121–27.

2 - Fogarty, 127–30.

3 - See, for example, Pope Eugene IV, Bull, *Sicut dudum* (1435); Pope Paul III, Brief to the Archbishop of Toledo, *Pastorale officium* (1537): 1495–1496 in *Compendium of Creeds, Definitions, and Declarations on Matters of Faith and Morals,* eds. Peter Hunermann, Robert Fastiggi, Anne Englund Nash, and Heinrich

Denzinger (San Francisco: Ignatius Press, 2012), hereafter Denzinger; Bull, *Sublimus Dei* (1537); Pope Gregory XIV, Bull to the Bishop of Manilla, *Cum sicuti* (1591); Pope Urban VIII, Bull to the Juridical Delegate of the Apostolic Camera in Portugal, *Commissum nobis* (1639); Pope Benedict XIV, Apostolic Letter to the Bishops of Brazil, *Inmensa pastorum* (1741); Pope Gregory XVI, Constitution, *In supremo apostolatus* (1839): Denzinger 2745–2746. An explanation of these documents, and the text themselves, are found in Joel S. Panzer, *The Popes and Slavery* (New York: Alba House, 1996), 7–48, 75–102.

4 - Fogarty, *Commonwealth Catholicism*, 141–48.

5 - Fogarty, 177–79.

6 - Fogarty, 177.

7 - St. Joseph Catholic Church and St. Mary Star of the Sea Catholic Church, *Frontiers in Faith: History of Catholicism on the Peninsula* (n.p.: Hampton Bicentennial Committee and Syms-Eaton Museum, n.d.).

8 - Joseph Wuest, CSsR, *History of the Redemptorists at Annapolis, Md., from 1853 to 1903: With a Short Historical Sketch of the Preceding One Hundred and Fifty Years of Catholicity in the Capital of* Maryland (Ilchester, MD: College Press, 1904), 66.

9 - Bl. Francis Xavier Seelos, CSsR, to Ambrose Seelos, Annapolis, MD, December 3, 18, 1862, in *Sincerely, Seelos: The Collected Letters of Blessed Francis Xavier Seelos*, ed. and trans. Carl Hoegerl (New Orleans: Seelos Center, 2008), 324–26.

10 - Fogarty, *Commonwealth Catholicism*, 181–85.

11 - Fogarty, 148–76, 188.

12 - Fogarty, 201–202.

13 - Vatican Council I, First Dogmatic Constitution on the Church of Christ, *Pastor aeternus* (1870), chap. 4 and canon: Denzinger 3074.

Chapter V

1 - Fogarty, *Commonwealth Catholicism,* 196–98.

2 - Fogarty, 225–28.

3 - Fogarty, 221, 235.

Chapter VI

1 - Fogarty, 255–56, 265–67.

2 - Fogarty, 226–28, 319.

Chapter VII

1 - Fogarty, 324–28.

2 - Fogarty, 330–33.

3 - Fogarty, 318–21, 331–32, 334–36.

Chapter VIII

1 - Fogarty, 305–308.

2 - Vatican Council II, Declaration on Religious Freedom, *Dignitatis humanae* (1965), nos. 2 §1, 4 §1, http://www.vatican.va/archive/hist_councils/ii_vatican_council/documents/vat-ii_decl_19651207_dignitatis-humanae_en.html

3 - Fogarty, *Commonwealth Catholicism*, 346.

4 - Fogarty, 347.

5 - Fogarty, 359–62, 365–77.

6 - Fogarty, 415–18.

Chapter IX

1 - Fogarty, 405–407.

2 - Fogarty, 418–24.

3 - Fogarty, 68, 105, 148–49, 182–83.

4 - Fogarty, 433–35.

Chapter X

1 - Fogarty, 457–58, 461–62.

2 - Fogarty, 475–79, 480–81.

3 - Fogarty, 466–69, 474–75.

4 - Fogarty, 442–48.

5 - Fogarty, 450, 508–512.

Chapter XI

1 - Pope St. John XIII, Apostolic Constitution Proclaiming the Second Ecumenical Council of the Vatican, *Humanae salutis* (Salvation of Humanity) (1961), nos. 3, 5–7, 12, 23, http://w2.vatican.va/content/john-xxiii/es/apost constitutions/1961/documents/hf_j-xxiii_apc_19611225_humanae-salutis.html; there is no English-language translation on the Vatican website. Speech on the Solemn Opening of Vatican Council II, *Gaudet Mater Ecclesia* (Mother Church Rejoices) (1962), nos. 2, 6, 11–12, 14–15, trans. Joseph A. Komonchak, https://jakomonchak. files. wordpress.com/2012/10/john-xxiii-opening-speech.pdf, n.d.

2 - *Fogarty, Commonwealth Catholicism*, 487–88, 520, 523–25. One permanent deacon was ordained in 1972; seven were ordained in 1973, following Russell's retirement (Office of Archives, Diocese of Richmond, email messages to author, February 11, 26, 2019).

3 - *Fogarty, Commonwealth Catholicism*, 81–83, 525–26.

4 - Zoey Maraist, "Priests, Sisters Recall Wisdom, Kindness of Mother Bernadetta," *Catholic Virginian*, April 8, 2018, https://www.catholicvirginian.org/?p=9701

5 - Fogarty, Commonwealth Catholicism, 520, 523, 526–28, 544.

6 - Fogarty, 512–513, 533.

7 - Fogarty, 529–39.

8 - Pope St. Paul VI, Encyclical on the Regulation of Birth, *Humanae vitae* (1968), no. 14, http://w2.vatican.va/ content/paul-vi/en/encyclicals/documents/hf_p-vi_enc_25071968_humanae-vitae.html

Chapter XII

1 - Congregation for Bishops, Decree on the Changing of Boundaries (Prot. N. 271/74), *Richmondiensis-Vilmingtoniensis-Vhelingensis* (May 28, 1974), in the archives of the Diocese of Wheeling-Charleston; Pope St. Paul VI, Decree Creating the Diocese of Arlington, *Supernae Christifidelium* (August 13, 1974), in the archives of the Diocese of Arlington.

2 - Phyllis Theroux, *The Good Bishop: The Life of Walter F. Sullivan* (Maryknoll, NY: Orbis Books, 2013), 42–43.

3 - Theroux, *The Good Bishop*, 57–77, 96–101, 105–106, 111–12, 122–30, 133–64.

4 - Theroux, 165–93.

5 - The earliest statistics available (1995–1996) indicate 2,870 Hispanic Catholics in the diocese; by 2000–2001, the total had risen to 7,243 (Office of Archives, Diocese of Richmond, email message to author, February 25, 2019).

6 - The first permanent deacon was ordained in 1972, during Russell's tenure; 8 were ordained in 1973–1974, during Sullivan's time as administrator; 13 were ordained in 1981–2001; and 49 were ordained in 2003, before Sullivan's retirement (Office of Archives, Diocese of Richmond, email messages to author, February 11, 25, 2019).

Chapter XIII

1 - Office of Archives, Diocese of Richmond, email message to author, March 16, 2019. With one exception (12 ordinands in 1874), there were never more than 5 priests ordained per year from the beginning of the diocese (1820) until 1952; in many years, there were no ordinations or only 1. Ordinations began to increase in the 1950s, with relatively large classes of priests from 1958 to 1966 (between 8 and 17 ordinands per year); medium-size classes from 1967 through 1979 (between 3 and 12 ordinands per year); and small classes from 1980 through 2005 (0 to 9 ordinands per year, with several years without any ordinands, or only one). Between 2006 and 2019, there were 0 to 5 ordinands per year, but with fewer years when there were no ordinations or only one.

2 - Office of the Vicar for Clergy, Diocese of Richmond, email message to author, April 18, 2019; Ellen Robertson, "The Most Rev. Francis X. DiLorenzo, Bishop of the Catholic Diocese of Richmond, Dies at 75," *Richmond Times-Dispatch*, August 18, 2017, https://www.richmond.com/news/local/city-of-richmond/the-most-rev-francis-x-dilorenzo-bishop-of-the-catholic/ article_8d6f856f-dced-585c-afc6-7d157289369b.html

3 - Office of Archives, Catholic Diocese of Richmond. There were 37 permanent deacons ordained in 2012, 2 in 2013, 14 in 2015, and 19 in 2018.

4 - Robertson, "The Most Rev. Francis X. DiLorenzo"; "On the Passing of Francis X. DiLorenzo, 12th Bishop of the Diocese of Richmond," *Catholic Virginian*, August 23, 2017, https://www.catholicvirginian.org/?p=5696; Steve Neill, "Diocese Mourns the Passing of Its 12th Bishop, Francis X. DiLorenzo," *Catholic Virginian*, August 24, 2017, https://www.catholicvirginian.org/?p=5713

5 - "'Nones' on the Rise," Pew Research Center, October 9, 2012, http://www.pewforum.org/2012/10/09/nones-on-the-rise/

6 - Pope St. John Paul II, Opening Address of the 19th General Assembly of CELAM (1983), no. 9, in United States Conference of Catholic Bishops, Committee on Evangelization and Catechesis, *Disciples Called to Witness: The New Evangelization* (Washington, DC: United States Conference of Catholic Bishops, 2012), 6, http://www.usccb.org/beliefs-and-teachings/how-we-teach/new-evangelization/disciples-called-to-witness/upload/Disciples-Called-to-Witness-5-30-12.pdf. See also Apostolic Exhortation on the Vocation and the Mission of the Lay Faithful in the Church and in the World, *Christifideles laici* (1988), no. 34, http://w2.vatican.va/ content/john-paul-ii/en/apost_ exhortations/documents/hf_jp-ii_exh_30121988_christifideles-laici.html; Encyclical on the Permanent Validity of the Church's Missionary Mandate, *Redemptoris missio* (1990), no. 33 §4, http://w2.vatican.va/content/ john-paul-ii/en/encyclicals/documents/hf_jp-ii_enc_07121990_redemptoris-missio.html

7 - See, for example, Vatican Council II, Pastoral Constitution on the Church in the Modern World, *Gaudium et Spes* (1965), nos. 7 §2, 19, http://www.vatican.va/archive/hist_councils/ii_vatican_council/documents/vat-ii_cons_19651207_gaudium-et-spes_en.html

8 - See, for example, Pope St. Paul VI, Apostolic Exhortation on Evangelization in the Modern World, *Evangelii nuntiandi* (1975), nos. 2 §3, 4, 52, 54 §2, 55–56, 76, http://w2.vatican.va/content/paul-vi/en/apost_exhortations/ documents/hf_p-vi_exh_19751208_evangelii-nuntiandi.html

9 - See, for example, Pope Benedict XVI, Apostolic Letter (*motu propio*) Establishing the Pontifical Council for Promoting the New Evangelization, Ubicumque et semper (2010), http://w2.vatican.va/content/benedict-xvi/en/apost_letters/documents/hf_ben-xvi_apl_20100921_ubicumque-et-semper.html; Pope Francis, Apostolic Exhortation on the Proclamation of the Gospel in Today's World, *Evangelii gaudium* (2013), http://w2.vatican.va/ content/francesco/en/apost_exhortations/documents papa-francesco_esortazione-ap_20131124_evangelii-gaudium. html

10 - *Encounter the Joy of the Gospel: Pastoral Plan for the Catholic Diocese of Richmond* (Richmond, VA: Catholic Diocese of Richmond, 2014), 7–8, 16, 18–19, 24–26.

Chapter XIV

1 - Bishop Barry C. Knestout, *Decree Establishing a Deanery Structure for the Diocese of Richmond* (September 27, 2018), https://richmonddiocese.org/wp-content/uploads/2018/09/Letter-from-Bishop-Knestout-Establishing-Deaneries-September-2018.pdf

2 - Brian T. Olszewski, "Healing Begins," *Catholic Virginian*, February 21, 2019, https://www.catholicvirginian.org/?p=9416

3 - Bishop Barry C. Knestout, "*From Tragedy to Hope*": Pastoral Letter to the Clergy and Lay Faithful of the Diocese of Richmond (September 14, 2018), https://richmonddiocese.org/wp-content/uploads/2018/09/Pastoral-Letter-Sept-14-2018-FINAL.pdf

4 - Diocese of Richmond, *List of All Clergy With Credible and Substantiated Allegations of Sexual Abuse of Minors*, February 14, 2019 (updated June 27, 2019), https://richmonddiocese.org/list/

5 - Juan Rogel, SJ to Francis Borgia, SJ, Bay of the Mother of God, August 28, 1572, in Lewis and Loomie, *Spanish Jesuit Mission in Virginia*, 106. The author made the translation from the original document. Used with the permission of the Virginia Historical Society.

Acknowledgements

Engravings by Melchior Küsell, in Mathias Tanner, *Societas Jesu usque ad sanguinis et vitae profusionem militans, in Europa, Africa, Asia, et America, contra gentiles, Mahometanos, Judaeos, haereticos, impios, pro Deo, fide, Ecclesia, pietate* (Prague: Typis Universitatis Carolo-Ferdinandeae per Joannem Nicolaum Hampel factorem, 1675). Saint Louis University Libraries Special Collections. Material in the public domain.

Images of the apostolic brief founding the Diocese of Richmond used with the permission of the Vatican Secret Archives (2019).

Monsignor Robert Trisco, professor emeritus of Church history at the Catholic University of America (Washington, DC), made the translation of the apostolic brief (2018), which is based on the collated transcript that he also prepared.

Reproduction of the apostolic brief founding the Diocese of Richmond by Jayne E. Hushen (2019).

Publisher
Editions du Signe
1, rue Alfred Kastler
CS 10094 Eckbolsheim
F-67038 Strasbourg Cedex 2
France
Tel (33) 03 88 78 91 91
Fax (33) 03 88 78 91 90

Publishing Director: Christian Riehl

Director of Publications: Dr Claude-Bernard Costecalde

Author: Anthony Marques
Editors: Anne Edwards, Ann Niermeyer
Photographers: Frantisek Zvardon, Vy Barto, Michael Mickel
Layout: Sylvie Tusinski

Printed in China

Ref: 111347
ISBN 978-2-7468-3681-5